ONE DAY I'LL REMEMBER THIS

PRAISE FOR HELEN GARNER
AND *YELLOW NOTEBOOK*

'In some ways, the diaries are the apotheosis of her entire career, and the most exciting thing she has ever published.' *Literary Hub*

'A crafted work of autobiographical glimpses, acute observations and insights into the writer's psyche...Even in private her sentences sing with a strong, clear voice.' *Australian*

'*Yellow Notebook* is as replete as it is spare. It is brimful of a life that needs to be taken a sip at a time to enjoy all its flavours...There is so much wisdom in this book that we can be grateful that Garner has decided to share it around.' *Age*

'The sensory nature of her observations is glorious.' *Guardian*

'*Yellow Notebook* has the power of great fiction that the finest poetry has.' *Saturday Paper*

'Reading these snatches of life being lived is like being given a painting you love gleaming with the still-wet paint.' Helen Elliott

'The sharpest of observers capturing with nuance and detail the most telling interactions between friends, siblings, lovers and society.' *Canberra Times*

'The pleasure of the book is Garner's eye—the momentary event, the instant's feel, the texture of time...A book of heart-wrenching break-ups, growing friendships, tears and celebrations.' *Stuff.co.nz*

'Don't mistake Helen Garner's *Yellow Notebook* for "something sensational to read in the train", as an Oscar Wilde heroine characterised her own diaries. Garner's are spare, quiet, reflective: a portrait of the artist and her world, observed with scrupulous honesty.' Brenda Niall

'One of Australia's greatest writers at her most raw, unedited, and brilliant...*Yellow Notebook* is both entirely ordinary, and completely transfixing.' *Good Reading*

'Full of Helen Garner's trademark acerbic wit and razor-sharp observations, this is the sort of book you can either read in parts or let it wash over you all at once.' *Booktopia*

'Severe, unbending, falling about at the absurdity of the world—Helen Garner emerges as a moralist rippling with intent and mirth. The diary, clearly, is her true métier. And now we have successive volumes to anticipate.' *Australian Book Review*

PRAISE FOR HELEN GARNER

'Her prose is wiry, stark, precise, but to find her equal for the tone of generous humanity one has to call up writers like Isaac Babel and Anton Chekhov.' *Wall Street Journal*

'Garner is a natural storyteller.' James Wood, *New Yorker*

'This is the power of Garner's writing. She drills into experience and comes up with such clean, precise distillations of life, once you read them they enter into you. Successive generations of writers have felt the keen influence of her work and for this reason Garner has become part of us all.' *Australian*

'Helen Garner [is] our greatest contemporary practitioner of observation, self-interrogation and compassion. Everything she writes, in her candid, graceful prose, rings true, enlightens, stays.' Joan London

'Her use of language is sublime.' *Scotsman*

'Garner's stories share characteristics of the postcard: they flash before us carefully recorded images that remind us of harsher realities not pictured. And like postcards they are economically written, a bit of conversation is transcribed, a memory recalled, an event noted, scenes pass as if viewed from a train—momentarily, distinct and tantalising in their beauty.' *New York Times*

'There's no denying the force of her storytelling.' *Telegraph*

'Garner is one of those wonderful writers whose voice one hears and whose eyes one sees through. Her style, conversational but never slack, is natural, supple and exact, her way of seeing is acute and sympathetic, you receive an instant impression of being in the company of a congenial friend and it is impossible not to follow her as she brings to life the events and feelings she is exploring.' Diana Athill

'A voice of great honesty and energy.' Anne Enright

'Scrupulously objective and profoundly personal.' Kate Atkinson

'Garner's spare, clean style flowers into magnificent poetry.' *Australian Book Review*

'She has a Jane Austen–like ability to whizz an arrow straight into the truest depths of human nature, including her own.' *Life Sentence*

'Compassionate and dispassionate in equal measure…She writes with a profound understanding of human vulnerability, and of the subtle workings of love, memory and remorse.' *Economist*

'Garner's precise descriptions, her interest in minute shifts of emotion, and the ways in which we reveal ourselves to others are always at work in these books, and make them a real joy to read.' *Age*

'She watches, imagines, second-guesses, empathises, agonises. Her voice—intimate yet sharp, wry yet urgent—inspires trust.' *Atlantic*

'Garner's writing [is] so assured and compassionate that any reader will be enthralled and swept along.' *Books+Publishing*

'The words almost dance off the page.' *Launceston Examiner*

'Garner is a beautiful writer who winkles out difficult emotions from difficult hiding places.' *Sunday Telegraph*

'Garner writes with a fearsome, uplifting grace.' *Metro UK*

'A combination of wit and lyricism that is immensely alluring.' *Observer*

'Honest, unsparing and brave.' *New York Times*

ALSO BY HELEN GARNER

FICTION
Monkey Grip
Honour & Other People's Children
The Children's Bach
Postcards from Surfers
Cosmo Cosmolino
The Spare Room
Stories

NON-FICTION
The First Stone
The Feel of Steel
Joe Cinque's Consolation
This House of Grief
Everywhere I Look
True Stories
Yellow Notebook

FILM SCRIPTS
The Last Days of Chez Nous
Two Friends

HELEN GARNER

ONE DAY I'LL REMEMBER THIS
DIARIES VOLUME II 1987–1995

TEXT PUBLISHING
MELBOURNE AUSTRALIA

textpublishing.com.au

The Text Publishing Company
Swann House, 22 William Street, Melbourne Victoria 3000, Australia

The Text Publishing Company (UK) Ltd
130 Wood Street, London EC2V 6DL, United Kingdom

First published by The Text Publishing Company, 2020

Book design by Chong W. H.
Jacket photograph courtesy the author
Typeset by J&M Typesetting

Printed in Australia by Griffin Press, an accredited ISO/NZS 14001:2004 Environmental Management System printer.

ISBN: 9781922330277 (hardback)
ISBN: 9781925923704 (ebook)

A catalogue record for this book is available from the National Library of Australia.

This book is printed on paper certified against the Forest Stewardship Council® Standards. Griffin Press holds FSC chain-of-custody certification SGS-COC-005088. FSC promotes environmentally responsible, socially beneficial and economically viable management of the world's forests.

'But evidently I had not understood enough, or rather, as I was slowly finding out, everything that one thinks one understands has to be understood over and over again, in its different aspects, each time with the same new shock of discovery.'

MARION MILNER, *An Experiment in Leisure*

1987

'What do you write in your diary?'

'Everything. I try to write all the worst things. That's the hardest. The temptation to gloss it up. I force myself to put down the bad and stupid things I do, the idiotic fantasies I have.'

'And do you read back over it?'

'All the time.'

———

Lunch. The company of women. This is what I need. Light and silly conversation about how to keep canvas shoes white. 'People think the world is full of couples,' says E. 'In fact it is made up of triangles.'

———

V's quite a frumpy bloke, really. His body is neglected, his hair is going grey. The pale skin of his arms and shoulders is thickly freckled, those childish freckles you see on boys in primary school, a starry sky of freckles, densely packed.

———

Being in love makes me selfish and mean, puts blinkers on me. I get tunnel vision. I want, I want, I want. That's all that happens, when you're in love. Okay, I've said it. I'm in love.

———

O and I took a turn around the park near his house. Muggy night. A flea bite on my left side. A moon one-third full, some faint stars, a scarf of cloud drifting across the Centrepoint Tower, large fruit bats flapping between church steeple and Moreton Bay figs. We convulsed ourselves by saying '*andiamo*' in posh English accents. In a second-hand shop window I saw a pretty nightie I wanted to buy. Always, under whatever else is happening, a level of thought and fantasy about V and what is possible. I try out the idea of a *mistress*, some long-term thing running parallel to his marriage. I know my ego wouldn't accept this. When I've been with him I feel fed, and anxiety dies a little. Like a junkie after a hit, I am able to contemplate giving him up.

————

My story appears today in the *Sydney Morning Herald*. On the front page: 'A new story from Helen Garner, plus how to avoid cholesterol.'

————

On the ferry V has brought a yellow plastic bag. He pretends it contains sandwiches but actually it's his bathers and a book on Wagner by Thomas Mann. 'I've got very strong ideas on individuality,' he says. 'I reckon the further you get from that, the less you are yourself, the more you blur.' I say nothing, but think, 'How does that sit with being married?' 'Course,' he says, 'that means anyone can do anything,' and gives a short, dismissive laugh.

————

At the beach O's wife teased him and he flung sand in her face, a lot, and hard. She sat up, brushed herself off and said, 'I suppose I asked for that.' She walked down to the water to rinse it off. O said when she was out of earshot, 'That wasn't very nice, was it. What can I do to make reparation?' I wanted to say, 'Get down on your knees to her, for openers,' but remained silent. He shook out her towel and rearranged it. She returned and lay down on it, looking ordinary, and we continued our conversation.

————

Dinner with the retired academics. I made a big effort and stayed with the conversation. Spare me from old men's calm assumption that anything they say, no matter how dull, slow or perfunctory, deserves and will have an audience. Their wives are still real, warm people, compared with these old blokes frozen in their own importance. The jerky little tales of eccentrics and their drinking. Sly innuendo about famous women they have known, one of whom was said to have had 'sixty-four lovers'. I sat quietly, thinking, 'You call that a lot?' Is this what V means when he says women never understand that men want to be with other men? Dread: he too will turn out to be *manly* in that way—looked after by a woman, no longer alive to her yet still drawing full benefits from her love and sacrifice...Is there hope for women and men?

———

I called home. M's lovely bright voice. Thank God I had a daughter. She tells me she's got a job as a cleaner in an office building. 'I started on Friday. $9.50 an hour. It's hard but I'll get used to it.' I was pleased it was a rough job and she had got it through her own contacts and not mine. She'll learn the connection between work and money.

———

These two men. I could say 'I love you' to each of them. To L in the most direct, old-fashioned and simple way: I know him, I like him, *he is like me*, we know each other without effort, two greedy, cheerful, sexy, sociable people, takers of foolish risks. To the other, how? A thinker, intellectual, contained, cautious, measured, hard-working, private. And *married*. This will have to be lived. It can't be walked away from.

———

'How greatly one needs declarations in love, and how greatly one fears them, as though they *used up* something that would otherwise survive longer.' —Elias Canetti, *The Human Province*

———

Awful evening at L's kitchen table. His attacks on me, the truth in them, but the way he strengthened their force, and ultimately weakened and undermined their truth, by the use of irony, or rather sarcasm. 'You're silent,' he says. 'I'm not like that. It's a powerful position, the silent one.' I put my head down on the table and cried with shame. Sadness, soreness, regret; relief.

———

M calls, laughing and high-voiced with excitement, to report her exam results. 'I knew the mail'd be there early. So I made myself some breakfast and strolled to the post office as if there was no hurry. I got two letters and I even made myself read the other one first.' I shower her with praise. 'Don't feel you have to move out as soon as you get back,' she says. 'It'd be good to spend some time with you in the house before we part. People have been staying over a lot. Some in your bed. But don't worry, I always make it nice again.'

———

V reads me some of his new novel. It's very good. Dry, completely *competent*, full of fancies that make me burst out laughing. He reads badly, in a stubbornly unemotional voice, as if gritting his teeth to do it.

———

Very, very hot day. I thought I was fine on the highway till I stopped at a motel in Yass and got out. Found myself almost unable to speak to the woman at reception. When she asked if I wanted dinner I just stared at her wildly. Trucks passed all night. Single bed, white cotton sheets. I was terribly thirsty. Drank eight cups of tea and a jug of orange juice. Wanted a beer desperately but was too stupefied to go out and find a pub.

———

At Albury I bought a Ry Cooder tape. Played it over and over, those instrumental songs, the leisure and sweetness of their hesitations. The quality of his music is goodness. Absence of straining ego.

———

Today I own a house. Got the key and rushed over. Hated it of course. No sun to show its many light sources. Phone went bung after one call. All windows seem to look on to brick walls. Plants in the garden ugly and neglected and worthy of euthanasia. I began to panic till I stood in the backyard and felt its space. Went again in the early evening, to water. Extreme quietness of the street, darkness beginning to cluster under the plane trees. In the backyard I stood holding the hose on yellowing grass. Sky in the west a paling orange. Above, a colourless clarity.

———

Moving house. One carload at a time. My room looks on to thousands of leaves. I lie on my bed and rest, looking up into the foliage. The dog lies in the hall and gazes out the front door. Back at the old house M's three friends are moving in. Their different types of bed. Nobody there looks at me. I have ceased to exist.

———

I feel, and have to force myself to write, that for the first time in my life I am able to stand up to, or with, a man of my own age whose strength of purpose and self-discipline are at least as great as mine. I'm prepared to behave with respect and patience.

———

Our father twists his head, red-faced, shouts, 'What I want to know is—what are you going to do with my money when I'm dead?' They've been drinking. Mum puts her head back against the armchair and laughs out loud. 'I think that's really funny! We won't *know*! 'Cause we'll be *dead*!'

———

At Manly V wouldn't take off anything but his sandals. He says that men don't like being looked at when they're naked.

———

Boy, can he write! Can he sling verbs around!

———

Paralysis, since I no longer live with M. Everyone I tell has a different analysis. 'It's a lack of structure! What you people all need,' says J, the Christian, 'is original sin. *That* gives you form and structure!

You won't be happy, but at least you'll know there's *shape*.' 'It's the abyss,' says R, the Jungian. 'A brand-new abyss. I envy you. Don't fill it up with old things.'

———

Me: 'This house is full of ants. But single ants. You look at a square foot of floor, and there'll be one ant just walking along vaguely. I think they're Argentinian ants.'

My sister: (*looking bored*) 'Long walk.'

———

Wind blew in the night: I thought I heard doors being opened and shut. Rain poured down. The house was waterproof. In the morning I hired a one-tonne flatbed truck to move the rest of my stuff. The pipsqueak at Hertz demanded incredible details from me—he rang the publisher and asked her to *describe* me. I told the guy who runs the Paragon that my old friend P is going to share the house with me. 'You women!' he said, handing me my coffee. 'You get together again, late in life! Have you noticed?' I was silent with shock. *Late in life?*

———

The black kitten that F palmed off on us is clawing up and down my leg. P accepted the offer of a cat eagerly, sight unseen, though when she did see it she was not *quite* sure about its colour. 'You can't go back on it now,' I said. She consulted one of her spiritual advisers, and returned saying black would be fine.

———

A letter that comes straight towards me with open arms.

———

Dreamt an old auntie told me that a woman 'always needs a good pair of stout brown lace-up walking boots'.

———

Sorted books for hours. At first I was ruthless, and culled, but as fatigue took over, all my decisions acquired a tone of angst, until I had to stop. Found an old literary magazine containing an interview with

V. His sentences were so dry as to be starchy, perfectly constructed in a way that made me feel exhausted and slightly panicky. He is married. He is an intellectual. He is only messing with me. And I have dropped my guard. Reading at random in Canetti: 'It seems that one cannot be *severe* all of a lifetime. It seems that something takes vengeance in one, and one becomes like everyone else.' Is this the sort of stuff V would write? Painful speculations, sometimes grinding, always trying to tackle the worst, the least attractive, what cannot be made beautiful?

———

The cheeky waiter at Notturno is the brother of a wildly erratic and endearing Italian boy I used to teach.

'Tell me, how's your brother?'

'He's gone.'

'Where?'

'Up there.' Points north. 'Carlton cemetery.'

'You're pulling my leg.'

'No. That's where he is.'

Pause.

'Are you having me on?'

'No.' He is calm, but his smart expression is gone. The freckles round his eyes are standing out. 'No. He died.' Looks at his watch. 'On the eighth.'

'*Why* did he die?'

'Heart attack.'

'*Heart* attack? How old was he?'

'Twenty-nine.'

'Did he have something wrong with his heart?'

'No. He had weak lungs. He smoked too much. He loved a bong. His wife came home and found him on the floor. They took him down to St Vincent's and the doctor said he'd be all right. But he said to my mother, "Take me jewellery off, Mum—I'm gonna die." And he died.'

At least I am not bound to anyone, hurting him with my obsession. Examination of fantasy state: it is not a series of clear pictures. Really it is more a stupefaction, a state of suspension.

Lunch in Fitzroy. The way friends, men and women, sit around a table, eating, drinking, telling little stories, making each other laugh. I dislike, and am shocked by, the spiteful sallies of one of the older men. I'd forgotten it. I'm used to living with teenagers. They have no bitterness.

My sister calls, the counsellor. 'How is it, living without M?'
    'Awful. I'm paralysed.'
    'Classic,' she says. 'Classic symptoms.'
    'What of?'
    'Grief. Starts with blankness, then that clears and it hurts more. It gets worse.'
    'And guilt?'
    'Yep. *Huge* discharge of guilt. Also—idealisation.'
    'Have you heard her HSC results?'
    We almost laugh.
    'Crying helps,' she says, 'if you can do it.'
    'But what should I *do*? My friend R says, "Go into it. Don't be busy. *Use* it."'
    'She's right. The sacrament of whatever's necessary.'
    'Who said *that*?'
    'Me.'

Agitated, stunned, in distress, all at once. Sobs won't form. I trudge about the house, hating the colours, ring up and order a deadlock, wait like a rabbit for *Cinema Papers* to call about my review. The cat has decided on a corner of my workroom as its lavatory.

Her first day at primary school, her eagerness, the way she gazed up at the teacher, my *jealousy* of the teacher. The heavy surf of guilt: times when she wanted my company, my attention, and I gave it but not with a full heart, or gave it briefly and soon let my mind wander in boredom with her childishness. I ran away from her. Once when he and I squabbled in the car she punched herself methodically in the head, she punched herself for some time *before I noticed*. I'm ashamed of feeling these things, it's an affliction I have to keep secret from her. Dull sky, cool wind, the side gate keeps banging. Voices in the street speaking another language. This state is like a second labour. I'm struggling to let her be born.

———

A Tchaikovsky piano concerto, on my own. The idea of it made me yawn but soon my skin began to crawl and various thoughts came to me with the music as background. If I go ahead with this, I will be spending a lot of time alone. That's something I am already good at, and often prefer. I will spend a lot of time waiting. And when I'm old I will be alone. How strange these thoughts are. They are serious thoughts. I am contemplating a course of action which at my age will have certain repercussions, important ones. Have I got, can I find in myself, the courage and strength to live like that? Would I want to be 'married'? I am notoriously bad at it. It does not suit me. The wife envies the passion her husband feels for the mistress. The mistress envies the steady companionship... 'The world is made up of triangles.'

———

H: 'I'm old-fashioned too.'

V: 'Oh you are not.'

H: 'You'd be surprised.'

V: 'Name one respect in which you're old-fashioned.'

H: 'I believe that children should be strictly brought up.'

V: 'Good. What else?'

H: 'Uhmmm…tablecloths. I like them, and I don't mind ironing them.'

———

My first cheerful day since I 'left home'. F called me and we went out to dinner. We spoke mainly French. I can still understand almost everything and can chatter away, but I get words wrong and some-times a blankness occurs. We had fun, drank a bit of wine and made ourselves laugh. On the way home we stopped at our old house—now M's and her friends'—to pick up my TV, a few pot plants and a ladder. The kitchen was full of the girls plus the law student and a debauched-looking, dense-faced boy I didn't know. They told me M was 'feeling ill' and had gone to bed. They were all stoned, stag-gering with it, especially the law student, whose face was puffy. He stumbled about in a red baseball jacket, hopelessly bombed, his eyes like eggs. He looked like a pampered, adolescent, middle-class boy and I hated it. He barely greeted me. We collected what we'd come for. A lot of jolly noise, loud wisecracks in US accents—they were waiting for us to be gone so they could stagger out to the Prince of Wales. The law student asked me if I was coming to M's party on Saturday night. 'No. I'm going to the country. Anyway she hasn't invited me.' 'She hasn't *invited* you?' 'Oh, it's all right,' I say, without looking at him or meaning it, already halfway out the door, full of sadness, shame, anger, a burst of disagreeable feelings that still ache with a light persistence. When I got home I looked at myself in the mirror. My top lip had twisted, higher on the left than the right. I looked bitter. Older and wiser. I suppose when your mother is 'old and wise' you have to be very tough to break away. You must have to *show no mercy*.

———

Dreamt that the married man was washing up at my sink. I came and put my arms round him from behind. He turned and wrapped himself around me *like a child*, twining, so that his feet were off the ground. I felt his lightness and smallness with amazement.

'Is *The Fatal Shore*,' says V, 'the kind of book you'd rush out and buy?'

'Course not. I've got no feeling for the past at all.'

'You've got a pretty strong sense of the present, though, haven't you.'

A character with no sense of the past but with such a sense of the present that she can be used as a gauge in any situation: 'What's going on in there? Send in the radar.'

I asked M out for coffee. She agreed eagerly. When I called for her the boys' dorm was still all over the lounge-room floor. The law student took me into the laundry and showed me a bong in a bucket of water. He explained its workings. I was bored, unimpressed, slightly shocked, basically contemptuous. In the cafe I told M about my ten miserable days. She was aghast: 'You should have come over!' She listened to my psychological account. I noticed she had tears in her eyes. 'I came home from work,' she says, 'and found them all bonging on just inside the back door, with the door open and fumes pouring out into the street. I walked straight through and went to bed.'

When we got back from the cafe we found the boys gone and one of the other girls, the opera singer, finishing a major clean-up. She told us she had put the kitchen radio on classical music and started the dishes. In the living room the boys put on one of their records so she closed the kitchen door. The law student burst in, turned off her radio with a violent movement, and shouted, 'Stop acting the martyr! *I'll* wash up later!' Telling us this, her face flushes dark red and huge tears spill out of her eyes and pour down her face. Boys who batten off girls, use their sense of order as something to sponge off and then desecrate. Girls who let them do this.

'I considered nothing. It happened. What will become of us?' At Primrose Gully, in the place where last year I painfully taught myself the discipline of solitude and learnt a kind of freedom, I recognise that I have given up freedom again, willingly let it go, exchanged it for *this bondage*, to time and another person, which is called LOVE.

———

Me: 'Oh, I wish I was an intellectual. But I'm not.'

My sister: 'You're doing a hell of a lot better than me. Or is it I.'

———

An unpleasant, scorching day with dry winds, then a cool change. I drank some beer and ate at the born-again Christian's place in St Kilda. We walked a long way in the dark and the south-westerly off the water, out the pier and on to the groin or whatever it's called. Coming back, we walked with our arms round each other. I said something and laughed and looked up at him and he kissed me, with open lips. I was stunned, thinking, 'This is *the wrong man*.' That thought did not even scrape the surface of the event. We walked on. I said, 'We never could walk in step,' and he said, 'That's how it is.' He told me that at work he had seen a beam of light pass through a concrete wall. 'Were you hallucinating?' 'I've heard the devil can appear as light, so I don't know.'

———

The flight to Sydney lasted only five minutes because I was reading Marguerite Duras' *La Douleur*. When her husband comes back after the war I cried so much my face twitched, I had to wipe my eyes on my skirt. 'I remember the sobbing all through the house, the tenants lingering on the stairs, the doors standing open.' Her writing is so physical. The movement of her sentences captures the movement of emotion and thought—it's real *women's writing*, shameless but never sloppy. Maybe she's what I'm looking for—to show me how to control emotion without being false to its power, how to be absent and fully present at once.

———

Reading in French slows me down, which is good, but there's always that veil, the absence in me of the complex vibrations that one's own language sets up. Vibrations of the past in the words and expressions, the echoing field of meaning in which one and one's own language can *play*. And yet the slowness makes it rich in another way.

————

From the hotel window I can see water, ferries in at the quay, but mostly asphalt and metal. The feelings I get from waiting are like an echo from the future. What is the technique for not waiting? Clearly it is not possible to develop one, while in a hotel room, taskless, homeless, workless, backyardless, carless, bikeless. This trip then is an aberration. From now on, discipline.

————

A letter to the law student. 'Also you are drinking too much and smoking too much dope. It is my prerogative to point this out. We shared a difficult year. Don't act like a fuckwit and spoil everything.'

————

What I miss about L is the sight of him at the Cretan's place, all brown and colourful on the sofa, talking practical talk about gardening.

————

V often fades out, halfway through a sentence.

————

When I sign my name, my first name, on a letter, I look at it and like it, and feel lucky to have been given it.

————

On Bondi Beach the moon, like a slice of lemon or a hunk of cheese, went down fast behind a peculiar tower. I thought about things I want to write. The healing sessions at the born-again church, the ragged doll at Primrose Gully, the bat, the rats, the Christian who wants to drown the cat, the sister planning an abortion, all the things I slid away from writing last year because I was scared.

———

One of the painter's favourite themes, said V, was mother and child. And yet he hated his own mother.

'There are other mothers in the world, aren't there.'

'Other than what?'

'Other than your own.'

———

I try hard to examine him, and him and me, for weak spots that might destroy my respect once the obsession wears off. Mostly I find areas of inadequacy in myself—mental laziness, ignorance, sloppy habits of mind, self-indulgence, while for him my respect grows as he shows himself to me. He is a knower of things. I know things too, but different things, and I know them differently. He loves to tell me things and sometimes I get bored. Why? Because it's a monologue. I have nothing to offer but my attention.

———

I can't stop crying, I'm so tired, and the building noise outside this room is making me crazy.

———

From a chaise longue outside my back door I survey my backyard, its complete stillness, the fine element of damp in the air, the stars thinly sprinkled above the shed.

———

Rosa Cappiello calls me from Sydney. I can hear her panting with the effort of speaking English. I am almost scared of her, she is so violently trying to be herself.

'Elen. Are you with a man?'

'No. Are you?'

'No. Because all the men I know are sick, and dirty. I want someone who is *clean inside*.'

———

Watched the Kundera doco on SBS at my sister's. She slept right through it. I walked home: light was leaving the sky, air clear, streets empty, air and sky perfectly empty. Walked along feeling overwrought, strange, as if some rusted mechanism in me were beginning, after a long stillness of disuse, to turn over again.

———

While the gynaecologist is examining my cunt she tells me that her old dog got cancer and had to be put down. 'I still cry when I think of it,' she says, doing so, burrowing away inside me. 'I've cried every day for two and a half months. He was like a child to me. Life is so empty without him.'

———

Great love I feel for T, her stubborn face and stubborn ability to laugh at the moment before despair. She's recovered from black lung, and is now convinced she's got MS. 'I keep bumping into things,' she says, heaving chairs in over the tailgate of the EH. 'And I've got a weakness which is TOTAL.' I diagnose a hangover. She's been on holiday with her bloke. 'We were together for several days. We were careful with each other, like two actors performing a play.' If she left him she would flourish as an artist. Easy for me to say.

———

The story about looking. I want it to have a curve in it. To come right back and tie itself to the very beginning.

———

P is very exercised domestically by what to me are minor matters: which kitchen table? She weighs this possibility against that, trotting from one room to another or standing in a thoughtful posture, finger against cheek. I adopt a good-humoured but blanked-out patience, like a man in a Maupassant short story with a garrulous wife whom he nonetheless loves. P is adorable, and faithful, with a delicacy that I completely lack.

———

The old journalist in an interview talks about her husband, how they lived a life of intense companionship along with surprising independence. 'So we both lied. I had twice been blindly and hopelessly in love, and I knew that he'd had two love affairs, but they were never discussed. I think the worst thing anyone can do to someone you love is to confess all, because I did love him more than anybody in the world. He was such a marvellous friend and he never bored me. We really suited each other down to the ground.' So even 'blindly and hopelessly in love' can't stand up against 'we suited each other down to the ground'.

———

What am I doing? He has been married for more than half his life on this earth. Why should it be any different from any other love affair? Why shouldn't it run through its phases, wither, and die? I'd better work if I want to survive this, and if I want to play my full and proper part in it. Who wants a lovesick, lazy drip, obsessed with her own emotions and full of resentment against fate?

———

Bad news. The owner of Primrose Gully calls to say he is putting it on the market. I have no money. I thought I could detach myself… but a moment ago, at sunset, the pinkish-gold light on the opposite ridge was so thick we might have been in Tuscany. Oh well. Kookaburras burst out in choruses from the gully. A full moon rises. P surveys it from the veranda couch, sitting yoga-style with her elbows propped gracefully on her knees. I have known her so long that I don't know any more where I end and she begins. I have been friends with her for more than half my life on earth. Like V and his wife. This simple thought is comforting. A corrective. Then she left the kero lamp on all night and burnt out the wick and mantle.

———

Schopenhauer is bracing. Things are about as bad as they can be, for humans, so we might as well recognise this and behave with 'tolerance, patience, forbearance and charity, which each of us needs and which each of us therefore owes'.

———

The born-again quotes Corinthians at me: 'Love seeketh not its own.'

'What's that mean?'

'*You* ought to be able to work that out.'

'How about "Love hath not an eye for the main chance"?'

He seems impressed, but perhaps is not.

———

Warm night, squashed moon, smell of dry grass as if from a plain. I read Kuznetsov's *Babi Yar* with bated breath. My story seemed paler and paler, its tiny thoughts, its peaceful world. All my mechanisms creaking and groaning. Doubt thins everything out, shows the void that always lies behind. Doubt that calls itself realism.

———

The law student and his dippy friend turn up very late at my door: 'We're tripping, Hel.' The friend is a talker, a joker, very tiring. The student's face is a screen on which waves of emotion are projected. I take them into the kitchen and devise small challenges: to get off on a plain white plate, and so on. Soon I'm getting a contact high. I begin to contemplate the flower pattern on the teapot spout, and a sound like distant music that is made by the motor of the fridge. I worry about being old and plain—then I think, 'They're probably seeing only light where I think I am.' The law student works hard at being courteous: 'The minute you feel like going back to bed, Hel…' He is meticulous about emptying the ashtray, but is waylaid by 'all these ants in the bin'. I rush to look, expecting an invasion, but find only two.

———

P and I drove to Albert Park for a swim at 10 pm. Dark water. I waded in. Wherever I moved there was a boiling light under the surface: phosphorescence. I cried out and she was scared—she thought it was pollution or radioactivity. I wanted to swim and gaze at my boiling accompaniment—off my hands came streams of it, in dense bubbling clouds—but the water smelled dirty and I was afraid of sharks. Out on the pier (lightning kept stabbing randomly behind the city) we sat in the breathless stillness and the air began to pour from the north, a wind *grew* as we sat there. P's towel, which had been hanging from the rail, was lifted on an angle and sustained it without flapping. People everywhere in the dark. We drove home yawning and as we walked in the front door it started to pour with rain.

———

After the movie, which I thought was sentimental, I got quite punchy, and mad at P for not arguing and for saying things like 'What's wrong with ending on a positive note?' As I Expounded My Views I felt (a) how *clever* and *articulate* I was being, then (b) disgusted with myself for priding myself on (a). P in her delicate and well-mannered way said that when a film makes 'one' furious it must be because it has touched on some sore point in 'one'. I was suddenly deflated by the truth in this. I was furious because *I'm* sentimental. Because in *my* work I am guilty of striking the sweet note when it should be sour.

———

I want to write a novel about the born-again. Shadow games. Premonitions. Where does the murder trial fit in? A helicopter passes, hovers, unremarked upon, during an important scene. I am a very *unlearned* woman.

———

The only way I can sit still for long periods is if I read and take notes. Maybe loneliness will save me after all. In these states I can listen with profit to music by Bartók, Schoenberg, weird and scary stuff. Except for Bach, other things seem too pleasant or even easy. Scared the shit out of myself by playing several times Bartók's 'Music for Strings, Percussion and Celesta' and his second quartet, and reading the *New Grove* entry about him. The spine-chilling impersonality of those biographies, it actually frightens me, I don't know why. And I can't help noticing the cold note: 'he divorced his first wife in the autumn and married his pupil Ditta Pásztory…' Oh hell. What will become of me?

———

A couple of beers at Little Reata with the law student. Loved his company, such a tenderness for him, his eager interest in life. He can't bear to think what might be in store for me. He puts his head on the table, holds my hands, groans. I laugh. One day I'll remember this.

———

If I write a movie I will be forced, by working with other people, to come out of my fantasy world and deliver the goods.

———

At Primrose Gully with R. Gas lamp hissing. Sky has cleared and is star-sprinkled. 'If I were you,' says R, 'I'd sell my soul to get hold of this place.'

———

During the wedding ceremony I asked myself why the simple hopes of these promises are so impossible when the complications of life fall on them like a collapsing wall. I do not understand marriage. V is always talking about *symmetry* but we are not symmetrical at all. I am offering everything and he is offering everything except the final thing, which in effect means that he is offering nothing. Is this true or is it just a smart crack? It is quite understandable to be stunned and even sick with fear when you're heading for a brick wall at 100 miles an hour.

———

'These soul things,' said R, 'they're on another level. They can't be legislated.'

———

'A girl at the supermarket gave me free coupons,' I said. 'She looked like Dolly Parton.'

   'Like who?' says V.

   'Like Dolly Parton.'

'Who's Dolly Pardon?'

———

Out to hear Washington Wives. I enjoyed moving, and staring at people. While dancing I fantasised what John Shaw Nielson called 'wonderful frocks' of a feminine style—big skirts with little socks—mutton dressed as lamb perhaps but I refuse to be middle-aged.

———

V quotes Degas quoting Delacroix: 'An artist must have no passion except his work and must sacrifice everything to it.' Privately I consider this to be bullshit.

———

Fantasy: I arrange to meet him in the US at the end of the writers' tour. He comes and we meet: but in the meantime I have met *a free man*. I see V coming towards me and I do not know him or want him any more. He is already in my past, a stranger, a finished phase.

———

A man with a habit of giving less information, and in a less coherently organised form, than one needs in order to be able to understand what he is talking about—almost as if he is trying to provoke one to ask puzzled questions so he can accuse one of not paying proper attention.

———

Alone at Primrose Gully. Sun pours in. Wind cool enough for a jumper. Stove quietly working. Could such a place be mine? I look at the cabin with a more critical, demanding eye: this must be cleaned, that painted. I walked along the road with the dog. Trees in their many dimensions flickered, like a Fred Williams painting. Intense beauty of the sparse bush. I tried to sing the Nielson song: 'And in that poor country, no pauper was I.' Floods of emotion passed through me: anticipation of work, ideas about a born-again novel, memories of the Mighty Force and its visitations. Walking on the road I felt my spine to be taller, more vertical. I thought, 'I will never be like V, or write like him, or use his methods. My value, to

him and to the world, in fact my JOB, is to work as I know how, as
is natural to me.' Terrific exhilaration of this.

———

A scene for a movie: two girls, young women, students, walk along
a road in the middle of a dry summer night. They take off their
blouses and walk bare-breasted. Wind blows on them. 'Do you
remember,' I say to P, 'the night at Merricks when we took our
blouses off, walking along the road? It was so hot!' 'I remember the
walk,' she says, 'but not the blouses.'

———

Last night I decided to 'sell my soul' to buy Primrose Gully. Today
I arrive home and find a cheque from Queensland for the exact
price of the property. I had not told her, or anyone, anything about
it. '*That*,' said the Jungian, 'is synchronicity.'

———

The healing session at the born-again's Pentecostalist church. 'What's
your need, sister?' 'It's my back.' He shouts over his shoulder, 'Get
her a chair.' A plastic chair is rushed up behind and I sit on it. The
pastor crouches in front of me, straightens my legs, seizes my ankles:
'Make sure you're sitting right back in the chair. See how this leg's
shorter than that one?' 'Yes.' He—what *did* he do?—pulls them, I
think, equally towards him, says, 'Feel that in your back? Thank you,
Lord! Thank you! Now see? They're the same length!' Grabs my
hands. 'Up! Now—run on the spot.' I do: 'It doesn't hurt.' I can feel
myself grinning. He's still holding my hands. 'And there's a fair bit
of tension, too,' he says, 'that makes the back sore.' He put his right
hand round my waist and presses it quickly against my lower spine,
exactly where the vertebra bulges out, and says, 'It's that vertebra
there, isn't it.' 'Yes.' I don't recall whether he laid his hands on my
head—but out of him bursts the word 'PEACE!'—hands catch me
behind and I'm on my back on the floor. I feel completely ordinary.
My face is turning red. I turn my head and see an old woman roll
over, scramble on to her hands and knees, and crawl out of the line

of bodies back towards the pews. I turn on to my side and lie there staring. Throughout all this there is a complete and total lack of ritual—no music, no set prayers, no *silence*—people chat quietly, the two catchers are laughing and talking in low voices about buying a secondhand Mazda only inches away from where the pastor is laying hands on one person after another and praying loudly and urgently. It's extremely casual, practical and relaxed. Small children are strolling about yelling to their mothers. I get to my feet and walk back to our pew. We leave before the end. In the lobby three little kids in Catholic primary-school uniforms are staring in: 'He's dead! See him push them over? The one in the red jumper's dead.' We walk away along the sunny street and speak of other things—about how he would like to marry, the puzzle of how to meet *girls*.

———

F showed me the bill from the Hôtel de la Plage at Fréhel in Brittany where we first had a holiday, in 1978. We laughed and laughed, in a fit of cheerful memories. 'That was back when you used to be nice,' he said. 'What? I still am!' He urged me, with hints, to recall the name of the next village, the last one on the road: PLURIEN. Laughed till we had tears in our eyes.

———

V: 'What'll you do tomorrow?'
  Me: (*genuinely surprised*) 'Work.'

———

M's been invited to join a theatre company and given (without having to audition) a part in *The Cherry Orchard*.

———

On the drive to the airport he has a cigar but no matches. I pull into a 7-Eleven.
  'What's this?'
  'The match shop.'
  He smokes the disgusting thing and talks like an American.

———

Rode lightless through the Fitzroy Gardens. Men on beat heading for the lavatories, I nearly knocked one flying. Home along Brunswick Street on the footpath. Wonderful summer night, half a moon hanging casually halfway up the sky, thick dry air, people out in the streets.

———

The pencil, and furthermore, it wore down. In another three months it'll be gone. There'll be nothing left of it at all.

———

'Called or not called, God shall be there.' —Above Jung's door.

———

I wonder what he thinks his rights are, in this? Has he the right to be jealous, to make demands? Have *I* got any 'rights'? What *is* a 'right'?

———

We open the front door at midnight. Someone's been here. The plastic box on the hall floor, the cheap jewellery spread as if at leisure. The living-room window's wide open, the blind still flapping over the sill. What's gone? TV still there: video, ghetto-blaster, stereo. In the hall my blue beret and a striped belt on the carpet. My basket's gone, the big light basket I bought in Vanuatu. *That* thing? Broken and torn? To carry away loot? But nothing that *big* has been taken. Ah, behind my bed a missingness: my CD Walkman. My wooden box with brass corners is open on the mantelpiece—oh, my pretty antique rings! But I never wore them. Nothing else missing: M's baby teeth and my wedding ring no. 2 still there but they've taken my first wedding ring. How did they choose? Come back and show me how it looks on you! On the floor where the Walkman was, a cheap gold pendant: a heart containing a pearl. I pick it up. Like a payment. Must've been girls. Dear girls! You've stripped me of a weight: take my things and wear them on your young hands and bodies.

———

Falling in love at this age is terrible because it makes you fear death.

———

'So this poor bitch,' says V, 'in glaring white shoes and a purple jumpsuit...' I flinch. He's one of those old-fashioned men who divide up women into poor bitches, molls, free spirits (Mirka Mora), and then their own women. Let's stop now, before I get so far in I forget where the exit is and have to blow up the building to get out.

———

Everything that can be called A SUBJECT he knows about. And I know about the rest.

———

The game I invent to entertain V when he's sick in bed. I put an object against his back under his T-shirt and he has to guess what it is. A hammer, half an apple. Aching paroxysms of noiseless laughter. When I put a candle there he thinks for ages and says uncertainly, 'Is it your watch?'

———

A savage taxi driver. His anger seethed out of his pores, he was sick and mad with it. 'Sydney's a dump. A bloody rubbish heap full of greedy sick pipple. Town Hall—in there's the biggest bunch of idiots. Wanting to change everything. Pedestrian malls in the middle of the city. Make everyone turn around and go the other way. Newtown. That's another bloody dump. If I had to live in Newtown or Erskineville I'd rather live in a *tent*. In a bloody *paddock*. The houses've got only one wall between 'em. You can hear the bloke next door talkin' to his missus. Where do *I* live? I've lived in plenty of places, lady. King Street—a dump. One lane of traffic. Blocked up for miles.' Battered by his bitter monologue. You only need a couple of thousand people like him to poison the entire population of the world. Considered saying, 'What happened? Why are you so angry?' but I knew he would massacre me.

———

'The first time I ever got into bed with a girl, starkers,' says V, 'I was

staggered by the softness. I was absolutely *staggered*.' I thought about
the three women I've been in bed with. The astounding softness
of their mouths and skin. I decide not to say, 'I know exactly what
you mean.'

———

I say, 'I'm no good at marriage. I think I'd be awful to be married to.'
 'Why? What makes you say that?'
 I look at my bare foot on the bed-end and think, 'Is it even *true*?'

———

The biographer sent me a copy of her letter to the subject's family,
dropping the project because of not wanting to 'hurt' them. She's
chickened out. I felt a roll of scorn. Then guilt. R and I discussed
possible reasons, and found plausible ones, which lowered my tone.
R says, 'She's closer to the precipice than most of us.' Once again I see
in myself an impatience with the suffering of others, an unpleasant
briskness.

———

Fear, at three in the morning after a storm, that I'll never write
anything again.

———

I weigh myself on the big machine at Coles. 'Eight stone four,' says
the man in charge of the scales. 'That's a good weight. You hang
around that weight and you'll be right.'

———

F tells me about a TV program he saw, about AIDS—junkies as
well as gays. Sudden rigid horror—what if I caught it in Paris in
1978? Staring at the chair leg I imagine the blood coming out of
my arm into the tube: 'You're positive.' I must have looked panic-
stricken. F says, 'I didn't mean to frighten you.' 'Should I get a blood
test?' 'You have to be careful, that's all.'
 David Bowie announces cheerfully that he has an AIDS test
every time he 'changes partners'.

———

At Mum and Dad's I sat sideways on my chair, staring out the window. Dad said, affectionately (for him), 'What are *you* thinking about, Helen?' 'Oh,' I said, 'just the meaning of the universe.' A true answer would have been, 'I've found the love of my life, and he's married to somebody else.'

———

I admire and want to imitate the way he looks at, say, a picture, and walks away. He shows me something and doesn't expect me to comment. He gives me time.

———

Kafka's letters to Felice. Struck by their dailiness, the intense detail he goes into about circumstance and feeling—and sometimes by a slicing sarcasm which makes me afraid of him.

———

The men on the excavation site next to the hotel arrive quietly, and go quietly about the tasks of preparation for work. I don't know what they're doing. Checking the huge pieces of equipment. Looking at gauges. Putting oil in things. Not seeming to communicate with each other, in their dark shorts and boots and socks.

———

My beautiful little indigo leather bag is not on my bed when I go to get a stamp out of it. I search my bedroom, the house—I go to search the car but the keys to it are in the bag. A hollow feeling. Where is it? $600 in cash, that P owed me and paid. My pen, my keycard, my bank book, door key, car key, PO box key, *my black notebook*—my notes for my movie, play, novel. I acknowledge it's gone, I call the cops. Two boys and a girl, all armed with pistols. Friendly, courteous, efficient. I wish I had a decent-sized teapot to make them all a cuppa. They leave, full of advice about security grilles, window bars etc. The robber must have taken the bag through my bedroom window, which was wide open to catch the breeze: it is a balmy night, the air is sweet with grass. I cursed and swore. I drank a glass of vodka.

How pretty U is, her clean cheek-line and small nose, her clear eye-whites, her thick curly forelock. She is upset in her self-esteem because a man she went to bed with last week subsequently behaved opaquely and then ceased to contact her. She rang him, left notes. What a terrible tactician, her ego all up-front and undisciplined. 'It's unfortunate,' I said, 'but you have to fake indifference until it becomes real; and then he'll be eating out of your hand. And you don't even *want* him, anyway.'

Are you comfortable, in me? Do you need a window opened, or cleaned? A night-light on your balcony? Are there enough bedclothes? The doors don't lock. The garden is endless and full of vegetables and flowers. Are you happy?

I will get only $4000 in royalties. So much for my fucking Subaru. Stop complaining and start working. Anyway the law student says that a Subaru is 'kitsch' and 'has no style'.

Pleasure of sitting by the fire. P was sewing, I was reading. We were silent for an hour at least. We know how to be silent. We are civilised.

'His Crockery'. First she stood in line at DJ's sale with half a dozen Arzberg plates in her hands. The queue was long. She lost patience and walked away, leaving them on the wrong display counter. Back at the house he said, 'You're a great little shopper, aren't you.' 'Not great enough. I was too mean to wait.' 'I don't care,' he said. 'I'm cooking. Sit down and read the paper.' Then he went away to Italy. Then she went to Grace Brothers and bought a whole set of the plainest white Australian china. She carried it on foot to his house. The other man there let her in. He was on his way to work. 'What's in the parcel?' 'Nothing. Just some stuff.' He closed the door behind him. She put the parcel on the kitchen table, went out to the shed for an axe, and started the job. I want it to have no particular *meaning*. Wherever there is a sign of character development, plot, explanation, I want to stamp on it.

———

An old man presents himself at my door: he found my Medicare card and licence in a neighbour's front garden while 'talking about roses', and returned them to our old house, where the dog attacked him and tore a great piece out of his jumper. He showed me the rip: 'Pure wool it was, and everything.'

———

Before the woman he was going to marry came back from New York, G told me, he understood then 'the black power of love'. Nightmares from which he woke sweating and stammering, mornings when he sang for joy.

———

I've kept myself for decades in a milieu of people younger than me.

———

Sun streams in. Stillness outside. Beans and potatoes boiling on the stove. Dog asleep nose to tail on the matting. Treetops open to air and light but their trunks deep in the darkness of autumn. Outside the window the koala is asleep in the crook of the branches. One foreleg grips, the other hangs loosely by its side. The great black shining claws.

———

I worked on my story. I pulled things out of thin air. I dragged stuff out of chaos. The moment when, working off diary material as a basis, I begin to invent: like the first moment on an unsupported two-wheeler, or ice skates, letting go, doing it on my own.

———

Dream of trying to help a briskly pragmatic old woman with her work of hostliness. The fish in the pond that she declines to notice. Her ostentatious refusal to remark on the fact that I am hopelessly, unstoppably weeping. Maybe R would say: the refusal to attend to the fish—what swims in water—the unconscious.

———

A beer takes the edge off this peculiar low-level…I want to write *suffering*. I worry about being mad, or unbalanced. Being 'brought undone'.

———

Final scene in *The Trial*: the two executioners who plunge the knife into him and then stand, cheeks together, watching him weaken and die; the attic window that is flung open, the figure that leans out with both arms extended in a large mysterious gesture. Both these images must have come straight out of a dream. I love this thought and feel freed by it.

———

There's stuff I *should* be reading, but I don't know what it is, and so I read just anything, and feel all the time that it's the wrong stuff.

———

What if the Mighty Force came back and stood behind me again, and this time demanded that I let V go? The Mighty Force never demanded anything. It stood. That's all. I knew that if I turned and acknowledged it I would not *be able* to continue with F. The thing with F was killing both of us, but I clung to it. The Mighty Force was offering me life. No, not offering. It offered nothing. It stood.

———

Lunchtime break from the Literature Board meeting. I eat then walk round the streets of North Sydney or sit in a park. In two days I'll go home, I'll work, I'll work in the garden with P, we'll go to Primrose Gully, I'll cook meals, paint the kitchen, I'll read, swim, see my friends. I have been neglecting my friends.

———

'Do you ever find,' says R, 'that someone's company, even though you love it, can completely exhaust you?'

———

The urge to blame V. To say, 'He is selfish. He wants to have everything, for the world to revolve around him. He will never choose me. He should never have begun this.' The cowardice of this urge. The old longing to play the victim. What's required here is a bracing of the self. After all, 'we' 'love' 'each other'. These hackneyed words. Who's we? What's love? Do we *know* each other? Or is each of us only a screen for the other's light show?

———

A warm night in Sydney. I don't belong here. A dog ran past in the street. It was sobbing—a voice like a man's—a lost creature, running and sobbing.

———

Taking the train to Central with R, I was shocked by the condition of Newtown station: Londonish, bombed-out, neglected, tumble-down. She says that when as a girl she would come up to Sydney from her small town and see these devastated house-backs, blackened chimneys and factories, it all seemed wonderful to her.

———

We talked about how men love to tell stories about *the famous*. 'They aren't really interested in hearing *our* stories,' she said. 'They can't even listen to what *we* think is poignant, or funny. Like that Down Syndrome woman saying she was 104.' 'But we give them our total attention.' 'Yes,' she said. 'That's the thing that turns women to feminism. Because it's intolerable, not to be recognised on that level.'

———

It doesn't matter how good a man is, he is not guaranteed love.

———

A letter that ends: 'Thanking you in anticipation and oblige, Love Dad.' We laugh and laugh.

———

Weird effect of Thomas Bernhard's blackness—the arrogance of his statements of despair, meaninglessness etc. Sometimes I feel impatient, as with a child in a tantrum or a 'depressed' person wallowing—sometimes want to laugh out loud—but all this is ultimately swamped by the high quality, the *brilliance*, of the writing, and by respect for the way he is able to confront and report the horrors of his childhood. I feel forced by his hopeless conclusions, however, into the area of myself I am most afraid to enter or to give credence to—the crack-up dept., the mind-skids, the blank-out, the flicker of madness. I don't know who I can talk to, about this. After Bernhard everything that's got lightness, beauty, humour in it seems almost wet—even self-indulgent. Bernhard's iron chords.

———

At home, P and I talk by the kitchen fire about the necessity to lose innocence in order to regain something for which innocence is the wrong word.

———

I call Mum. A high-pitched voice answers. I think I've dialled a wrong number. But it's her. She's sobbing. Dad has accused her of having 'something going' with their old, old friend—her best friend's husband.

'But—that's *mad*!'

'Yes! It's mad!'

'Do you want to talk about it? Or is he standing right there?'

'I don't care if he's "standing right there".'

'Where is he?'

'Oh, he's skulking around somewhere.'

She says she'd thrown a handful of cutlery across the kitchen at him at the exact moment I rang.

'I didn't recognise your voice when you answered. I thought it was a stranger.'

'I can tell you, I *feel* like a stranger.'

This is the saddest, cleverest, truest thing I've ever heard my mother say.

———

Y came over to see my house. Showing it to her, I saw only its shabbiness, its temporary arrangements of furniture, its devastated backyard.

———

Reading an old diary. I cannot remember, even in the thinnest or most fragmentary moment, how it felt to 'love' the man I was in love with, back then. All that hideous torment, everyone suffering, and for WHAT? What would I remember of NOW? This one works, steadily, quietly. His mind does not take the easy way out. I can only live the thing to its fullest extent. This is what life is. It's not for saying no.

———

The weird silence of Easter Sunday. Beautiful autumn morning. A wind in restless gusts, sun comes and goes, I take photos of its patterns on the wall above my desk. Sick, been sick for a fortnight, a ghastly cold, coughing up yellow stuff. I can't seem to get better. Phone never rings. I get up and stand at the window staring out between brown slats. Sometimes I feel I should be lonely but I'm not. I wish someone would bring me an Easter egg, or that P would wake up and come in with a cup of tea so I could say, 'He is risen.'

———

Fantasy: V's dead. No one close to him, of course, thinks to tell me. Finally, a day or two later, R calls: 'H, I've got some very bad news…' Odd feeling that he may as well be dead, he may as well never have existed. His existence is purely intellectual. I can't even write him a letter. Because he doesn't exist.

———

I heard on the radio that Primo Levi died last week and maybe on purpose. I got out *The Periodic Table* and turned its pages. Listened for his voice.

———

V: 'If you didn't like my new book, would you say so?'
   H: 'I'd *want* to tell the truth. I want to be able to be blunt.'

V: 'I'd expect you to tell me what you really thought.'
(What if I don't think anything?)

———

His being married is saving me from my own worst faults: he is a perfect example of the kind of man I could go to water for—clever, harsh, super-critical, remote; and once the thrill of it wore off I'd be fighting (myself) to remain myself. I depend on his marriage. For balance, and for my freedom.

———

Ripped through Joyce Johnston's *Minor Characters*. What a bunch of windbags, mamma's boys, manipulators!

———

How F used to read English poetry to me—Keats, Shakespeare—stumbling, putting the stresses all wrong. It was electrifying. The power of the work came bursting through—his utter lack of pretension, acting, expression—nothing there but WORD.

———

A letter comes from L, a dear, friendly one. Just sticking his head over the wall, to see if I'm still here. And I am.

———

At Primrose Gully, a night of the most perfect stillness, hardly a sound, colossal wheeling fields of stars, and very late a small bright moon, lying on its back.

———

Reading Judges 5, a murder story with wonderful repetitions: 'At her feet he bowed, he fell, he lay down: at her feet he bowed, he fell: where he bowed, there he fell down dead...'

———

Woke slowly from a fading dream. It seemed that what woke me was a long, calm, sweet note, as from a bell. I lay there, still, in a state of perfect calm, joy, wellbeing.

———

Two Frenchmen chattering about sausages. One says he knows a

butcher who makes andouillettes. The other jumps in the air and
runs for his pen to write down the address.

'I'm not sure...'

'I'll find it. I'll find it if it takes all day.'

First time I've ever heard French people talking about food
without getting cranky.

———

After seeing M in *The Cherry Orchard* I woke up wanting to write
Chekhov a tremendous and humble fan letter. An excruciating love
for the play: its moods, its changes of tone, the appalling funniness
of its non sequiturs.

———

There must be something seriously the matter with me, that I go
on and *on* being sick. I finally went to the STD clinic and asked for
an AIDS test. Spent hours there, saw a doctor and a counsellor and
was comforted, then a skilful girl jabbed me. I watched. The blood,
surprisingly liquid, like ink, filled the tube. I saw all my prominent
veins. Away I bounced, with new virtue.

———

Windy day, ragged grey clouds flee across a denser grey ceiling, no
sun. Still sick. Made a soup.

———

Reading V's new book. I find it quite mystifying—much less 'funny'
than the earlier one—I don't know what the hell he's doing in it.
And as I read I get the weird feeling that one day I simply won't
know him any more: not that we will 'part', but that he will go
back to being him and I will go back to being me, our contact will
cease to exist; thus, that it has never existed except in our separate
imaginations. Thoughts neither pleasant nor unpleasant. *Do* I know
him? It's all mutual simultaneous projection. I've never seen and
will never see his bed, his table, his chair. How strange.

———

But the bright freshness of his writing, its muscle, its dazzling turns. Carved free of cliché. Scrubbed till it hurts. There is nothing spontaneous about it. Everything is worked, tense, intense; compressed, packed hard. 'Evidence of struggle', he calls it. His incredible detachment. I'm the opposite: I'm close in all the time.

———

'People who are scared of going into therapy,' says S's husband, 'have an image of all their repressed stuff as volcanic—as if it would explode out as soon as they took the lid off. But really it's geological, like those diagrams of rock formations we had to draw at school. You have to dig your way in.'

———

The *Sydney Morning Herald* reports that 'two yellowing envelopes containing the dusty remains' of Dante have gone missing from the National Library in Florence. No one seems to remember having seen them since 1929.

———

I suppose that in my work he doesn't really understand what I'm talking about.

———

At the library I worked for an hour and a half. Every few minutes I felt an urge to bolt but I gritted my teeth and slogged on. After a while the stiff brain began to move, and to produce ideas.

———

Puzzling in the car about a woman we know who left her small children and ran away with another guy. O says, 'I don't judge her for it. I think that one's first duty is to oneself, but—' 'But with children that young,' says R, 'they're still an extension of oneself.' In the back seat I am quiet, but astonished again at people's ability to say things like 'One's first duty is to oneself' or 'I've got very strong ideas about individuality'. I suppose I too live according to certain beliefs, without ever stating them clearly to myself or to others.

———

Hard to remain in *integrity* while waiting.

———

He fell asleep with his face almost touching mine: face to face on the pillow: the little cool wind of his breath.

———

'I've realised,' said R, 'that everything that's beyond the physical world, all those moments of illumination or insight—*that's* God. That's what God *is*. And dogma gets in the way.' The born-again would say that some of those moments were the devil.

———

I got off the plane at 5.15 to find a perfect autumn evening. I feel like a wayward woman who returns to her normally grouchy husband and finds him charming, after all and for no apparent reason. I mean Melbourne, this place I seem to be tying myself to with *property* when all my real urges push me north to where he is.

———

I dinked M home after lunch. We laughed at memories of my dinking her to kinder as a very little girl—singing behind me about witches and 'a very dang'rous frog'.

———

'By soul I mean, first of all, a perspective rather than a substance, a viewpoint towards things rather than a thing itself.' —James Hillman, *Archetypal Psychology*

———

The panic of starting a piece of work. I can't sit still. Any distraction will do.

———

At my kitchen table G talks at length about a young woman with whom he is about to have an affair.

'What do you want?'

'I want to own her.'

———

Men sweeping the street. The plane trees drop immense drifts of large, brown, twisted, claw-like leaves. The men sweep without speaking, but when the truck comes they all begin to yell and roar.

———

There's no laughter between lovers that's as precise and deep and full of genuine mirth as that between two people who are no longer a couple.

———

My new black lace-ups. One man calls them 'gumshoes', another says they look like 'two little Cadillacs'.

———

Back to the VD clinic where I'm told that my AIDS test was negative. Felt less elation than I did upon skipping down the clinic steps after the blood had left my arm.

———

Dreamt that a man came and sat opposite me in a cafe booth. He handed me his very small child. It sat peacefully on my knee.

———

Review of V's book: 'a triumph'.

———

On my way up the stairs to the party in Brunswick I heard someone sloppily playing an acoustic guitar and a girl singing a Beatles song. Reached the top and found that the player was G. He is a wonderful guitarist but was too drunk or stoned to use his fingers, also what on earth was he doing at this academics' jamboree? When I left he came with me. Rain was pouring. He was on a roll, raving unstoppably. In Lygon Street I picked up two hitchhikers. The girl was 'a beautiful blonde'. I saw G register her appearance. The air pressure in the car palpably changed. The two kids hopped out but G continued to rave: what bar should we go to, what club? I drove on with a scornful grin: 'I'm not going to any fucking club. I'm bored. I want to go home.' 'Oh yes, but you're in love,' he said crossly. At my place I put on my hideous flannelette nightie and crawled under the doona. He tucked me in and lay down beside me on top of the bedclothes in his suit and shoes, talking non-stop, laughing and making me laugh. 'Ah, Hel. I love the way you remember things. When I was last in Paris,' he said, 'I went to look at that street you used to live in, back in the 70s, rue du Docteur Heulin, remember when I came and visited you there?' He kept stroking my forehead and making much of me and saying, 'Don't *frown*.' Just as I was slipping off to sleep he sprang up and said, 'I'm gonna call a cab.' Next thing I knew it was morning and his wife was ringing from Sydney and he was nowhere to be seen.

———

Dreamt I met some black people in a sloping garden. Women made me welcome, but in a reserved manner. We all got out our scissors and sewing gear and began to perform small stitching, snipping and mending tasks together. I felt honoured to be accepted by them.

———

These ridiculous interviews V's doing about his novel. *I* should interview him. I'd ask him, 'What is an idea? What is a large idea and what is a small one? Which are the structural ones and which ones is the structure carrying?'

———

Awake in the early morning, fears about this movie—that there won't be enough *events*, that my idea is only a framework, that it lacks *flesh*. I love tiny little scenes, barely a paragraph on paper but on screen an image of power and meaning: the sky through the struts of the Harbour Bridge, or in *Heimat* the soldier's fine hair flying up on the wind of the explosion, or Maria riding towards the camera on her bike. Small, small, small. Irritation of not knowing who I am aiming the outline at makes it harder to do. I am tempted to pull back all requests for funding and to write it quietly on my own—so I can shape it as I like, and as *it* wants. To do this I will have to be poor or else grab some journalism. 'You could write something for the *Age*, couldn't you?' says V. 'Yes,' I say, 'except I only like doing journalism that involves dead bodies.'

———

'Give me a lecture on structure, quick.' 'Structure. Right.' I feel him go into his favourite mode: advice. 'Structure should be like a birdcage. Light, strong, big enough to hold everything you need to put in it. But you have to be able to see straight through it.' The elegance of this image conceals its lack of practical instructiveness.

———

M did not introduce the boy to me but I was struck by his friendly manner, frequent eye contact etc. He is a very Teutonic-looking boy. Or rather *man*. The other girls arrived, great shrieks, I faded out their back door and rode away, the superfluous mother. A bit painful, but I have other fish to fry.

———

Three women in the kitchen, a long conversation about hair, should P have hers cut or not? I broke into our engrossment and said, 'Is this neurotic?' 'No!' said P. 'It means something. A circle means something different from a triangle. The shape of your hair affects the outline of your body, where it connects with the rest of the world.' I would give large sums for a tape of that conversation, its movement, tones, pauses; our concentration. Could I ever invent it?

———

I am labouring with groans, tears and blank spots on this screenplay. The father offers her the tank water and she gracelessly refuses. Less afraid, after a morning's work. In the street, looking at ordinary people working, driving, going about their business, I thought, 'This is my job. This awful, painful struggle is *what I do*, it is my part and I must play it, it is the price I pay for months of *not* working, the luxury of freedom. No one can give me orders. I must do it all myself.' The loneliness of this.

———

A happy and cheerful day visiting my parents at Ocean Grove. Dad and I chopped wood and went for a '2.5 km walk'. M and dog and I drove to the beach, dark sky, strong cold wind, long waves breaking and throwing back huge manes of spray. We sang all the way home. Felt blessed, fortunate, optimistic.

———

In a book on intimacy and marriage I read remarks on affairs. The introduction of a lover, unbeknownst to one partner, gives the ailing relationship a short breathing space...then, if the affair is serious, it either repairs the marriage or pushes it to dissolve.

———

A walk in a country town. The quieter the place and the happier the day, the softer our voices when we speak. Man: 'I won't live as long as you. I just know I won't live to be old. I'll be lucky to reach sixty—' Woman: 'Oh, look! Rollerskating! And they've got *music*!'

———

Daydreaming is necessary. In float the objects, the patterns and thoughts. Peculiar material rises to the surface. I see where I can use my dreams. I'm surprised by what appears on the page: it's like poetry, coming from somewhere my thinking mind doesn't know about.

———

At R's house I take a mandarin and go out into the yard. A child's voice somewhere above me: 'Hello!' I look up and see a small blond boy high in a sapling that looks hardly strong enough to bear his weight. He says he is waiting for his brother and R's daughter to come back from the library. I hand him the mandarin and say, 'They're already back. They're inside, reading. How come you didn't go?'

'I don't like Tintin books. I'm going to stay up here and wait for them to come and find me.'

'I won't say a word,' I reply, but I think, 'They won't come looking for you. You are a gooseberry.'

———

A very sexy, very good-looking woman strolls past, in cowboy boots with metal trimmings. Women like her walk *really slowly*. Whereas women like me walk as fast as they can, with the aim of becoming a blur.

R shows me an account of philosophy's 'moral man', whose qualities (according to Kant and Schopenhauer, she says) include the belief that women are unable to make moral judgments but act only according to what pleases them. It is quite clear however that men who espouse these stern views *would die* unless women did their emotional living for them. Is this why some men go berserk when their wives leave them? Because they are unable to perform for themselves certain functions of living?

Lindy Chamberlain is pardoned.

A fresh, clear morning: pink light on buildings: an edge on the air.

The producer came to talk with me about this movie. I find her useful in that she is not ashamed to ask the really obvious questions—the kind of necessary, grounding questions that I don't ask myself for fear of *losing height*.

The bus to the city wound its slow route along streets full of trees, and up through the Cross and down William Street, on which it picked up a young couple, dark, curly-haired, foreign-looking, cheerful, liking each other, the woman holding a small boy of six months or so. The mood of the bus lightened and lightened, to a point where *'dans mon euphorie'* I thought it would take off into the sunny air and roar into the sky on the combined beams of the passengers' high spirits.

Hearing that my letters have all been thrown away—a blast of liberation—even *that* past is gone, whisked away from behind me almost as soon as it happens—everything is now now NOW.

He spoke of himself as only men can: as if he were speaking of someone else. 'The power, the intensity that's in my work…' Would a woman ever speak with such detachment, or use such words, about her own work?

———

Yesterday I felt lonely. I knew that he would not leave her. I forgot that I did not want to be his wife. A failure of imagination. I did not feel beautiful. I longed to be asleep. Woke, heard rain falling quietly outside, felt the desolation of my position. I thought about Primrose Gully, the room with the table, hearing rain there, looking out at rain falling, the healing of it. I need to go home.

———

The speakers in the movie mustn't answer each other. Not directly. There's always a little slide, every time. And a subtext. It's so *hard*.

———

'Whenever I get to a dream in a novel,' says V, 'I lose interest.'

———

Went to Gas & Fuel to order a new hot water service. Girl: 'Is it urgent? I'll see if it can be done this week.' (*Returns*) 'The lady said, "Is it the writer?" She's read one of your books. We can deliver it tomorrow.'

———

Lindy Chamberlain interviewed on TV. We sat forward. Her face is thin, extremely good-looking—a wide range of expressions— a very attractive mouth, pretty nose, good strong white regular teeth—striking eyes—very skilfully made-up—and out of this chic and elegant face issues an Australian woman's voice, flat-vowelled, nasal, harsh, with oddly self-dramatising inflections and aggressive intonations. At times she wept and this moved me. I admired her courage in continuing but it also frightened me. Her eyes show a tremendous power. At a distance they seem to darken and narrow. When she laughs, though, she is just a pretty woman laughing—a lovely sight—and her wrinkles fan out from her eye corners in an attractive way.

P took me to Heide to see a show of paintings about childhood. Mostly Blackmans, but some fabulous Joy Hester ink things, some Fred Williams which I loved, and notably a couple of thick, juicy, dark, frightening paintings by Albert Tucker of his son—on a trike, in a high chair, his eyes lazy, almost evil, his cheeks dark red and puffy, his hair flopping thickly. 'There,' said P, 'is a man who hates children.'

'God, I had a hangover,' says the man in the cafe. 'When I took the dog for a walk I spewed in the gutter. The dog tried to eat it but I kicked him in the guts.'

I heard a gospel song in the car and a rush of Christian moral scruples came over me: 'If I gave him up I would be a more virtuous person, more correct, more calm, more blessed.' This kind of thing, which attracts me at times, is almost a death wish, a nothing wish, a blankness wish—like wishing that we could all *like each other's work*, that there should be no *conflict*. The LIFE of life. No laws apply.

My father strides past the window. I know it's him because of the coins jingling in his pockets.

At Primrose Gully shooting with a visitor's .22. The high-velocity bullets passed straight through a beer can on a post without even setting it rocking. We thought we'd missed. Went to take it off the post and saw three holes in it. Question: who fired the shots that struck it? We go inside laughing. A moon rises. P is driving up tonight. I've left a candle for her in the small window, though the moon is so bright she'll hardly need it.

I would like to know how to give an injection, stop bleeding, deal with snakebite, set limbs. Just in case.

A koala is climbing out on a thin branch not far from my desk window. Pleasant stink of kero heater. Crickets. As evening approaches the sky clears, except for pink and lavender streaks low down over the farmer's place. There'll be a strong moon tonight. Since the visitor got rid of the rat, the mice have returned. Their meek shuffle and pit-a-pat.

————

Think I've broken the back of the screenplay draft. The speed and force of the thing's arrival, when it comes. When will I learn and accept that the anguish phase is a necessary part of the process?

————

I began Bernhard's *Concrete* and to my surprise find it hilarious. The cover blurb says, 'His views on life are fascinatingly introspective, profoundly human and strikingly provocative.' They are also cranky, evil-tempered, pathetic, unstable, choleric, mad, and so exaggerated as to be comical, but no hint of this is given on the cover.

————

P asked me what I thought was the purpose of life.
   'Do you mean each person's life, or life in general?'
   'Any way you like.'
   An answer rose smoothly to my mind.
   'I reckon it's everyone's responsibility to clean up their act. To do some work on themselves. So they won't be an obstruction to the progress of the good. Does that sound...?'
   Astonished, now, by this statement. Is it glib? What's 'the good'? And is it making progress?

————

P comes home from work, her mouth all hard with tiredness. I make a fire and cook a meal. I enjoy 'making things nice' for her. We eat, listen to *Scripsi of the Air*, play a record.

————

I paid for Primrose Gully with a bank cheque. A woman in ridiculous boots stood beside me at a cafe counter and I was so elated about owning three acres that I wanted to kneel down and put my forehead on their pointy toes. Everything I saw was beautiful, the sun was shining in air so cold I was still wearing gloves at lunchtime. I felt berserk, as if I should be very careful. Not to go mad. How on earth can I thank my self-effacing benefactor for this gift? I'll write to her: 'Dear Queensland. The days are sunny, the nights are white with stars. I don't know why you're doing this, but I rejoice, I am ever in your debt.'

———

A reading last night with Gerald Murnane. He is brilliant: a terrific density of personality. He reads those long complex sentences with a tremendous concentrated energy. The *inwardness* of what he writes. Overwhelmed with respect.

———

At lunchtime drove M to Dimmey's and bought her a double doona. Adored her company: she had a little hangover, chattered at length, an account of the evening before: 'I don't know how I can be hungover—I only had a glass of red wine and four pots.' She breaks off, after half an hour of rambling, vivid discourse, and says, 'It's not really a story—I'm just telling you what we did.' This seemed a sophisticated remark about narrative and I wrote it down.

———

Today, or maybe yesterday, was the first time I began to think about death. I mean *my* death: being dead, in a closed box, buried. I did not like this thought at all, and was afraid of rotting.

———

The strongly and seriously married couple invited me to dinner. I am old enough to be their mother. I belong to a different species—like a wild beast, scarred with loneliness and nasty experiences. I often have to bite my lip not to say cynical things about sex and couples. Perhaps they think I'm a lost soul. Perhaps I am. I lay on their sofa and watched her cooking: her smooth skin, contented sober expression of concentration, her pretty lavender cotton top—felt a little bliss, watching her and being looked after.

———

The awful attraction of cop shops, those hard-faced men, their comfortless echoing rooms, the lost and disappeared children notices with their tragic blurred snaps. I could loiter there all day, staring and sucking it in.

———

Dreamt I tried on a beautiful coat with perfect shoulder pads. Into the back of it were set irregularly shaped panels of something red and glassy that shone. I looked fabulous in it. I tried it on with a hat of the same colour, also with a sparkling jewel.

———

We went up the river in the boat. River the colour of tea. Sound of the ocean on the other side of the bar like the sounds of war.

———

The wife reports a dream: 'I met a man whom I loved instantly. This man had the power to stop time.'

———

It's easy for me to get lost. I wander in peculiar minefields of doubt and anxiety, arguing with myself, training and disciplining myself, thinking up worst things and planning how I will assimilate them without bitterness.

———

The former politician dies in a hotel room, at sixty, of a heart attack. A cop tells *Truth* he died with a 'loaded' condom on: 'he died happy'. On the plane I sit beside an eighty-year-old lady who tells me she's his sister-in-law, on her way to his funeral. A nice, funny, direct old woman. I long to say, 'Listen. I love a man. He's married to someone else. What will become of me?' But why would she know?

———

Someone showed me how to fax my copy to the magazine. 'How long will it take?' 'It's already there.' I was struck dumb with wonder.

F reads the screenplay. His comments are very frank, very open, a painful picture of me as I was in that marriage. His generosity: 'You know you have my imprimatur, whatever you do or write.' Now I'm aware of sadness under everything, the churning up of old matter, and the realisation that the draft is very rough and that it will need a good deal of hard, concentrated work, both technical and emotional, before it's done.

Uncle Vanya at Anthill. The closedness of the play, the imprisoned characters, the wild despair of Vanya's outburst.

Mild sunlight on grass that's blond in winter, flattened in patches as if roos had been lying on it with their great awkward haunches. Stillness on the opposite ridge when I tramped over it with the dog. Sound of the river getting louder the higher we went. Over the spur to its other curve. The logic that leads you to the river. If I were with V, living together, would I still have this occasional, very powerful sense of freedom? And self?

From a review of Jessica Anderson's short stories: '...we are made to see the futility of trying to prolong an affair beyond its natural limits, and how little an outsider—even an ardent lover—can ever know of what actually binds a husband and wife together.'

When the coffin was brought in at the front of the church the man beside me said in a horrified whisper, 'Is that *it*? Is that the *coffin*?' 'Yes.' He turned paler and paler, in his black coat. 'I didn't know they brought it *in*. Will you stay next to me all through?'

V says he 'doesn't believe in jealousy'. This can only mean that he has (a) never experienced it or (b) managed always to give it some other name.

———

Dreamt that on a big ship, a liner, some rats were a nuisance. A campaign against them, but then, moulting and half stunned, they stood about nonchalantly on the carpets. I threw one overboard. It turned on its back, gave me a calm, insolent look, and was towed away by a girl in a boat.

———

F's notes on the movie give a very disagreeable picture of me: 'the artificial turbulence she needs in order to function'. I see myself as tense, fast, always moving—screechy. How awful. For years I went on behaving exactly as if I *wasn't* married. And then later when I started to try to be married it was too late. I became pathetic. A pathetic creature.

———

A woman calls her sister. 'What are you doing?'
    'Threading a needle.'

———

'Don't drop that on the floor or I'll drop *you*.' Man behind me to his three-year-old daughter.

———

Willpower is required to keep pathos from aggregating around certain symbolic objects: *an open suitcase*. 'I only ever saw her in rented or borrowed rooms, the small suitcase neatly packed, the cotton clothes folded.'

———

Is it possible to develop a voice in writing with such coherence and quiet authority that I can do away with narrative structure? (Plot?) In the dream story, all that's holding it together now is the voice, and maybe the imagery—holding it together against its own tendency to fragment, to fly apart. The pieces want to return to *some other order*—not with each other—but I compel them quite quietly to hold together *my way*.

———

My heart feels too light, as if it were growing too high in my chest. It keeps giving spasms of high fluttering. I wonder if I am ill and about to die.

———

I go to Z's house, it's got a new front door with a mail slot. I bend down and see him sitting there on the couch in the sun, neatly reading—he hears my knock, hops up to let me in. 'I was about to make some coffee and eat an orange.' We do this together.

———

V says every man is a moral coward. He's trapped. Trapped between two forms of partial death. How *fascinating*.

———

Gerald Murnane in a review: 'Of those three distinctively human activities, laughing, crying and thinking, the third is most often ranked highest, and books that provoke thought likewise. I do not agree with these rankings. I even wonder, as Robert Musil wondered, whether the best kind of thinking is only a subtle kind of feeling.' These remarks make me think that one writes only *as one can*, as one's character allows and equips one to…that theories and beliefs are superimposed, almost irrelevant.

———

'I've already told you about Cubism,' says V.
    'Yes,' I say, 'but I've forgotten.'
    He raises his eyes to heaven.
    'I know it's terrible, but think about it this way—you'll never bore me because I forget everything you say.'
    He takes a deep breath. 'Well. You know how you *look* at something…'
    I can't help it. I laugh out loud.

———

R was awake and came downstairs saying, 'If you think I was waiting up for you, I was.' I don't know how she does it but I always feel, within three minutes of arriving in her presence, as if she's said,

'Here. Give me that *huge bundle* you're carrying, put it down here and we'll have a look at what's in it.'

———

The born-again had an asthma attack at 4 am, very bad, taken to hospital in an ambulance—masks, drips, the full catastrophe. At 9 am, having made a fast recovery, he was sent home wearing pyjamas and a jumper, that's *all*. Bare feet! In this weather! He looked awful when I got there—white, with dopy eyes, lying bereft under his wretched Christian single doona, on his Christian single bed. He said, 'Give us a hug?' I took off my runners and got under the bedclothes and cuddled him from behind for an hour or so while he told me what had happened. We both had our feet on the hot water bottle; it was really quite nice. Every now and then he'd give a sigh and say, 'Thanks, Hel.' At a certain point he dozed off and I lay there thinking, 'What am I *doing* here? Lying fully dressed in a single bed in a furnished room in St Kilda with a born-again Christian at 12 o'clock on a weekday?' His budgie's cage was beside the bed. It kept making its fidgety little noises, ringing its bells, whistling tunes.

———

Dreamt I was in a little country town. Its streets were running and filling with water. 'A flood!' I shouted. 'Isn't it beautiful! I've never seen one before!' Shining water dripped off roofs, the streets were flowing.

———

Went to lunch with a feminist academic. Odd to feel so at ease with someone who proudly declared that she had never read Chekhov, and advised me to 'give Dostoyevsky a miss'.

———

The biographer's falsely courteous, reasonable manner while she's destroying my character: by means of her sweet tone, her disarming smile, she makes me ashamed of the violent emotions her words are provoking in me. She says that if she'd been one of the people I've written about she would have sued me. 'It could be thought that I can't bear your success, but I think your books are outrageous. They should never have been published.' My left cheek begins to burn. I go on listening, nodding, saying 'Mmmm,' when truly I want to upend the cafe table and throw her against the wall. 'Can you listen to any more of this?' she asks, in that sweet voice. 'Are you feeling…glazed?' She moves to the chair beside me, seizes my wrist in one gloved hand and holds it firmly, turning her face away and looking out the window. 'I'm only saying these things because I'm so *fond* of you. I'm feeling *fondness* for you.' A curtain of red descends before my eyes. 'You said that to me once before—remember? On the phone one night, ten years ago? You told me all my faults. That I was a bad mother. That you didn't want your daughter to play with mine any more—that my daughter smelt. And you kept interrupting yourself by saying, "I'm only saying this because I'm *so fond of you*."' She lets go my hand, stands up, begins to put on her coat, looking down at her buttons as she fastens them. 'That's awful,' she says. 'That was disgusting.' She has had nothing to eat or drink. I pay for my coffee. Out on the street we stand looking helplessly at each other. I say, 'Let's shake hands.' 'Of course.' Her hand in its soft glove is all knobbly, from the arthritis. This hurts me. I turn, she turns, we walk away in opposite directions. As I walk I think, 'She's right. What I do is bad and wrong. I'll have to learn some other way of writing.'

———

'You are a vulnerable person,' writes the old professor on a postcard, 'to people like her, who need to…who are drawn to HURT others to EASE the pain in their own hearts, who see you as a rewarding TARGET, i.e. you are a CREATIVE PERSON—you are so sensitive that they believe they will get from your response the satisfaction they CRAVE. Keep out of the way. Never reply. Listen to Prelude No. 24 in B Minor of Book I of the *48 Preludes and Fugues* by J. S. Bach. It says everything.'

'You've got a reputation,' says O, 'as a bitch and a slob, and a lot of other things. I won't tell you some of the things that have been said to me. Fuck 'em. Just keep going. But don't think your friends aren't jealous of you. *I* am.'

The Nolans at the NGV. First time I ever cared about Ned Kelly. Peculiar effect of the clusters of brass buttons on the policemen's uniforms. They glow, and seem to mean something to me.

In George's import department with G. We saw a fabulous big stiff black shirt with white spots. H: 'Guess how much.' G: 'Ummm...a thousand?' H: (*triumphantly*) '$3245.' He sat near the window on a curlicued gilt chair and I stood beside him, we looked down at Collins Street, spoke as intimately as if we were in a private living room. No one bothered us. I kept thinking, 'This would be a terrific scene in a movie.' 'I don't remember my dreams at all,' he says, 'at the moment. I feel as if I'm going through all sorts of parallel experiences that I know nothing about.' He confesses to something I don't even want to write down. 'Nobody knows. You're the only one.' This strange connection between us. *Mon semblable, mon frère.* When I let him off with his bag at Bourke Street he takes my face in both hands and kisses me.

Radio Days at the Rivoli with my sister. We laughed and cried. The girl comes out of the bathroom with a towel round her head and mimes the Cuban song on the radio. The two men come in and watch, she performs for them, they sing the chorus and mime the actions—how much fun they're having, playing and fooling around. It's true, TV's ruined everything: it's smashed the family, nobody looks at each other any more.

At the International, two Italian men stand at the huge window on to St Georges Road, talking quietly. Their voices, bass and baritone, are inflected more beautifully and casually than any Australian's could ever be: our voices are made for explanation and argument, theirs for song. The world outside is dry and bright, as if there were no air—the houses *exist*, in purest clarity, radiant and perfect, as they would exist to someone about to fall down in an epileptic fit, or to die.

Reading accounts that writers send to the Literature Board of their promotion of self and of 'Australian literature', I shrivel up, long to disappear and work silently in some unnoticed corner. Will I have to make 'pronouncements' on this flamin' US tour?

T's got a job sewing costumes at the opera. 'Five twelve-metre curtains made of some slithery synthetic substance. It was like trying to carry armloads of water.'

Couldn't fall asleep for hours last night. I had too many shoulders and hips, my breathing was too noisy and in the wrong rhythm.

On the plane a businessman's wife: she is working hard at being with him, dancing attendance—dressed up, anxious, not relaxed, very focused on her husband—wanting to do the right thing, to be an asset, but not knowing how, not being part of his world: afraid of losing his attention, which anyway she has not got. She's there on sufferance, as a favour.

The literature professor, before he fell asleep at the dinner table, invited me to be writer-in-residence at Sydney University next year. I have also been invited to ANU, and to the Defence Force Academy.

'There are plenty of people,' says V, 'I mean really good, really *top class* people—who won't have a bar of psychoanalysis.' A chill comes over me. Afraid of his mind. Sadly I imagine the deflation of this love, its collapse into something bumpy, discourteous, disappointing, regretful.

———

Up at Primrose Gully O, who has a cold, lies under the doona all day. While I busy myself looking after him, making things clean and nice, lighting the stove to make him a soup, he says in a tone I can't quite describe, 'The story of how you got the money to buy this place is too good to be true.'

———

The mezzo in the Mahler is slim and stately in a strange black dress with a fitted top in metallic material and a long velvet skirt. V: 'Why don't *you* get a dress like that?' He carries on with a joke that all the women present must be green with envy of her. How peculiar men are—they like to sow discontent.

———

Horrible massacre in Clifton Hill. A young man who lives behind the station runs amok with weapons, kills six people, injures a dozen. I see his photo and get a creepy feeling that I know him or once even taught him, though this is impossible.

———

How on earth could he leave her, this blameless, kind, funny, faithful woman?

———

'I love intellectuals who *hesitate*,' says the nun.

———

Will the woman who's meeting my plane in Wellington recognise me? I should have said, 'I'm a small, crabby-looking woman in a cheap black suit.'

———

The old poet's house was at the top of a very high hill. I had to puff and pant to climb the steps. In her pretty living room we drank wine from pottery cups and looked out over a harbour, a mountain and a great deal of sky. She was intensely likeable, a grandmother, very intelligent, very powerful. Tall, a big face with a big mouth and teeth, lipstick. I felt very lucky to have met her, and glad not to have chickened out of the visit. Talking about a difficult man we both knew, she wondered if his solitary and very privileged upbringing had left him without what most people learn in bigger families—'the experience of defeat'.

From the plane, broken cloud like blips in hot porridge. Clouds white but in their folds a fine grey-blue, and on the sun side a delicate pink flush.

Romeo and Juliet. What a play. Bodies strewn about (one of them my daughter's), huge speeches, and in all that worked language such simple lines as 'Any man who can write can answer a letter.'

The indignity of a mammogram: one's breasts squashed flat between two pieces of hard plastic. Upset by it, and frightened.

Ate twelve oysters and went to see *Lohengrin* at the Opera House. A very clear, very cold evening, a ragged half-moon in an inky sky. The old professor was in one of his weird moods about sex and women. 'Look at that pretty girl,' I say, 'sitting on the steps. The one in the white dress and black pillbox hat.' He looks. Pauses. 'Do you think she'd eat a man up?' '*Tsk*. No. I think she's a pretty girl. That's all.'

I'd like to write something with weird time-pockets, layers etc. I know a bit about children. Funny how when I come to Sydney my mind works in a different way. I have better, freer ideas. Must remind myself that this is *because* I don't live here, rather than a reason for me to move here.

————

Headline: 'Man gets life for strangling musician.'

————

I'm crazy, moving around as much as I do. I must make this a RULE: do not accept invitations to GO anywhere.

————

I won a prize for the *Two Friends* screenplay. The cheque is made out by the Housing Department.

————

Ben Chifley used to say, 'Always make your decisions on moral grounds, and the details will fall into place.' Thus, 'if you go down, you go down on something you believe in.'

————

Awake at 4 am. Somewhere in the street a dog moans and yelps. I want to go out, find it, *shut it up.*

————

The hosts of the dinner party were eager to show me their word processor. I enjoyed this but was horrified to see the *alarm clock* that is necessary so people won't become too fascinated and get RSI— one of them already has it. At the table a woman talked about her sister, a nightclub dancer in Europe, who recently came home for a visit. 'She has a wonderful body,' she said, 'but she can't walk. Her muscles are all wrongly developed, for walking. She couldn't walk up the hill to the Kew library. She just couldn't.' 'I'd rather be able to do the cancan,' said another guest, 'than walk up the hill to the Kew Library.'

————

I made a speech at P's exhibition opening. I keep thinking about her new paintings, feeling wonderstruck. She left me a note on the kitchen table: 'I think we do such equivalent things in our respective ways, it was so nice having the paths cross as they did tonight; dovetailing together then off again.'

————

I saw at once that the small, exhausted schoolboy in the Fitzroy High jumper was coming to the end of a pretty rocky form-one year. He stood in the crowded tram at peak hour when kids aren't allowed to sit down and kept looking with secret longing at the empty seat beside me. I suffered from appalling maternal pangs, wanted to adopt him on the spot or at least be his foster mother for a couple of months until he grew a bit and got used to being in high school. Finally I said, 'Hey. Sit here.' He shot into that seat like a ferret down a rabbit's burrow.

———

Weird feeling, when I look at a photo of V that I took, that once again he does not exist, I have never met him, I have invented him, he is a FIGMENT. If a long enough silence should fall between us we would forget each other and slip back into our previous lives. Does he exist? No particular emotion accompanies these fancies. In fact it's a breathing space between bouts of reality. I don't miss him. How could I miss a flicker, a quick darkness. It would be easier if we never had any further contact with each other, but left each other's lives alone. He won't leave his wife, they'll live out the rest of their lives together, side by side, without passion but with a strong famili-arity, *used to each other*. What'll I do? I'll take up piano lessons again, learn to make plants grow, write novels. Summer will come. I'll grow older. I'll be happy. If I could be this calm, when we're apart, then we could live it properly, honour it, without causing smash-up, pain, grief, humiliation. On the other hand, this state seems unreal to me, a kind of nothing state, an interim—or like sleep, or death. '*First—chill—then stupor—then the letting go—*'

———

Breakfast with M on her eighteenth birthday. She keeps watching for 9.03 am, her 'birth minute', and when it comes we kiss each other on the lips. Later I buy her a strapless linen dress in which she is so beautiful that I gaze. My Mastercard is declined, I burst into a rage, we go for cash.

————

I'm cleaning the house. Even if V doesn't come, the place will be spotless. Coldish night. Scent of pittosporum and other blossoming plants stabs the air.

————

These nights I sometimes wake with a jolt for no apparent reason and lie here with my heart crashing and my limbs trembling.

————

Finally I tell G the identity of V. He says he's not surprised. 'I couldn't finish his book. I didn't care about the character.'

'It took him seven years to write that book.'

'Seven *years?*'

————

While I'm in America, V is going to Africa. My fantasy: he doesn't come back. I find out from someone that he's lost. I fly to Sydney and say to his wife, 'Come on. We've got to go and find him.' She won't come, flatly refuses, but when the me character gets to the airport, there she is. The two women set out. The conversations they could have! The silences, resentments, outbursts. And quieter passages: they have to share a bedroom in some shit hotel, two single beds, they lie parallel, like sisters, exhausted, angry, frightened. One begins to talk...would there be flashbacks? Voice-over? Flashbacks that don't match what's being related in the voice-over because each of them is having to embroider the truth.

————

Seeing V's raincoat on my hall chair. He makes a phone call in my kitchen while I'm washing my shirt in a bucket. I keep looking back over my shoulder through the window. He is holding the phone *in my kitchen*.

————

Early in the morning P and I meet at the open back door. Outside it a bird is singing, very loud. We look at each other happily.

————

Gerald Murnane gives a speech in which he describes an experiment he performed on himself: he takes off the shelf books he's read and sets himself to recall as much as he can of each one. Often his memories are, he says, no more than moods, or what he calls 'the memory not of the book itself but of the experience of reading'.

'That's exactly how *I* remember books I've read,' I say. 'I always thought it meant I was a sloppy reader.'

'But surely,' says V, 'he's only talking about minor works. Think about something really great. Proust for example. I remember all kinds of absolutely specific things.'

'Like a woman changing her shoes?'

'Yes, or Charlus arriving.'

'Or the page whose head's like a tomato.'

'Or an experience of time passing. See? He's only talking about *minor* stuff.'

At Abu Dhabi airport. As I emerge from the tunnel into the weird tiled womb of the airport transit and duty-free I wish I had someone with me to whom I could say, 'Look! A stately pleasure dome.'

Heathrow. At security a grey-haired Sikh woman turned to go back through the beeper arch. All the white guards, male and female, set up a cry: 'Stay! Stay here! Go back! Stay here!' The one who was holding my bag continued to call out, long after the woman had grasped and corrected her mistake, 'STAY. STAY. SIT. SIT. STAY.' One of his colleagues said affably, 'She's not a collie, you know.'

Paris. A knock on door at 7.30 am, three young men looking for my host. I go down the hall to wake him. At his bedroom door I realise they're right behind me in their soft shoes. H: *'C'est pour quoi?'* 'Police,' says the second one, showing his ID. My host springs out of bed, making unconvincing gestures of innocence—rolled eyes, widespread arms. Two of the detectives are pleasant, the other who follows me everywhere and watches me with a dull, aggressive eye is an expressionless thug, broken nose etc. I sit on the couch in my nightie, he loiters by the door, suddenly says *'Vous aussi, vous faîtes l'usage de drogues?'* *'Moi? Bien sûr que non.'* The cute one with the dark brown curly hair tries on my host's hat, admires himself in the big poofy gold-framed mirror: *'Ça me va?'* He asks for my passport, copies details into his notebook. Sense of unreality, yet familiarity. Their extreme Frenchness; except for the broken-nosed one they are courteous in a blunt way. The leader even waves me goodbye as they take my host out the door. *'Mais c'est pour quoi?'* I say. The cute one says, *'Oh .. des stupéfiants. C'est une affaire.'* All the while, though rather palpitating, I can't wait to tell this to my sister.

———

Terrible Paris. The four-digit price tags at Galeries Lafayette, the overkill of display. One feels one lacks some essential female quality. So much elegance and beauty: fine limbs, perfect skin, hairless legs, massed hair. How plain I am: big-footed, small-mouthed: a sense of having to summon up other resources. I long for Australia, the thinness and modesty of things. I gnash my teeth to be missing the lilacs at Primrose Gully. When I get back it'll be snake season. Still, walking along rue Vieille du Temple last night, tired, sad, lonely, pointless, I heard music from a record shop—a piano, someone playing Bach, the *Little Notebook* pieces, I thought—didn't recognise the pianist, stood in a doorway almost bawling—whoever it was used a lot more dynamics than say Glenn Gould would—asked the woman, she said, *'C'est Dinu Lipatti.'*

———

To Des Femmes, who published *Monkey Grip*. Beautiful office, wisteria trying to work its way in through the window frames. The manager tried to roll us but I couldn't help liking her because in spite of her glamorous and rather good-looking face, chic clothes etc, she had clunky ankles, large feet and bare legs that were dry and peeling.

'Les Murray, for example,' said the Australian politician's wife at the reception. 'He's called a poet. Not a writer, not a novelist, but a *poet*. You read his work, but what do you remember of it? Nothing. You couldn't quote a single line.' Stunned by her stupidity and ignorance.

Picasso Museum. I found the mentions of his many women frustrating because I couldn't know *what really happened*. The sequence of them alarmed me, the painful stories that must underlie the bland facts ('secretly accompanied by Marie-Thérèse'). I liked very much the little drypoint illustrations to Ovid's *Metamorphoses*—especially I loved the tiny sketch he'd put in the frame of each one—a face, an arm, two schematic bodies.

On TV a video clip of Mick Jagger and a beautiful brown girl actually (or apparently) fucking. I found it repellent, his revolting scrawny body, huge wriggling tongue—the attempt to shock in this lâche period of history—I kept thinking, 'He's too old to be behaving like this—it's undignified.'

Los Angeles. First newspaper headline we see: 'Hungry sailors barbecue mermaid.'

Before breakfast the agent and I were walking across the hotel's enormous garden towards the swimming pool when from our right came a loud, harsh, whirring sound—like a helicopter—getting louder and louder—it was the rattling of hundreds of windows in their frames, fifteen floors of them. The garden began to blur, the roses were a shivering red streak, the ground heaved under our feet. We stood still and threw our arms round each other. Sirens began to scream. We continued to the pool, laughing and running. A smiling old Japanese couple in kimono waved gaily to us from the other side of the garden; the woman spread her arms and mimicked swaying, the man climbed a tree and hung from a low branch by his four limbs like a sloth.

―――――

The poet praised my work. His praise made me ashamed, for I felt it was false.

―――――

Physical loneliness can derange a person.

―――――

I try to imagine V and me in New York. Two tiny figures arm in arm at the bottom of 'canyons of steel'.

―――――

The editor is terribly homesick: his wife has just given birth to their first child. We sit in an Ethiopian restaurant and begin to become friends. We speak of emotional things. I say, 'I've got this man. He's married. He lives in another town. I only see him every few weeks. Sometimes between those times I get the weird feeling that I've invented him, that he's a figment—and then when I see him again I'm shocked by his three-dimensionality, and his warmth, and the fact that he's got colours.'

 'Yes,' he says. 'When I rang my wife today I was amazed by how sweet her voice was.'

―――――

The cab turned into Stanford and passed through a small forest of eucalypts. The smell of them in the dry heat was intoxicating. I hung out the window with a lump in my throat.

―――――

The kind of artist V admires sets himself up with a wife, a companion who cushions him; he puts his head down and *works*. The awful privileges artists claim for themselves: to be waited on and for, protected, tolerated, and at the same time to be *left alone*.

―――――

For hours fighter planes have been screaming round in the sky over San Francisco and the water. The tearing noise they make—ripping the air—it makes my heart crash and I go trembly. In the street men look up, impassive; women look up and then at each other—some shake their heads, some smile, or laugh, or frown—meaning, 'They can't help themselves; but I don't like it.' Even when I'm lying on my bed mid-afternoon, their roaring and tearing makes me feel sick, my body seems to shrivel as they pass. In the post office, news passes as dotted letters on a screen: the US has sunk several Iranian ships in the Persian Gulf. Woman beside me in line follows the news with downturned mouth, then nods, as if to agree that *of course* Congress must not make the US Air Force withdraw within sixty days. I get a terrible desire to burst out sobbing with fear and ignorance.

I went into the poet's bedroom so he could brush fluff off my black jacket. I stood there in a little daze of luxury as he brushed and brushed. A photo on a shelf: two very young boys dressed for baseball, one plainly the poet himself, a face like a landscape, grinning, looking up adoringly at the other who is older, taller, his face half hidden by the peak of his cap. 'Is that your brother?' 'Yep.' 'What happened to him?' 'Oh, he killed himself. In 1971.' I remain silent. He keeps on firmly brushing.

I took hold of V's upper arm and felt the skin, the roll of relaxed muscle, *the bone*. The horror of death came to me: one day *he will die.* Is this why I suffer so stupidly when he is late? Because it's a rehearsal for his death? Is this what being an adult is? To grasp what death is? He will be put in a box, the box in a hole, dirt will be shovelled on him, and his body will become meat. Meanwhile I will be walking around in air, breathing it, moving in it, thinking of him in the dark rotting. Appalling horror of these thoughts, incoherence in the face of them. Dumb, stricken, dazed.

When he introduced me to his friend, the adventurous beauty, I felt humble and afraid. People like me, who aren't beautiful, fear beauty because it seems to be a guarantee of love. She and V and I walked together as far as the corner of the street, and she continued alone. Why is she alone and unhappy? I see that even beauty as stunning as hers is no guarantee of anything. Perhaps not even of itself.

———

Before he left he made sure I knew where the hotel's fire exits were. A room now without meaning. I lie awake hour after hour, listening to the ridiculous drama of sirens in empty streets—the classic crying and wailing, then the brusque blurting of the deeper, more urgent, the 'real' emergency horn.

———

Bus trip through the Bronx. Empty streets because of the rain. Great blocks of gutted buildings.

———

Dreamt I put my black jacket on a hanger over a car's windscreen. When I returned, pollen had collected on the jacket so thickly that it looked like gold braid.

———

Middletown, Connecticut. Sitting here in a 'clean, well-lighted place' with a window opening on to masses of turning leaves, the agent sitting quietly reading and smoking at the window; black branches, sky clearing; writing down what happened, trying to describe people. I love, and am loved. 'The sun is up/ and death is far away.'

———

On the Greyhound bus between Boston and Waltham a semi-comatose young man with a plastic hospital ID bracelet on his wrist, foam coming out of his nostrils, his eyes half-closed, crawls on all fours down the aisle.

———

The cab driver ripped us off and we had to hurry along Wooster Street to the theatre. Some boys in bovver boots were yelling *Sieg heil*! outside the building. We thought it was the play itself, then one of them turned towards us a white face crazed with something violent and I saw that it was real. Someone opened a door: 'Come in here.' We did, she pulled it shut and a crashing blow landed on it from outside: *Fucking faggots*!' The cops arrived with sirens whooping. The audience sat in rows rolling their eyes at each other, and the show began.

———

At the Rockefeller Center skaters were told to clear the rink while a man in an ice-mowing machine moved across the frozen surface in smooth, perfectly oblong sweeps. The treated path looked as I'd always imagined ice would look before I ever saw any: deep, a greenish silver.

———

Rain, in Chicago; and the black worker sings loudly a song about rain as he enters the clubroom he is about to clean.

———

A letter from F: 'Each time I hear the tunes of the *Little Notebook* I think of you struggling with the notes in that attitude of panic and "application" that you had in front of the piano, with your little head marking the beat, and it makes me a bit sad. I could have been more encouraging.'

———

I had my hair cut in Chicago by a guy called Benny Casino. As usual a haircut removed, distorted and replaced askew my self-image. When he finished I said, 'Can I take your photo?' This restored my power as looker.

———

I want to be home, writing.

———

A silver mist rises off the river.

———

I blew $200 on the most beautiful pair of brown boots. I rushed straight into a bar, threw myself on to a stool and ordered a margarita. The barman, Saleem, was from Karachi. Turns out he was a fellow shoe fetishist. He darted out the back and returned with a bag containing a pair he'd bought yesterday. We had a short but pointed colloquium on *heel height*.

———

A muggy, cool morning. Empty streets, the weird clustered skyline, the jade water of the Chicago River clashing with the grass-green of its banks.

———

Waiting, in silence, and in full knowledge and acceptance that what one is waiting for one may never get.

———

At Indianapolis airport this morning I pulled out of my head a single white hair.

———

After dinner the four of us, homesick, watched porn on the hotel room video. All these youthful healthy bodies jigging in fierce, mindless rhythms, faces gaping, mouths emitting stupid grunts or foul words. We laughed most at the dialogue. The sex itself made us sad.

———

'Either sit in the carriage or get out of it.' —Chekhov, *Notebook*

———

The flight home. Occasionally a town or city will appear miles below. One, through broken cloud, gave an impression of being a dozen or so comets, randomly scattered, moving in the same direction. After the Hawaii stopover a pleasant Australian girl called Libby takes the seat beside me. We talk quietly. I say, 'It's my birthday. Nobody knows. You can wish me—' She laughs and does. We both doze. When we wake to eat she says, 'I had a dream. You were in it.' Later I got a blood nose. Three oyster-sized clots ran down into my mouth and I spat them into a paper towel.

———

Home. Rain falling softly. Mad spring growth everywhere. Trees in my street heavy with leaves, a green tunnel. Thick greenness outside my window. I can put on a record. I can walk from room to room. Spent the entire day answering mail. I wrote thirty-nine letters.

———

How I know I have been to New York. A cold, rude tram conductor refused to change my $20 note. I took it back and sat down. He tried to put me off the tram. I said, 'I've offered to pay. You refused it. I'm not going to *walk*.' He went into a flurry of rule-stating and finger-pointing. I sat tight, astonished to find I neither blushed nor had heart palpitations. Small silence. Me: 'Do you have a system whereby I can give my name and address and pay later?' Conductor: (*still huffy but seizing at straw*) 'Yes.' Thus honour was satisfied.

———

Don't want to leave my house—sun enters it quietly, on angles which I have forgotten, then retreats to clouds and a wind shifts in damp leaves. I look at old notebooks, feel the freshness and usefulness of their contents: so I *am* working all the time, after all.

———

Saw M play Irina in *Three Sisters* at Anthill. Oh, its funniness, its awful sadness. She has presence, and power.

———

Dreamt I saw a line of trees along a fence, on a piece of land that was mine but that I had neglected. The trees fell over, all at once, sending up a cloud of dust and leaving a desolate landscape with little figures running about in dismay.

———

At the sink, washing up, I glance behind me as wind puffs in through the open back door; some cloth moves behind the table, at knee level, and I think there's a little girl in the room. But it's only the tablecloth, on the breath of air.

———

The Fatal Shore, about cannibalism in Tasmania: '...also off the thick part of the arms, which the inhuman wretch declared was the most delicious food'. The part of V in touching which I apprehended death.

———

Gardening at Primrose Gully. Sun, but fresh wind blowing. Walked to the eagle's nest carrying spade (snakes) and lump of wood (magpies)—saw none of either, though something whisked itself very fast back into the woodpile when I approached the tank. There's a nest in the hanging terracotta pot near the kitchen window. I climbed on a chair. Three speckled eggs, white with brownish-black markings like brushstrokes. A bird sang and sang in the tree near the veranda: an imitable song that I could almost whistle back to it, though less melodiously—a crude mimicry.

———

A review by Elwyn Lynn of Max Kreijn: 'He can let fractured light flicker across pale stone…The wall of hot rust; the paler ginger of the open trapdoor…' Art critics are obliged to work hard on *colour*.

———

P and I sunbake actively in the backyard. 'I'm going to get brown this summer,' she says. 'I don't care about the ozone layer.'

———

The desk girl says, 'Your friend's waiting up in your room.' The door is ajar. I push it open. He's asleep on the bed. Before I can even look at him he springs up, cheeks flushed, hair on end. I throw down my bag and leap on him.

———

Rain pours down. Lightning. A huge roll of thunder. He's telling me about his famous friend in England and his 'flat-chested, pug-nosed, short-sighted wife, a real sweetheart. She serves him.' I want to say, 'Does your wife serve you?'—not meanly, but because I need to know. I'm afraid that if she does, that this is what he needs and will continue to need so he can work. And before long he's saying, 'Do you think two writers can ever live together?' I hardly know what load this question is carrying.

———

Possibilities: this will run its course and subside. He'll sink back into his married life, its comfort, taking with him whatever he's learnt from this. But what about me? I tend this seed of fear, water it, *want* it to sprout.

———

I walk through shops, I look in windows, I am happy. Maybe this is what life *is*: constant change, constant attempt to balance one's needs with what is possible.

———

I notice that I have a menstrual cycle of about twenty-two days, lately. I do not want menopause to happen to me until it absolutely has to.

———

Dinner with the Little Sisters of Jesus, two French and one American, in their Richmond Housing Commission flat. Hot night, beautiful sky. Small cockroaches in the kitchen sink. Awful wine decanted from a cask into a Schweppes dry ginger bottle; a mound of food. One tells of a bag search at Customs: 'I was *red*! Like these carrots!' Another sang *'Je ne regrette rien'*, and we did special dancing. I was wearing my new dress with fishtail, they applauded when I twirled to make the peplum fly out. We had *fun*. By 9.30 we were all yawning.

———

Each time I go to see *Three Sisters* at Anthill the same thing happens: when Masha makes her confession of love and asks rhetorically, '*Is it wrong?*' the audience holds its breath. Everyone wants an answer to this question—even perhaps an absolution—but Chekhov won't give one. *There isn't one*. 'These things cannot be legislated.'

———

Clouds today like a layer of pale grey cream. And a north wind.

———

F's cat gets run over, but not killed. "E is in pieces. 'E is 'orrible to look at. 'E 'ad no—'is 'ead is in shambles.'

––––––

In a gutter I found an X-ray of somebody's…knee? A joint, anyway. Its shadowy bones. Painful that such an intimate photo should have been dropped in the street.

––––––

All V's jokes about men hating 'messes', 'trouble' etc. (Should I let him lend me $1000?)

––––––

Playing with their baby. His head as billiard ball: ivory colour, perfect smoothness. His alert look and profound, mature expressions.

––––––

I come home and find the gas on under the pea soup, the house full of a burning stink, back door wide open. At ten P and my sister burst in, hysterical with excitement, wearing crudely printed lapel stickers with made-up names: 'Blue Sapphire' and 'Ruby Rose'. They've been at a meeting of a New Age money-making scheme called the Golden Aeroplane. Blue Sapphire rushes straight to the phone to recruit another friend. Ruby Rose reports: 'There were people there stuffing money into their pockets. Someone asked me if I'd mind standing hand in hand in a ring going *OMMMM*. I said, "Look, I don't care *what* I do."'

––––––

The only way I can tell that time is passing is by noticing that my hair and fingernails are growing.

––––––

Women can endure things and keep going because our lives are made up of small practical physical tasks, and no matter how lonely or sad or humiliated you are you *do the dishes*, or wash the clothes, and you come to the end of a small task and see a small result.

––––––

There's a tremendous weight coming from somewhere, pushing me towards feeling that I'm being short-changed, that there's something humiliating in my situation. I hate it. I think it's wrong. I fight it. Because I'm happy, when I don't think about it in that way.

———

Two tasks: 1) to accept that someone loves me, and 2) to accept that at the same time I can be free.

———

In a *Times Literary Supplement* overview of Australian writing my work is described as 'Mills and Boon for bohemians'.

———

We argue about beauty, what it is. I try to explain my ideas about looking: how men have control of it, how in order to be an artist or a writer a woman has to overcome her sense of herself as an object, has to usurp something. V's opinion is that in visual art, depicted figures 'dematerialise' and become shape, line and form, and that what results from this dematerialisation of the female form is more beautiful than the male. 'Listen,' I say. 'I stand at this window. I look out at the blokes working on the building site, and what I see is *beautiful*.'

———

A man can strip his wife's friends away from her over the years, by teasing or mockery or lack of interest, and leave her nothing but himself. Then one day she might find that even this is not completely hers. Small cold wind of this thought.

———

Driving me back after dinner the husband begins to tell me about a 'numbness' he has noticed in my work. I ask very carefully where exactly *is* the numbness? Is it in the story, the characters, the prose? He says he can't really say. He presses on—the words get worse and worse—numbness, a frozen waste, blasted, devastated—all the way to the hotel. As the car goes under a bridge I remember the last time someone gave his opinion on that same book. *He* said my work was too nice, that it doesn't really say what's bad about people, it always looks on the bright side, is not about real life. We part awkwardly.

———

Dreamt that in Melbourne, in a long street quivering with plane trees in full leaf, a man stands with me outside a shop with a deep Victorian veranda, and says with a shudder, 'Melbourne! This endless peacefulness.'

———

The Golden Aeroplane is about to crash. Ruby Rose and Blue Sapphire are going to lose their money—in Ruby Rose's case, half of the thousand bucks I gave her last week to bail her out of a mess. 'It's a scam,' I say. 'No, it's not,' says P. She is very upset. She had believed she was breaking through barriers of mistrust: that she was freeing something in herself. 'You went into it,' I say, 'with a freight of idealism. But I bet most people are like Ruby Rose and only go in because they *want money*.' As I whack down my points I see her face hardening and becoming sharper, and I realise we aren't even talking about the same thing.

———

'Are you going to *Les Misérables*?'

'No,' says my sister. 'I hate going to spectacles and enjoying them in spite of myself.'

———

Our sister's coming home from New York. 'Dad's rapt.' 'I know. It means he hasn't lost another daughter to some scumbag or other.' Waiting for her at the airport I turned all red from trying not to cry while watching scenes of reunion. I noticed a strange, intense silence that surrounds the reunion of an old woman and her son. Once the cries of greeting and laughter die down and the touching begins, there is a density to it—no one speaks, it's almost visible, the meaning of *mother and child*.

———

V was awkward in a household of women. He said he had felt left out. 'When we were eating in the kitchen you all kept laughing and putting your heads on the table. Like flowers at night.'

———

I walked into the change rooms at Brunswick baths and came upon two fat women in their thirties, naked, drying themselves. Sun coming down from high windows lit their white flesh and it was like walking into the world of two Picasso women, slow, pale, solid, utterly present.

———

'I have come to like a melancholy tone,' says the young writer in a letter, 'because it softens the embarrassment one feels about being ridiculously well-off and happy.'

———

'I once,' says V, 'introduced her to Fred Williams and Arthur Boyd. Together. She gushed.' 'So what,' I say. 'She was shy. Some people gush to hide their shyness. Others turn into silent, dry sticks.'

———

The law student's twenty-first. All the young men singing, talking, laughing, whispering, heads together, their girlfriends mostly forgotten.

———

Huge train strikes, trams packed solid, a party atmosphere. One young bloke so drunk his face was shining with sweat. Afraid he'd spew on me. The handsome young Greek conductor took his hand to keep him upright.

Conductor: (*in loud, merry voice*) 'I'm not a poof, mate, but I'll hold your hand.'

Drunk: (*faintly*) 'You don't *look* like a poof.'

———

My sister says her first memory of me as an adult was when she and our parents drove to my house 'after you'd had a baby. Mum went inside and Dad and I stayed in the car.' There are things in my past so excruciating that I have forgotten them. No wonder Dad keeps offering to lend me money.

We drink some champagne. I put on *Graceland* and we all start to dance. The doors and windows are open and a wind is rushing down the hall, F has the colander on his head and we dance, spontaneously but always trying to form patterns: forward and back in step, arms high and pumping, criss-cross paths through doorways, apart with our backs to each other, back again and pass with inscrutable faces.

Kath Walker, to an interviewer in *ABR*: 'When the kids come to me all dewy-eyed I say, "What you look for in a man is mateship. Forget about this love thing. I've told at least thirty-five men in my lifetime that I'll love them forever."'

'I shouldn't read as much,' says V, 'and yet I should read more.'

Church. My sister is one of the servers. Unaware that I'm there, she approaches the spot at the altar rail where I'm kneeling with my hands out. She stops in front me, carrying the big silver chalice, looks down, recognises me. She rocks back on her heels, her face is still with astonishment, then she smiles and I have to keep my eyes on her black shoes. My lips quiver against the rim of the chalice so hard that I'm afraid I won't be able to swallow.

F had prepared for us a beautiful little meal, pretty things arranged in patterns: a lot of vegetables; some prosciutto; mango and red currants; champagne. Everything went cheerfully. When we got up to leave he said, 'I wasn't intellectual enough for you. That's what the problem was.' 'No!' I said. 'You were *too* intellectual, *that* was the problem!'

Report from Paris: 'This cop smashed me in the mouth, twice. That's all. Nothing special.'

Alone on the Hume I listened to Bach violin partitas and Beethoven's third symphony. The ego that's working very hard in Beethoven, the battle he's waging, while Bach sports impersonally in the empyrean. Is this the difference between Romantic and Baroque? Mind filled, emptied, filled again with brilliant things I'd write if only I were brilliant.

––––––

The attractive, calm reasonableness of Elaine Showalter in *Towards a Feminist Poetics*: 'It is because we have studied women writers in isolation that we have never grasped the connections between them.' Part of my current unhappiness, frustration, unease must be due to the *absence of mothers* that I feel, in work—uncertainty, fear, a floating feeling. I haven't paid proper attention to what women write, have written. I've been tagging along on men's coat-tails, watching for their approval, and look where it's got me.

––––––

'Why are you embarrassed about your car?' says V.
   'Because it's new.'
   'That's a hippie way of thinking about cars.'

––––––

Z lambasts a new biography of Hemingway for its ignorant assumptions and 'psychologising'. Compares Hemingway's photo on the cover ('that terrible face—but *good*') to the biographer's on the back ('isn't he *awful*—so smug—and it's taken by his wife, dear little woman'). 'These bastards,' he says, 'they've never *written* a novel, they don't have a *clue* about the writer's life. They live all their lives safe in a university, with a wife and kids. They've got *no idea* of the risks writers take—I don't just mean the risks on the page but the way we make ourselves *uncomfortable* in life, so we'll *learn* things.'

––––––

M talks about a 2 am death freak-out she had in the motel at Numurkah where we shared a room. 'I kept looking at things in the room—chairs, a table—and thinking, "What are they *for*?"'

Why didn't she wake me? My punishment for her arms-length upbringing is her powerful independence, her resolute not-need of me. But when I told my friend with cancer this story he said, 'Two things. First, she's able to get through a dark night of the soul without needing to wake anyone. Second, dark nights of the soul are *personal*. You feel you want to go right to the end of it, and afterwards you're proud of yourself for getting through it alone.'

———

Two boys passing, on New Year's Eve:

One: 'Eddy, Eddy's not allowed to go anywhere near any girls, whatsoever.'

Two: (*voice breaking*) '*Bull*sheet!'

One: "'E says girls make you weak.'

———

V: 'You're very good, very sharp at *noticing* things, but don't you have any...beliefs, or thoughts, or arguments that you want to convince people of?'

Me: 'No. Not in the abstract. Only when something arises out of a practical circumstance.'

———

People keep telling me I look healthy, fit, purposeful. Must be the shoulder pads, which quite drastically suit me.

———

I met an arson engineer in an art-supplies shop. He smelt strongly of pipe tobacco and his lower lip was yellowed, almost charred. 'I've been on call for a fortnight. Three people burned to death between Christmas and New Year. One had left his deadlock key in the bedroom. We found his body against the front door.' I begin to think of violence, death, burning, what people do to each other, to their children. And to think that I need to find out about these things.

———

In the Leichhardt cafe we ran into two old friends of mine. Their simplicity and kindness made me feel very warmly towards them but V was withdrawn, reticent, not curious, and I wanted to kick him. I thought, I don't even *know* you. Who are you? Do you even *exist*?

———

He reads me a lovely piece of Goethe's conversations with Eckermann. 'He must have cleaned that up a bit when he wrote it down,' I say. 'It's not really the Studs Terkel approach, is it.' He stares at me in silence, even more shocked than he was when I said that a certain pink iced bun at Bondi looked like a Fairweather.

———

A storm was smashing over the Opera House when we emerged at interval. Great wide sheets of sepia lightning, sometimes with a hairline fracture down the centre. The bridge sprang towards us on a burst of light then jumped back into the dark. At the end of the show as we left the building we thought the rain had stopped, until we saw an upward-pointed fluorescent street-light squirting what looked like snow into the darkness.

———

Mending my skirt. Even putting a few stitches in something lightens this feeling of uselessness, of not really existing, which I believe I can identify as homesickness.

———

In the borrowed bedroom in the borrowed house, I felt a slowly growing peacefulness which became happiness and then joy. As I pulled the sheet tight and tucked it in, I remembered R once telling me of a 'bliss' that had come over her, a joy so strong that she had to sit down, cross-legged, on the ground and let it fill her completely—I did this, on her gritty bedroom floor, hands on knees, eyes closed, facing her shelf of poetry; and I thought about the dark column of meaning (behind my left shoulder, where it used to manifest) and I let it step forward and enter me—it became me, I mean it fused with my spine, and I was full of such powerful joy that tears ran down my cheeks. Writing this now I'm still shaking with the force of it.

It was my spine that took the meaning. Meaning entered me and became me. It was the Mighty Force. I wasn't afraid of it, in fact I summoned it, I called it and it *came*.

———

The house on Dangar Island. 'Sometimes in spring,' said the host, 'the light reflects off the river on to this wall, and it's *sickening*, it's so bright and dappled.' We ate, I asked to have a nap, he showed me to a hanging bed under the house, and tucked in a mosquito net around me. I read a few pages of Pablo Neruda's memoir. His first poem. He wrote it to his stepmother when he was very small, in a rush of intense emotion, then copied it out neatly on to a small scrap of paper and, still trembling, took it to his parents and handed it silently to them where they sat talking. The father scans it, hands it back and says, 'Where did you copy that from?'

———

The cat next door is going to have kittens. The little girl hangs out the upstairs window and shouts down to us: 'Mummy, ask Helen her opinion of Ginger's pregnancy.'

———

The ten-year-old boy and I share a room. He is charming, clever, friendly. We talk so much in our two narrow beds that we don't get to sleep till after midnight. 'I've realised,' he says, 'that it's possible not to *like* someone in your own family. For example, I respect my grandmother but sometimes she says cruel and hurtful things about people, and when she does that I don't like her. I like my other grandmother more, but I don't respect her.'

———

At my agent's I signed two contracts. I will get an advance that I can use to PAY MY TAXES.

———

'All the…most important problems of life are fundamentally insoluble…They can never be solved, but only out-grown.' —Jung (in Harding's interview book)

Our attempts to discipline this tremendously powerful *thing*. It can't ever supplant his marriage. If we can't discipline it then one day it will have to be put down. Perhaps there *is* no mode that can integrate this kind of love into a structure. Maybe that's the whole *point* of it: that it blasts structure sky-high; that it's all or nothing.

My old friend, with his wife close behind, enters their kitchen where I am cooking. 'My wife looks wonderfully beautiful,' he said, 'while *you* look—' My fear of what he might say, what *ranking* I might be subjected to—then relief when he doesn't finish his sentence.

Alone in their house. Rain falling quietly, a small choir of crickets. It was still light. Sparrows were hopping about in the branches. Rain collected in curved upturned leaves with frilled edges; and in different spots, now here, now there, a load of rain would become too heavy for its leaf, which would suddenly sag and let the water pour down in a quick stream, as suddenly cut off. I tried to call home. No answer. Played the piano. Got somewhere. Opened the front door, stood by it watching the rain. Remembered M when I picked her up from that crèche in Kew. The lady says, 'Your daughter's sitting on the back doorstep watching the rain.' At *two*. This thought made me suffer. What was I *doing* to that little girl? I was so absorbed in love and escape.

Some bloke reviews *Postcards from Surfers* in an American university magazine. I am taken to task for 'transcribing: it appears that she never invents anything'. Even in *The Children's Bach*, says the critic, occurs this Philip character who appears in so much of my work that 'he is almost surely based on a particular man'. *Pfff.* I thought he was an archetype.

We walk into the ward. A rhythmic moaning, is it an instrument or a human voice? An 'operation', one thinks of it as mechanical, a neat metal process, and can't conceive of the brutality, the violence of metal on bone, the force it must take and the body's frantic fighting back: blood, coldness, temperature up and down, shivering, unconsciousness, sleep—*dreams*.

People who can't stop talking. Their monologues work as fences (and they must always ride the boundaries) around things that cannot be spoken of.

Dreamt that a Vietnamese man was torturing me by digging his fingers hard into my back muscles. I was kneeling in front of him in a sparse public room. I was obliged to conceal my pain. When I woke my back went on hurting in the exact spots into which he'd been sinking his fingers. Tonight when I pulled my nightie from under the pillow to put it on I found it was torn right across the back.

———

Tremendous dry heat. Not even a sheet over me, till morning.

———

At his cousin's funeral Dad failed to recognise his own sister. Listening to the priest reading Corinthians on life and death, I felt again quite sure that—well, I even thought 'There is no such *thing* as death.' All right—Cambodia, blue plastic bags, Babi Yar, Anita Cobby. And yet. Even so. All those souls struggling to stay a while in this world...

———

P: 'The heat! How will we get through this *night*?'
   H: 'It's nearly over. It's already midnight.'
   P: 'But how will we get through the wee hours?'

———

Ian Buruma on 'Oriental' cinema, for example Ray and Mizoguchi: 'The emotions under the surface, the long spells of apparent calm, suddenly interrupted by an emotional climax: a look of terrible grief, a stifled scream, a burst of silent tears. The image of the woman betrayed by weaker men, biting her sari or kimono in anguish…'

———

This is the hardest thing I've ever taken on, in my whole life. Its huge demands: self-discipline, solitude, secrecy; the frustrated longing to speak about it. I pick up his moods. His wind blows on me and I shiver and tinkle. And yet I like my life, perhaps better than he likes his. I don't have to tell lies.

———

Swam twenty laps. Worked merrily on the movie, shuffling the order of scenes and writing more in—enjoying *making things up*. Gee I'm good at dialogue sometimes. The rhythm of it is my natural element. Worked out what to write for *Good Weekend* ($300) and began it.

———

Dreamt I was in a pitch-dark house, feeling my way around a bedroom. When it got light I realised I must have my period: the room was covered with bloody palm prints. Clothes hanging over a chair-back were stained.

———

Mass in the Little Sisters' Housing Commission flat. A dozen people sitting on the floor. Someone read the Gospel. Jesus said to shake the dust from your feet. Is it a curse? No, said a big woman in a corner: shake off rejection, rather than dragging it along with you to the next experience. Bread was a large scone. Wine was passed round in a wooden cup. At the sign of peace everyone got up and milled about, hugging and shaking hands. A window was half-open and a breeze kept puffing the synthetic curtains into the room. Outside, noise rose and fell: shouts, an explosion, a radio on somewhere, traffic. I thought, 'This is real life, this is better than church, it's not even religious.'

———

'Do you think people can ever avoid betraying each other?'
'No. Because promises can't stop everything from moving and changing.'

———

My sister wants me to give her grammar lessons. We get a couple of textbooks and I tentatively begin. 'Come on!' she says. 'You're the teacher! Teach!' We do nouns, verbs—begin to parse. I feel the terms coming back.

———

Drinking coffee as I write, I feel optimism begin to run quietly along my veins.

———

I keep thinking about the children in *28 Up*, the tension of their faces. The seven-year-old in his boarding-school blazer: 'Mai hawt's desayre is to see my fawther, whoo's in Chaina'—his little face hollow-cheeked from the stress of dancing. The roughness of the working-class kids, their ability to change, improvise, *flex*—their readiness to laugh and give a shrug.

———

In the hotel I work happily all morning on the movie. I order tea, they bring it. Men work outside my window on the building site next door. Rain starts, then stops; clouds form, shed water, part again. Drills, hammers. Clanging of pipes. My self-confidence in work waxes and wanes, but never sinks below the level of function. Later in the afternoons he visits me.
    'Don't you ever get bored,' he says, 'loafing about like this?'
    'Never. Do you?'
    'Not bored, but it does seem strange, to spend a whole afternoon...Do you think it's lazy? Shouldn't we be doing something?'
    'We are.'
    'What?'
    'Reading. Talking about adjectives.'

———

He goes home to his life. I will always be displaced by it. And here I am again in this room, calm, half-sleepy, looking forward to going back to *my* life. We will never be a couple. One day we will find the sexual passion gone and a friendship taking its place. And through it all his marriage will have sailed serenely on. A radio's on, somewhere out there, a woman singing wildly. A train passes. I don't care. Nothing can touch me. The power of *work*. Art, and the huge, quiet power it gives.

———

Sitting on a bench, laughing at the mean wit that is so amusing if one is not the butt of it.

———

My friend's home from hospital. Smaller-headed, hair growing back in a convict's prickles. Like an actor playing him, but they haven't quite got it right.

———

On the dark building site after a night of heavy rain a man in a blue, almost-black boilersuit and leather belt walks across the ground floor carrying a folder and a plastic cup. Now someone's whistling in there, like Dexter, a bright whippy little tune. Someone else begins to whack metal with metal, and the night's over.

———

O and R's vast new fridge. It dominates the kitchen and, like the decrepit one before it, hums all the time as if faulty. It looks anomalous there, with its shining surface and squared corners, its aggressive whiteness.

———

A fantasy: I call his number, his wife answers, I identify myself and ask to speak to him; she says, 'Do you know what you are doing to me?' and I say, 'Do you want to tell me?'

———

Walked with R through Hyde Park at dusk. Bud lights along the boughs. She said, 'Why are people afraid of getting married?' I said, surprising myself with the clarity of the thought, 'Because they're afraid they won't find it in themselves to go on loving the other person once the obstacles to their relationship are removed.'

———

To church. At the peace greeting R and I turned to each other and whispered simultaneously. She said, 'I hate this part—I find it *excruciating*.' I said, 'I love this bit. It's my favourite.' She laughed and said, 'You little extrovert!'

———

The children encounter a flasher/masturbator in the churchyard opposite their house, and flee in disarray, leaving a valued skipping rope behind. They call me into their bedroom and whisper their tale. Later their uncle offers to go back with them for the rope. They decline, then a little while later they ask me to accompany them. Very flattered by this. We trudge over there. The perv's long gone of course, but the old churchyard is very beautiful under the thick grey sky: a creamy wind blows across wet grass; the gravestones are crumbling sandstone, one has a sailing ship carved into it.

———

What about a small short story: the flasher gone, leaving the churchyard in a state of strange beauty.

———

Started the structurally very difficult job of cutting the home scenes into the desert trip. It was hard but I was very happy doing it. I cut with confidence, though some things I sadly miss as I toss them over my shoulder on to the floor. The process of tightening the net is exhilarating. And nutting out ways of putting in pieces of factual information unobtrusively.

———

Last time V was supposed to be coming I cleaned all the windows so that if he didn't turn up I'd at least have clean windows.

———

Why is my torso changing shape so radically? I don't like it—a thickening.

———

'But,' said U, 'I really can't bear what I become as soon as I'm involved with a man—this simpering creature. I like myself much better when I'm with my kids and my friends, just doing practical things and trying to be nice to people.'

———

Anyway, I drove P to the Sydney bus at 7 am—her masses of luggage, her little skirt and jacket, pretty legs, pretty golden shoes. Then I went to F's to pick up my uke, which he had lent to some visiting Tahitians. I played until told, 'Shut up, or else play something with a progression, at least.'

———

The nun talked about a man sitting opposite her on a tram: 'I liked his face because it reminded me of my own.'

———

M and F came over to our place at 10.30 pm after his birthday dinner. We played a stupid game of me pretending they weren't welcome and yelling GO HOME! Pretending to attack them with a carving knife. M hurled herself on to my bed and I dragged her off by the ankles. After they left we were ashamed. I had to call F to apologise and wish him bon voyage to Tahiti.

———

An extremely intense conversation with the nun, no small talk, just a driving urge in each of us to *get to the point*. She tells me about the Jesuit: 'We didn't get as far as actually making love, but we got very close to it, and for the first time—you see—years ago when I was working in a very bad ghetto in Boston, I was raped. I was walking home at night and a black man dragged me into a deserted building. I thought he was going to kill me. He was strangling me, and I thought, "He's gonna have to kill me before he gets my body"—and so I was fighting him really hard—but then I thought, "If it gets out, in Boston, that a nun *with a name like McDermott* was raped and murdered in the ghetto, the Irish—'cause the Irish are the ones that hate the blacks the most—the Irish are gonna come in here and burn the whole place down. So I said, "OK, do what you have to and get out." So he did. And it was a really…revolting experience. And between that day and this, with the Jesuit, there hadn't been—so you see'—she sits forward and brings her face, lit up and smiling, closer to me—'for the first time I felt *my body was a sacrament.*'

———

Sometimes at night, when I'm the last to go to bed and I walk down the hall towards my room, seeing the other doors closed or ajar with sleep or undressing or reading or emptiness occurring behind them, this house seems a mansion to me, full of possibilities and a kind of private freedom. I'm so happy, in this attenuated state, that I barely dream of resolution. In fact I'm afraid of it. Because I might lose this happiness. By being greedy.

———

Fragment of a dream: two people, a man and a woman, in profile, sitting facing one another, as if going along in a carriage, not quite but almost in dark silhouette.

———

Late summer morning. Swam. Pool very beautiful. Sun giving out long, oblique rays of pink and gold.

———

At the kitchen table I ate my solitary chop and lettuce leaves and read Sally Morgan's *My Place*. I surprised myself by starting to sob out loud: ashamed of being a twerp, ignorant, an intellectual snob. What would I know about such suffering?

———

I called the born-again on his building site ('Want me to get him for you on the walkie-talkie?' says a bloke eagerly). He nearly fainted when I revealed that the tickets to the Manning Clark musical were $29 each. When we walked into the old Princess Theatre he looked

around him aghast and said, 'I'd like to run a bulldozer through this.'
I told him that when I went to the nuns' Eucharist the priest drank all
the wine and the rest of us got only bread: 'Is that because it's Lent?'

'No. That's Catholic. Didn't you know?'

'WHAT?'

'That was one of Luther's complaints that he nailed to the door.'

'But that's APPALLING. It's a fucking SCANDAL.'

'Good on you, Hel.'

To Primrose Gully with T. We sawed branches off a half-dead tree
and planned a big bonfire for the winter. Next: fill in those stupid
ponds. She said, 'I'm a Baptist. I like hell-like activities. How about
we start now, using buckets?' I said, 'No, I have to finish this thing
I'm writing.' So she began to tear meat off a chicken and stuff it into
her mouth. A mild night, with scented air. After tea we walked for
hours: a thirteen-kilometre 'evening stroll'. I had the little torch that
F gave me but it was easier to walk by the faint light from the sky,
which was quite covered, after having turned on a stylish display
of stepping-stone clouds at sunset. Slept with the tomahawk beside
my bed. In the morning we woke and gardened: a lot of destruction.
Bare lines everywhere. Now I'm burnt, cut, blistered and stiff, and
sore from laughing. That is my idea of a weekend.

Out to dinner with C at the Siam, where the beautiful Thai waitress
addressed each of us as 'sir'. Back at C's place we loafed about on
the pillows and gossiped. She remarked on my frequent trips to
Sydney—did I have a bloke up there? 'Yes.' 'Does he ever get down
here?' 'Not much.' (*In very small voice*) 'He's married.' 'Oh.' She
smiles and nods, and the subject is pleasantly changed.

Worked for hours, slowly and painfully, on the movie. Fearfully,
slowly, obliquely. Wrote another scene, stitched my squares and
oblongs together.

The boys from St Joseph's go roaring and rending the gardens as they pass.

'I don't want him to die. I'd be furious with him if he died.'
   My sister, impatiently: 'He *will*.'

I walked down Brunswick Street and bought a wooden towel rack in a secondhand shop. It's got a little heart carved into each end. Now I'm going to paint it white.

So close to finishing the screenplay that I've been half-stunned all afternoon, roaming round the city. I actually wrote what I think will be the final scene. I don't know whether a camera can do what I want it to but I wrote it down anyway.

My sister, asking for the hinged egg-slicer, called it 'the little harp'.

Dancers' bodies, rehearsing. Their stretchableness, length of neck. Their feet in soft laced shoes. Some have regal bearing, others are chunkier. One man very strong and blocky: he can lift, but he is also graceful and has a well-set head. The choreographer tries to explain certain movements to me. I pay attention but fail to grasp her point. She walks off towards the dancers and I say to the composer, 'It's hard to put into words, isn't it.' He says, 'That's why people dance.'

Washed and de-flea'd the dog.

My sister tells us her son wants his golf clubs buried with him, and he wants 'Hello, Is It Me You're Looking For?' to be sung at his funeral.

Replaced the disgusting shower curtain, painted the towel rack, cleaned the bath, raked the garden, ironed the tablecloths, made a soup, picked up things off my bedroom floor, washed my clothes, and sat down to read the Literature Board papers.

———

Someone stole M's bag, she comes over to tell me about it, puts her head in my neck and bursts into tears. 'When I got a new key cut I had to get rid of that old Lockwood one I've had for *six years*—and now I've got this great big *silver* one.' She sobbed and sobbed.

———

Adelaide Writers' Week. Hearing certain British writers speak I realise how scandalously little I have ever *thought* about my own work.

———

I just received the first fax of my life. A procedural matter about an interview.

———

V introduces me to his friend W: her beauty, and somewhere coming from deep inside her, her lostness. She and I take to each other at once, we can't get away on our own quick enough. H: 'I was looking for you when I came in, but I only had his description to go by.' She: 'What did he say I looked like?' H: 'He said you were beautiful, that your hair was white, and that you wore terrific clothes that you just threw on.' She laughs out loud, with happiness. We talk very fast about our experiences alone in our respective bush dwellings. Hers she can only get to by boat.

———

We hired a car and drove to a beach. He clowned at the wheel, making the tyres scatter gravel and keeping a deadpan face. Swam in flat water. Girl in the dunnies was smoking a joint. Beautiful country, clean-looking properties. We saw a dead snake. He backed up so we could have a look.

———

At breakfast the Cretan's fig was bursting with ants.

———

I read her story. It had three marvellous moments in it. But driving along later I thought that what was missing from it was something hard, sparse, distant and impersonal. I think that what I'm trying to do is stand back from telling the story *myself*, and let the language tell the story. Is this what poetry does? It doesn't preclude at all a first-person narrative; but it means that all cosiness, all *comfort* must be excised—everything easy, chatty, loose.

———

J says his wife 'bakes the sort of bread you want to peel open and lie down in'.

———

Sudden money problems: tax $6000, royalties $1500. I was hoping they'd balance out.

———

A fox at Primrose Gully. 'It came flying,' said my sister, 'straight down the hill from the corral, absolutely *streaking* along. It saw us, and swerved for a second then decided to go straight on. It flew past us so fast that some of us didn't even see it. It had a *huge* brush, a beautiful russet colour, with a white band around it near the tip. It turned its head to look at me and it had a perfect fox's face—a sharp triangle.'

———

E in Sydney offers me her spare room this winter. A friendly, un-pressing invitation.

———

The young woman answers the phone in a soft, dreamy voice.
  'I didn't wake you from a nap, did I?'
  'No...I've got this lovely little baby on my lap.'

———

György Ligeti's 'Chamber Concerto'. *Corrente; calmo; sostenuto; movimento preciso e mecanico; presto.* All kinds of weird pluckings, knockings, tickling of strings, and a flowing feeling.

———

On the tram a strange couple, young, a bit lumpen. The girl had untidy red hair and freckles, and a rather dignified and thoughtful expression. She sat half turned away from the boy, not touching, lost in thought. He kept glancing at her, then after a moment, feeling unnoticed, he gave her knee a firm sideways whack with his. Her eyes focused and she looked at him. He said nothing. She got the message: put her arm through his and sat closer to him so their sides touched all the way down. Then she laid her head on his shoulder. All this without changing the expression on her face one iota. He, on the other hand, looked almost pretty with happiness. His eyes shone. Hard to imagine their future. Or anyone's, for that matter. What a stupid remark.

———

'Don't buy the jacket,' said my sister. 'It makes you look like a businesswoman.'

———

To a comedy night with M and my mother. Mum loves to inveigh against 'city drivers' and tells endless boring stories. I'm ashamed of my reaction but I can't help it and I know she's afraid of me. Writing this my eyes fill with tears—a pathetic and useless response. M's terrible beauty: it too frightens me and makes me sad—and with Mum it becomes almost too much. Is Mum what I will become? No—because she's afraid of everything and I'm less afraid. But I'll *look* like her; and right now I'm skating along a middle line between them, slightly further on her side than on M's.

———

'We meet someone at the right moment, I thought, we take everything we need from them, and then we leave them, again at the right moment.' —Thomas Bernhard, *Woodcutters*
    It makes me feel cold, he's so bilious and splenetic.

———

The extreme *structural* pleasure I get out of pulling a long interview together: trying to make it move like a real conversation, though in fact I have deconstructed it completely.

———

My mother was in my dream, but stronger, freer, cleverer, more alert and focused—I explained to M that Mum's name had been changed to Paradiffy, 'because it was *Paradise* and she was *Different*'. Won't this *ever* end?

———

And now my nun's got leukemia. Stunned by this news. No emotional reaction.

———

There is nothing I can do to get V into my life, or myself into his. Having drunk two glasses of wine I am not feeling any pain.

———

As soon as she grew some pubic hair, said the woman, her mother explained what it was and told her that men were animals.

———

V showed me a shocking photo of his father as a young man: spectacles, hair cut short and combed back, his face thin, hard, clamped, full of some terrible inward-turned power—like someone who could have died of a broken heart, or of bottled-up emotion.

———

A hilarious evening of play and foolery with R and her kids. V played poker with them, examined a broken billycart. Driving away I say, 'It was fun with the kids, wasn't it.' 'Yes,' he said, 'but they take over. Nothing *happened*. Nothing got *said*.' 'Of *course* something happened. We *played*.'

———

One day, sitting at the table in this hotel with the construction workers battering and yelling away outside, I will feel a big wave rush over me, and I'll pack up my things and go home. I'll ring him up or write to him and I'll say, 'If you want me you'll have to come and find me; because I can't keep this up any more. It breaks my life into small pieces and I can't feel whole.' In other words I will find a place to stand, and I'll stand on it.

———

When in doubt, V heads for a bookshop.

———

'What I meant, when I said I was like a Catholic,' says V, 'was that I'm bound. By some inviolable rule.'

———

What I'm learning from this is how to be a grown-up. That life's not as simple as I thought it was. That people are good at not being happy. And that the kind of selfishness I used to function by is simply *not appropriate* in this situation. I'm starting to understand why it's been necessary for people to invent concepts like original sin, to try to explain why we're so good at making ourselves unhappy.

———

Window and blind open, room lit like a black-and-white movie by reflections from high buildings nearby. Our faces must look smoothed of lines but also dramatic, as if enacting a drama, dramatically boned and planed.

———

On the lunchtime ferry a man of seventy or so who seemed to need a witness directed his discourse at me. He'd left Sydney twenty years ago to live in Tasmania and was here now on a visit. He was in distress. 'See that?' he said, pointing at a sandstone building we were passing. 'That was a pub. I used to drink in there. I dunno what it is now—but they'da done better to pull it down and use the sandstone for something else—don't you reckon?' He had been in the city: 'It's all changed—it's terrible what they're doing.' 'What about the quay? They've spent a lot of money on it.' 'Ah, they've spent money, but it's a bloody abortion.' His voice trembled and he turned away to hide the fact that under his glasses tears were running out.

———

At 6 am the air of the harbour is cool, misty, about to be bright. Ships slide past in silence. I'm floating here in this cheap hotel with its outrageous view, cut off from daily life, watching other people's lives going on around me. In my room I haven't even got a table. When I get back later an old man with a suitcase is standing in confusion in the hall: 'Where's room 13?' 'Over there.' He opens it with his key. 'How's it look?' 'Well,' he says, 'it's got a bed in it.'

———

Greek Independence Day celebrations outside the Opera House. Boys dancing. They slouch about clumsily in their extravagant white-frilled skirts, white stockings and pompoms, then at the moment they form their line they stand up straight and strike out in splendour, turning their whole torsos when they turn their heads. The leader holds up his free hand as beautifully as if he were a woman. One Cretan boy dances wildly and with skill, his arms and shoulders open wide—the music tense and repetitive, about to explode—also the smaller children, the preoccupied girls, one round tub of a boy, 'Spiro', working gracefully nonetheless.

———

The girl standing on her own in the street, watched through the window by the four others, holding the dead cat in the bag. This is the central image of her character and role. If V had written this, would he have worked *back* from that idea? I can't plan. I can only work on feeling. He told me that when he saw *Two Friends*, before we met, he thought, 'This person knows about a world that I know absolutely nothing about.'

———

In Ariel I picked up Art Spiegelman's *Maus* and held it out to him: 'Look—it's a cartoon about Auschw—' and he cut across me, 'Oh, look! Steiner!' I stepped back. He said his formula for these moments: 'Sorry to interrupt'—and to my horror I heard myself utter a sharp and bitter laugh. He stood there holding Steiner's novel, I stood there holding *Maus*, three feet apart and facing each other. He said, 'I didn't mean to be rude.' I said, 'Oh, stop it.' I could have sat down (by Grand Central Station) and wept. Instead we both recovered, and he said something about Steiner's novels being no good, and I listened; and then we left the shop.

———

The superstitiously gloomy beams that one casts on love: as if wanting to smash it oneself so that fate won't have to bother.

———

As if I could change myself in any way, at this age. All I can do is try to know myself and apply discipline.

———

A postcard from G, newly married, so recently ecstatically in love: 'I'm missing being able to talk to you. It seems to be the only way sometimes to get to those things in the back of the mind. At my centre is a lack that I keep trying to fill with women. You included, I suppose.'

———

Strange bright clouds of rain are falling but the colours of everything are as if the sun were shining.

———

A box of old papers. Love letters by the score. And two horrible letters from Mum and Dad in 1967 when I was in London and told them I was going to travel home overland with a man. The coldness of their rejection—I was never to contact them or my brother and sisters again if I went ahead with this—once more I felt my world grind against theirs.

———

P and I talked about men we'd been with, their effects on us. She told me about the one who vigorously undermined her as an artist. He said, 'I don't want you to paint. It feels like competition. Do pots, or something.' She did, made two she liked, and in one fight he smashed her second-favourite one, and in another she smashed her best one. 'I did it to *myself*,' she said, 'worse than he did it to me.'

———

I think I must be insufferable. I feel as if I'm beaming out impatience and nastiness. Everything one may have is lustreless because there is one thing that one may not have.

———

Collected from the old house several boxes of spirax notebooks in a neurotically regular round hand, and in a tone that fancies itself as *writing*: self-dramatising, taking its emotions very seriously; little set-pieces on the weather—quite embarrassing but no doubt full of information. I could sell them. I could probably pay for fixing my shabby kitchen. 'Do you want to buy the series of notebooks on which *Monkey Grip* is based?'

———

Our dog, left behind in our separation into three houses, I now have to take with me everywhere I go. She lies in silence behind me as I work and is pleasant company. I feel sorry for her glum sadness. Yesterday I took her to get clipped and felt free, as if she'd gone to kinder for an afternoon.

———

Cranky at Primrose Gully. Broken hurricane lamp still not replaced.

———

In the Smith Street post office I was served by a frizzy-haired woman in a hand-knitted pink jumper. The fingers of her left hand had bandaids over their tips. She had a very small, dry smile, barely a change in her features, but it gave a short glimpse into an interior that (I sensed) was extremely experienced and morally unrestricted. She drummed her fingers lightly and firmly on my name on the envelope.

'Is this you?'

'Yes.'

'I've read all your books, many times. That one about the junkie. That's my favourite.'

———

When the born-again was leaving Primrose Gully we said goodbye under a sky 'weak with stars'. I said, 'What's that white patch up there?' 'That's another galaxy.' A corridor of terror opens and closes. Terror of the cosmos.

———

Two women were talking about a young mother they knew who was furious no one had told her how much it hurts to have a baby. Surely she must have read novels and seen movies? Let alone heard other women *talk*?

———

A night's good sleep at Primrose Gully, beside a window full of stars. Later a strong moon, so bright it woke me and I had to draw the curtain. Towards morning, a mopoke. Drove to the opposite ridge and picked up wood. Saw a large kangaroo crash away between the trees; and surprised two eagles. They blustered up from a tree and flapped away very fast. Why shouldn't I live up here? No TV. Only radio. No piano. No power. Very little water for washing clothes. Would I be lonely? I'd start talking to myself. (I do that already.) The pretty little kelpie that followed me home from the stud—she wanted to stay, refused to get out of the car when I drove her back. Old man comes out in the dark to see who's there: his white hair blows up in a crest.

———

'To die is only to be as we were before we were born; yet no one feels any remorse, or regret, or repugnance, in contemplating this last idea...It seems to have been holiday-time with us then: we were not called to appear upon the stage of life, to wear robes or tatters, to laugh or cry, be hooted or applauded; we had lain *perdu* all this while, snug, out of harm's way; and had slept out our thousands of centuries without wanting to be waked up; at peace and free from care, in a long nonage, in a sleep deeper and calmer than that of infancy, wrapped in the softest and finest dust...' —Hazlitt, *On the Fear of Death*

———

R and I talked excitedly on the phone about prose and 'what moves behind it'. 'It's as if,' she said, 'even if all I write is fragments, I'm getting ready for the moment when I'll have something to say.' 'That's it. That's it exactly. That's what my life's about.'

———

I like this cheap paper because it's got exactly the right amount of *drag*, and because sometimes the point of my pen goes straight through it.

———

In recent literary magazines I see that my name begins to be mentioned in a manner that leads me to believe my 'dream run' is over. I'm glad about the relative anonymity of screenwriting. People watch a movie and never ask themselves who wrote it. I'm tired. I worked. Even if I'm 'not experimental' I can still work.

———

'There are feminine garments so lovely that one could tear them to shreds.' —Cesare Pavese's diary

———

I call G in his recording studio. 'Are you busy?'
   'Yes, but…'
   'I want you to do me a favour.'
   'Of course.'
   'I want to send you a letter for the love of my life, and I want you to ring him up and arrange for him to come and get it from you.'
   'Ooh, I *love* this.'

———

My sister puts on the record of Bartók's *Mikrokosmos* and I see it gives exactly the mood I want for *The Last Days of Chez Nous*: dry, thoughtful, slightly manic, slightly out of whack.

———

Typed up the final draft of the movie. It looks solid, as big as a novel. Walked home with the dog, squinting in autumn sunshine. Lay on my bed under a body-temperature waterfall of fatigue. It's done. I've finished it. It's taken me nearly a year and it's actually quite good.

———

I sat in Marios with the two painters. They talked about materials. 'Medium.' It was pleasantly impenetrable. One of them had a very weird style and presence. Her discourse was a series of collapses and reconstitutions.

———

Dinner in Camberwell with my angry sister. She arrived full of bitterness against the tax department, and against me for having lived on a supporting mother's benefit when M was very small. Went to see Huston's *The Dead* at the Rivoli. She fell asleep twenty minutes in. The middle-aged couple on my other side talked all the way through. When Gabriel sees his wife on the staircase, the bloke said, 'Look at that wallpaper. It's peeling.' And during the great monologue at the end about the snow 'faintly falling' all over Ireland, the woman said, 'Huh. Depressing. Bit depressing.' All the way home I felt a violent hatred for *common sense*.

———

'Jesus,' said my nun, 'must have been the sexiest man the world had ever known. Once you've got your*self* worked out, then you know the most important thing is *relationship*. They had to get rid of him. He was *too sexy*.'

———

V meets G and is very taken with him. 'He's a very worked-out, worked-on person. He's strongly shaped and individual. And— have you noticed? Oh, of course you have—he's got extraordinary oval-shaped fingernails.'

———

Mice on the rampage in the Primrose kitchen. Constant scrabblings, comical gambollings in pairs, and whenever I open a drawer I'm confronted by bright eyes, furry faces and pink ears. I set two traps but they got the Weetbix out without springing them, and now I feel attached to them.

———

'Thin turquoise and delicious musk pink.' —Elwyn Lynn

———

I ask G if he had liked V. 'Yes. We disagreed, but we seemed to enjoy
to disagree. He twists around in his chair while he speaks.'

———

While I was washing my face I thought that one day I will say to
someone, 'Once I was in love with him. We loved each other. It was
a great passion.' I imagined myself speaking of it painlessly and
without regret, in the past tense.

———

Not far from my road at Primrose Gully someone has found the
badly decomposed body, in two plastic bags, of a man who had been
shot twice in the head. It's been there for about three years. This
find, rather than spooking me, confirms my previously unexamined
impression that the world is full of the results of secret deeds. The
bodies that are found are only the accidents, I mean the ones stumbled on. There must be others, everywhere.

———

Today they're wrecking my kitchen to make it bigger. Traumatic
chaos. I can hear them grinding and gnashing away. As if part of my
body were being violently dealt with and altered. Teeth, perhaps.

———

At my agent's in Double Bay we sat on her balcony and watched
the rain on the water, the cloud rolling along the surface from the
Heads towards us. The paths wind makes on water—rippleless,
uncertain tracks. She was affectionate, pleased with my screenplay.
I felt approved of. Someone I love is proud of me.

———

O cooked the dinner and during his labours such a fit of frustration
exploded in him that the frying pan twisted into the air and six
small schnitzels flew about the room. He found five of them but the
sixth remained a mystery. He even went out into the yard, in case

it had sailed through the narrow opening at the top of the window and landed among the bikes. Later he called us and showed us the missing piece of meat resting against the lid of the shopping trolley in the passage between the kitchen and the living room.

———

This terrifying Sydney rain. It goes on all day, all night, always the rattle and hiss. This morning R took me to the front door and pointed out a small bird which had taken shelter on the first-floor window of the flats opposite: 'Look at this image of pathos.' We stood in silence on the doorstep and stared at the bird, and the rain kept on gushing down, running two inches deep across the front garden and pouring away into the street.

———

He turns up at last, in a wet raincoat, looking pale. We spend an hour in the car down at the Point, talking, our eternal conversation which flows solidly on, despite these repeated interruptions. Rain drizzles, pours, thunders, falls steadily again. Lights on singly in the shipyard across the narrow arm of water. A gutter spouting up over an obstruction. Tonight, outside my window, a single cricket is trying to chirp, feebly and without enthusiasm or energy—as if only learning.

———

Lately in my dreams my girl is a child again.

———

A married woman asked me about my life, whether I was content with solitude. 'Don't say yes! Or I might feel desperate.' I searched for something negative to offer. I found this very hard to do. Because I love my room, arranged according to my needs, and the way I'm 'beholden to nobody'. But I came up with, 'Sometimes when I see two people who are going home together I long for some sort of domestic intimacy.'

———

Do I want resolution? So I can stop all this travelling? I keep wanting to start a novel. It's starting itself and the only thing stopping it is me.

———

His whole life he has been cosseted by women. A few years between mother and wife. He can't cook, though he (says he) does the shopping and washing. 'I've never made a salad in my life, actually.'

———

'Men handle money differently from women,' says the film director. 'They're *playful* with money, whereas we have little purses, and we count it out—"This is for the rent, and this for the 'lectricity"—but they chuck it around.'

———

Because they could not live together in the world she knew best and inhabited, he detached her from it, very gradually and subtly, and drew her into *his* world, 'the world of ideas and books'. Superman takes Lois Lane flying, holding her firmly by the hand.

———

Why should he love me, or think of me, when at home he has a 'happy, generous, sometimes very funny' wife who knows him, loves him and wants to serve him? In other words, what's the point of me? But on the quay, walking round the curve of it, for a moment I took his arm and felt proud of him, and joyful in his company.

———

Dreamt I was in the driver's seat of a very large, luxurious station wagon, and in charge of a charming little boy. The car swooped along very fast and I panicked, not knowing whether its expensive sophistication meant it didn't need a driver. I yelled, 'Am I driving this thing? *Am* I?' The adults just laughed.

———

Driving along Racecourse Road near the creek M and I saw a little white foxy veer off the footpath and tear across the road. The car in front of us hit it, paused and drove on. We both shrieked. I pulled over and parked. I could hear the dog crying out, it was lying on the road, no blood or guts, just squealing and thrashing. We ran back to it. A lady hopped out of a parked car and we stood around it keeping cars from running over it, and watched it die. I'd never seen that before—the life leave a creature—no, I've seen fish, and insects of course, but not a warm thing. I was horrified that I didn't know what to *do*, though some sense that everyone must have was informing me that it *was* dying and could not be saved. It stopped squealing, but its body was convulsing, big twitching shudders ran from its head down its torso and into its legs. Its eyes and mouth were open, the shudders became less frequent till I had to squat right down to make sure it wasn't just the wind of passing trucks making its hair riffle, and that's when I noticed that its eyes were quite still, wide open (brown) but not registering any response at all to the trucks and cars whizzing past only a few feet away. All this took about three minutes. When we saw that it was dead I was afraid to touch it. I was revolted by it and scared that it might still be alive, that if I picked it up I would hurt its broken spine terribly, and it might turn in pain and bite me. I thought, 'Am I too cowardly to pick up a little dead dog? How *disgusting*.' I got a jumper out of the boot and rolled him up in it. This was the worst part, because he was as warm as a live animal and yet *completely limp*. I've lifted up sleeping children a million times and thought I knew what limpness was but even a sleeping baby is springy compared with this dead dog. I carried him to a patch of grass and laid him on it. When I drew the jumper out from under him he flopped on his side and his face disappeared into the blades of grass. He didn't have a collar, yet he wasn't scruffy like a stray. We left him there and drove on. So that's what death looks like when it comes. His eyes so quickly lost their lustre.

———

A man is digging some boulders out of my front yard. Light flickers through the plane leaves and bounces off his faded pink windcheater. The dirt he is digging sends waves of a smell like mushrooms through my bedroom window.

Our dog has run away. I went to the Lost Dogs' Home. Awful pathos of the *sorting* of the dogs: small brown ones in one enclosure, big browns in another, whites and greys elsewhere: they will rush up to any visitor, even tilt their heads as if about to be photographed for a calendar.

In DJ's I found a good black coat for $425. I did not buy it because I can't afford it. Apropos black coats, P came out of *Wings of Desire* and spoke of it as if it had been a treatise on angelic powers, a topic she probably knows more about than did Wim Wenders.

I could write a novel about optimism, though maybe only a scientist could do it, for it seems to be metabolic, like a substance secreted by a gland so far undiscovered. I fall asleep tragic, but wake picaresque and humanist.

He lives in a squat monolith, and I live in an extremely tall, thin and airy tower. I've got a little mattress and blanket up near the top, and some binoculars through which I examine the bunker for signs of his life.

'I have read somewhere,' said the Polish philosopher, '—perhaps it was Jesus who said this—"You would not be looking for me if you had not already found me."'

I moved my bookshelf so I can have the big dictionary beside my desk.

'Illicit love between a married man and a married woman. The man abandons his wife and daughter in order to join the woman with whom he has fallen in love. Yet the deserted wife—a teacher who sincerely loves and admires her runaway husband—refuses to be broken by what has happened. "Not a single day shall be spoiled! They all belong to me. And that is that!'" —Chekhov, *Notebook*

———

Cholesterol test this morning. My arms were so cold that my veins were 'too fine', and the young technician could not draw blood. While she struggled I was afraid I might get an embolism and die in this ugly cubicle. She had to call in the other woman, who filled the tube from my left elbow-crook. I saw the red fill the tube and said, 'Bullseye.' 'Not bullseye,' replied the second technician. 'I had to shift it.' The first kept saying to me, 'Look away! Look away!' 'It's all right,' I said grandly. 'I'm not squeamish.'

———

To church. The best part was when my sister, all vested in white, stood up at the end, threw out her arms and cried, 'Go in peace, to love and serve the Lord!'

———

Such a late autumn that the Armenian lady next door is hitting the branches of her apricot tree with a broom to try to make its leaves come down.

———

The Polish philosopher and I sat in the front row at Melba Hall to hear Yvonne Loriod play (her husband) Olivier Messiaen's *Vingt regards sur l'enfant-Jésus*. She looked 'like any old housewife,' whispered my philosopher—loose, ageing skin, faded hair in a bun, pale-rimmed specs—a frumpish figure in a dress like a translucent Bedouin tent and old-fashioned gold sandals. She sat down with a lot of fussy rearranging of draperies, and placed several folded Kleenex under the piano's open lid: she dabbed at her nose with these between movements. Her hands and wrists showed great power. The music was difficult and rather wild: many times she laid down a grid of severe chords, which were then decorated or even assaulted by unresonant explosions in the upper registers. We enjoyed it very much indeed. At the end Olivier Messiaen himself stumbled on to the stage, a heavy-set, white-haired old man in a huge grey suit whose trouser top came up to his nipples. He kissed Loriod on both cheeks.

———

V's letter consists almost entirely of quotes from what he's been reading—Walter Benjamin, whom he describes several times as 'the true intellectual'. This irritates me, for some reason. I want to shake him and say, 'What does this silly phrase *M E A N*?' I wish that instead of copying out Benjamin's recherché compliments and examining this amazing new feeling ('love') which I have somehow caused him to experience, he would materialise down here and *be a companion* to me. He's become a figment. I don't believe in him at the moment. I know he won't leave his wife. He would be wrong to, on every count, because I don't know if I want him to, because I may be finally unmarriageable, because I dread the death of sex and romantic love that domestic life entails, and because I don't know if I can handle the strain of our life as we are now living it. Fantasy: I say, 'Look, this is going nowhere. Let's decide to part,' or 'This isn't a life, for me. It's too difficult. I'm alone so much that I feel a bit crazy. Tell me what chance there is of our ever being together. If there's none, I'm saying goodbye, now, today.'

———

'So,' writes G, 'I find myself married and at the same time in a state of jealous panic because my "best friend", M-C, the object of my love, is going to marry her boyfriend. She said that the next night we spend together will be the last. "Why?!" I asked, dumbfounded. "What's different?" "I have to at least start this thing off on the right foot," she replied.'

———

My sister comes home from a day's emergency ESL teaching and tells me about the Vietnamese student who, when she asks the demoralised class to write a paragraph, writes, 'I do not understand the teacher. I damn myself. I feel like a mad and crazy lunatic.' When, distressed,

she shows this to their regular teacher he shrugs and says, 'Oh—
Hoah—he sits at the back. He's always quiet and well-behaved.'

———

A mild night at Primrose Gully. Koalas in the night made a colossal
racket, and something wailed. Mice nibbled patiently at food scraps
on the dirty dishes—a slide and a rustle when I went out to piss.
Many stars but very high, in huge wraiths of milky light, not bright,
not crackling, though perfectly clear. How small they were, how
far away.

———

Dreamt R had fallen asleep sitting on a sofa, her head on her arm.
I called her and like a mother she answered me before she was
properly awake. She was angry. Her eyes had a red glow.

———

Last night P and I quarrelled, perhaps for the first time in our
lives. A painful explosion. My sister overheard us shouting in the
kitchen and made a dash for the front door. We calmed down and
exchanged criticisms of each other's hurtful behaviours. We went to
bed chastened and sore. In the morning I heard her moving around
getting ready for church. Saw her through the venetians, all dressed
in white, hurrying out to her car. On the kitchen table she'd left me
a note, in her beautiful swooping hand: 'This is a new day. (Just
thought I would write something.)'

———

We watched *A Passage to India* by the fire. P told the story of her year
(1960) as an exchange student in Kansas City. She shook hands with
both Eisenhower and Kennedy. My sister very envious.

———

My emotional life is in suspension. The metal of it is dull, it doesn't
ring. Till I can slog my way to where he is.

———

The builder took off the old pergola. Suddenly the backyard is full
of sky.

———

At the hairdresser a young, plain, thin girl with a lot of make-up covering bad skin said to me as she rubbed away at my head over the basin, 'I love the way you dress.' 'Beg your pardon?' 'That long skirt with socks and flat shoes. It's like something out of a magazine.'

———

In Neilsen Park the astonishing beauty of Sydney in early winter: tremendous towers of cloud coloured delicately in greys and pinks, boats sliding or toiling, clear cool air. How can that hard-looking mouth be so soft?

———

After the reading, R and I had a long conversation with a poet about child abuse. The poet ran a very strong line against state interference in families. He said that the family is such a mysterious entity that what one family considers a normal expression of affection another would see as an intrusion on private space. He said that if the high percentage of women interviewed in a recent study who claim to have been sexually abused as children are telling the truth then we need either to redefine the word 'abused' or to realise that some things are simply part of 'the give and take of life' and as such should be accepted and chalked up. 'If all these people have really been abused, or if what happened to them were really psychologically damaging, then the whole fabric of *society* would have collapsed by now.' We tried to tell the poet that a woman or a girl deals with unwanted sexual attention by the unfortunate process of ceasing, during the moments when her body is submitting to the handling, to *inhabit herself.* We said we did not believe this process to be *a good thing*. Later, walking home, R said, 'He's on the side of the abuser, isn't he.'

———

An expression I heard a man use, in ironic quote marks but I don't know who if anyone he was quoting: 'the corrupt flexibility of women—the *diplomacy* of women'.

Marriage, in O's world-picture, has such a dense constellation of importance around it, such a thick cluster of *idées reçues*, of holiness, that my mind will never penetrate these galaxies of reverence.

Is it a dead end when you lose hope that the other still has the power to surprise you? And what does loyalty require of you, when in spite of this dead-end view you must acknowledge that what you are, what you have become, is to a large extent the outcome of what the other has given you—of their devotion to you, to your growth and your wellbeing?

I think I must *do voices* when I report direct speech: V shouts with laughter, doubles up in a silent paroxysm. I probably describe things in such a way that he feels we are closing ranks against the world.

At the exhibition some pictures that V liked left me completely without response, while a painting by a New Zealand woman of two overflowing vessels, which I 'understood' immediately without even having to think, did not touch him at all. I found it impossible to tell him why the painting meant something to me. Is this because I'm ignorant and inexperienced, or because I'm afraid he'll tease me and laugh at me, or because the language for talking about paintings is formed in such a way (i.e. by men) as to make my thoughts foreign to it? I suppose he doesn't need to worry about these things, since nothing he wants to say is excluded by its awkward form from the established discourse.

The English department gives me a big, pleasant office, but no typewriter. I sit down and write two pages of a story with a pencil sharpened by a machine to a long slender point. I am taken to morning tea and introduced to the famously domineering professor who of course (though I've heard I was not her choice of writer-in-residence) is charming, in a pale-blue fake suede jacket, with a confidence-inspiring handshake.

———

As dark fell, a sharp green evening light seemed to rise and rise into the upper registers of sky, leaving us *struggling mortals* down below.

———

I was about to write, 'This is a bad time of my life' then thought no, it's merely a short period of upheaval. Seeing the eagerly begun but unfinished Hildesheimer biography of Mozart beside my bed I fantasised V reproaching me for starting and not finishing a 'great book' and me bursting out at him, 'How can you expect me to read calmly, steadily, moving smoothly forward book after book as you do? Your life is stable. You sleep in the same house, the same bed every night, your hours are regular—but my life is fragmented, always moving and changing, and can't be otherwise if *yours* is to maintain its equilibrium.'

———

La Forza del Destino. Oh, to write such *fierce* events as are the domain of opera—murders, revenge, divine interventions!

———

I've learnt how to wait, and how to be alone, two very useful skills but which must be constantly and consciously *attended to*.

———

'His father went to jail.'
  'What for?'
'Theft, I think. Embezzling, maybe.'
'Embezzling's creepy, isn't it,' I said. 'Worse than straight-out theft. It's the betrayal of someone's trust over a long period.'
  Horrified that he might think I was referring obliquely to his behaviour towards his wife. But he didn't seem to notice, and went on talking.

———

Why are his thoughts so silent and oblique?

Because he is trying to behave loyally to her even while he betrays her.

———

G says his lungs are playing up again. He's giving up grog, coffee, cigarettes etc.

———

A dream of a neglected garden that stubbornly still bore fruit. Did it *belong* to me? I got to work clearing away weeds and grass.

———

Watching the gum trees go black while the sky is still full of light.

———

A dream about a middle-aged man in a boat? The boat capsizes? Then rights itself?

———

Night falls. In my small borrowed suburban flat with its shelves of uninteresting paperbacks (Leon Uris) I finish reading the Bellow and begin to cook a chop. I should think about the novel that keeps patiently presenting itself to me—fear that if I don't take up its offer soon it will give up on me and *go elsewhere*.

———

'Prayer is the contemplation of the facts of life from the highest point of view…It is the soliloquy of a beholding and jubilant soul.' —Emerson, *Self-Reliance*

———

R says that what gives one power is needing people less than they need you. 'Most people seem prepared to fritter away their time in socialising. To me it's always been a matter of the utmost urgency to get away by myself and read a book.' We couldn't stop laughing.

———

We fly in and out of moments of declaration with a kind of terrified speed and lightness.

———

My sister on the phone: 'When your postcard came and I read the last line it made me cry.'

'What the hell did I write?'

'About dreaming of a neglected garden that still bore fruit. I lay on the couch and cried for *hours*. I got slug eyes and everything.'

———

Me and V at the Brasserie with G who is thin and handsome, hair lying in its shining blond curls, dressed in a beautiful suit and a *white* white shirt whose cuffs were unbuttoned. G says, 'I want to be rich by the time I'm fifty-five.' 'Why do you want to be rich?' says V. 'Oh, I don't just want money. I want to get rich through record sales, or ticket sales. Through having done something good.'

———

Feeling ill, V puts his head in my lap while I'm driving. It's surprisingly heavy. The Yourcenar story about the outlaw and the priest's wife: she carries his severed head away wrapped in her apron.

———

The flowers in Nolan's *Boy in Township*. When I stare at them I feel like fainting, and want their colours to swallow me up.

———

By being decent, you only extend your own period of suffering. I said, 'I'm not waiting for you to leave. That's not what I'm doing.' But the truth is more like: 'Tell me whether you ever will, or whether I must accept that the rest of my life will involve this complicated, delicate balancing act. What hurts me is the suspense.' I didn't say this. But I must.

———

Biographies in which artists change wives without apparent outrage or destruction (because the tale is told from the artist's point of view) give the false impression that it can be done cleanly, without the charred flesh and gouged innards.

———

Worked clumsily all morning, fumbling and feeling my way, hating some of it, respecting some, trying to balance the sentences and make them flow.

———

W's small tinny, the dash with which she pilots it across from Palm Beach wharf. She says she has learnt to see in the dark and never needs a torch. I slept on a low, comfortable bed with pale-pink sheets, a dark-pink eiderdown, an ancient wool blanket of the most beautiful dark green. A proper reading lamp. Three well-chosen books.

———

Seeing one of her yoga commentaries on the bedside table and a photo of her guru on the wall, I resolve that I will never be scornful of someone else's spiritual struggles or moments of enlightenment— not even gently dreamy ones like P's or stiff, forbidding ones like the born-again's. I can be sceptical but never scornful. And if I want to write about them, I bloody well *will*. Get rid of the biographer and her threats.

———

A wonderful TV remake of *The Shiralee*. The little girl trotting gamely after the uncompromising man—this is how I dragged my girl through her childhood, paying no attention to her complaints.

———

At dinner the men shouted about 'the regional' in Australian art. One of them ran a patriot's line. The other said that any art had to pass over the barrier between the regional and the universal—he roared about Henry Lawson: 'He drags us down.'

———

'Till you pointed it out to me, I thought people still wore their shirt collar *out* of a round-necked jumper.'

———

This English department office is the wrong place for me to work. Every time I write something on a piece of paper I look at it and think, gee, that's not very sophisticated. I've got to get out of here.

Late in the afternoon a moon (full) bounced in a sky powdered with green and pink. Water like yellow silk, like aluminium. At Bondi some satisfying sand-coloured stones were being picked up in mouthfuls by a machine and arranged in baskets made of cyclone wire, which were then laid in a freshly dug hole against the sea wall. A man welded. His cold spark.

Is it menopausal that (1) I often wake up at night damp with sweat? (2) my period comes six days early and lasts two days and nights, then abruptly stops?

Rang Mum for her birthday. When I heard Dad call her to the phone a heavy sense of their marriage crashed over me. This *arrangement* that has lasted nearly half a century, produced six kids, is indispensable to both of them—but what has it done for them? Crushed my mother and made her spirit weak, and frustrated my father: made each of them less than they might otherwise have been. And yet it has survived many periods of unhappiness and cruelty. By comparison I feel my life to be once again light, transparent, almost gauzy, composed of filaments rather than blocks of concrete.

Five people in a room this evening told me I was 'extremely pale'. I'd been quite faint and wild with pleasure all day long, shaping sentences, juggling the pages, trying to get sense and pace into them without flattening the imagery or becoming even the smallest bit explanatory—trying to trim adjectives without losing the sensuous detail they afford—and feeling the shape of the story changing under my attentions—it expands, becomes richer, more leisured and yet still *packed*. I ate things, cleaned up, walked from room to room, thought, wrote again. In my absences from it I could sense its faults of structure, pace and narrative. Got to stop it from galloping away.

Maybe, if we have to part, what I'll miss most of all is talking with him about what we're reading. Always ready to bear a parting. We compete to be the more stoical, I think.

———

Mooching through the Macquarie I come upon 'ablative absolute', a Latin case. The example given is: '*via facta*—the road having been made.' The blunt brevity and portmanteau power of this two-word clause convulse me with envy and frustration.

———

Dreamt of a sturdy, bright shrub, waist-high, that was growing on the extreme lip of a precipice near which I stood, some feet back from the edge. Beyond this plant was empty air, a chasm I couldn't see but whose presence was palpable and which contained a huge, smoke-blue hum of significance. I was trying in this dream to compose a sentence that would encapsulate the existence of this plant: its flowers were an explosive red, it grew with vigour, its branches sprang out from its stem in a satisfying, meaningful shape. The fact that it grew on the very rim of nothingness was of no concern to it. It grew, it was firmly rooted, it blossomed, it *was*.

———

Mozart and Mahler at the Opera House. I tell Z I've bought us the cheap tickets. He props in the kitchen: 'In the *orchestra*? You'll get deafened!'—as if he were suddenly no longer of the party. The seats turn out to be perfectly adequate. The Mahler I did not know. I liked its stereo effect—cowbells, knocking percussion, terrific horns; but though it carried me away I could see why people make jokes about it—all that torment. A colossal rainstorm exploded overhead as we were leaving. Every rubbish bin we stumbled past contained at least one broken umbrella. Water lashed across the road as if a powerful hose were being played from the top of a building.

———

The jumping force field of *interest* between V and me, both mutual and outward, that makes the world seem so rich and teeming with spectacle. His pen moves fast and light across a sheet of paper. The way he can physically put words down makes my pen seem a log.

———

I am always reminding myself that he is not mine, that he belongs to somebody else, that it's not safe to fantasise being with him always. This is the precipice; but on its lip the bush flowers fiercely, *taking no thought for the morrow*.

———

I know, from my own experience, that people can recover from things. And I can't see the end of a marriage as the end of a life. 'Life goes on,' says R. 'It *must* go on. It can't stop.' 'And it can't go back?' I say. 'No,' she says, 'it can't go back.' In a blighted cafe in Rozelle V and I share a small bottle of mineral water. I feel deeply appalled that he's started the process of extrication. My thighs on the seat feel weak. I'm not seeing properly. Terror of the magnitude of these events. And grief. For *them*, and their marriage.

———

Bartók's second string quartet. Some of those harmonies sound like brown wood.

———

Men's horror of the *unreasonableness* of our emotions, the tidal nature of our moods, the way they expand and explode. Men are afraid of losing the *shape* of things, even momentarily.

———

What am I blithely handing over, here? Tonight, walking to give my lecture, carrying my briefcase and feeling unmarriageable and neutrally solitary, I felt a dropping heart at the idea of becoming half of a middle-aged couple. Comfort myself by remembering nonsense and play with F—how even now, after everything that's happened, we can still *have fun* together.

———

'They that have power to hurt and will do none.'

———

Moments of terrible, groggy shock. And yet underneath it the sense of something logically unfolding. It doesn't feel bad, or wrong, to me. The wake slaps me around but the pain I'm getting is vicarious.

———

What am I doing this evening? A trifling question. Doing the ironing. Listening to some music. Reading. Hoovering white fluff off the carpet. Upstairs, muffled, a choir is singing the Lacrimosa from Mozart's *Requiem*.

———

Chicken pieces (?). Cold Power $3.75. Two chops $1.19. Coloured clouds in a low bank over the city, packed there as if to act as dense padding for the bridge's tough curve. The pretty young woman serving in the grocery shop made me feel her fingertips, to show how cold they were.

———

R calls, I give a shout of joy. My dear friend. It's taken me years of work on myself to become worthy of her. I often doubt that I am.

———

A whole life can be spent quietly and patiently drawing nearer to something important. It can't be hurried. This is why there is no such thing as boredom.

———

Violets grow in a pot on the porch of this apartment. I picked some and put them in a glass. At the moment of picking they have no scent, but half an hour later, sitting here, I notice something faintly delicious and turn around. The violets have opened further, become purpler, are in their small way terribly beautiful.

———

Every morning I wake in a sweat. Where one of my knees has rested on the mattress there's a little round pool.

———

The dying man's shaven head is resting on a blue gauze pad. His wife and I go out to the lift so she can fiercely smoke. She lets tears pour. The smoke bumps its way across the thick curls of her permed hair. I ask, 'Is there any comfort? What are you living on?' 'I believe certain things,' she says. 'They're useful to me. I believe there's a chance of more than one life. I believe this because for there to be one thing in nature which made no sense and contradicted itself would be illogical.' We are sitting in two chairs, talking intently, tears running off our cheeks. Our voices are low, but audible to anyone who cares to listen. A teenage girl comes out of the lift and sits down facing us, very close, her forearms along the armrests of her chair. She sits like a judge or a witness, and gazes straight at us. Neither of us takes any notice. When his wife stops crying, her eyes are very widely spaced, full of life and feeling. I walk out through the huge front entrance. Late in the afternoon. Birds are calling very loudly in the trees along Missenden Road. A quick shot of *being alive*. Their song is so loud, it's as if my lively ears had magnified it. Walk along sobbing and gasping.

The Queen's drawing collection at the gallery. Appalled to see the little ER stamp of ownership in the corner of each one—on a *Leonardo*! A *Michelangelo*! What a hide these people have got. An Annunciation: an angel with arms spread and knees still flexed from landing. Glad to have gone alone.

I told R that even in a ghastly split-up there are certain moments of truce, where both people laugh freely, as if for that moment seeing each other truly and deeply and without rancour. She said, 'How interesting.'

In Melbourne our dog has run away twice. She trotted all the way from North Melbourne to Fitzroy and arrived drenched and dirty at F's front door, behind which he was at his desk reworking somebody's terrible French translation of *Monkey Grip*: 'The rhythm of the French sentence is different from the English and with not enough words to play with it is at times difficult to get the music right.'

———————

A teenage girl gets knocked off her bike at a crossing, in front of a bunch of pedestrians. She goes flying. She is wearing a helmet and has only skinned her elbow, but she sobs with anger and fright, sweating, trembling, a dark red flush down one side of her neck and shoulder. The driver, an old man grey with shock, gets out of his car and approaches. She yells at him in a studenty, self-righteous way, tears and dirt streaking her round cheeks. As soon as he sees she is not seriously hurt he makes as if to return to his car, but an Arab truck driver pulls up and the old man is returned by the combined moral force of the silent group to face the raging girl. 'You don't even *care*!' 'I *do* care!' he cries. 'I care very much! I have two daughters!' He says it was her fault. We all say no, it was his, and he becomes greyer and smaller, mumbling, 'I'm sorry, I'm sorry. Thank you.' 'Those wheels,' she shouts, shaking and sobbing, 'cost *one hundred and seventy-five dollars!*' I keep my hand on her shoulder: 'Don't ride home. You're in shock.' The truckie offers to drive her home. She refuses, and wheels her beautiful (undamaged) bike away. 'It was an accident,' says a man, and we all go about our business.

———————

Babette's Feast. The artist's cry: 'Let it be possible for me to do the very best I can!' I went home smaller, ashamed of my agitated idleness, my unfinished story.

———————

The officer-students at the Australian Defence Force Academy, their trim heads and uniforms, their marching gait with high-swinging arms: they have to fall into step if they walk anywhere in groups of two or more. The only place they don't have to salute is *in the library*. At breakfast in the hotel my father was the only man not in uniform. I said, 'You want to look out someone doesn't hand you a white feather.'

Watching the TV news my father says, 'What's the point of showing us Israeli soldiers shooting round corners? They see the cameras. They're just putting on an act.'

'You mustn't pity her,' I said to V. 'Your pity will weaken her. What she needs is your respect.'

My mother knitted as we talked, showing the best of herself—talkative, but not droning. V was sweet to her, asking her the direct questions he's so good at: 'Do you like having so many children?' 'How did they let you know your brother had been killed?' She told him things I'd never heard before. She mentioned a childhood friend called Florrie Beanland. He threw back his head and shouted with laughter: '*Nobody's* called *Florrie Beanland*!'

V said that women look 'ugly and old' when they cry. R to my surprise agreed. I protested. I said that once I'd cried for three days and then got out of bed, looked in the mirror, and found I looked 'gorgeous—all soft and young'. They burst out laughing, having expected 'raddled', I suppose. We agreed that the final effect of crying was often relief and that this could take away ageing tensions.

I took Mum to the Opera House, to see *Otello*. We both had to wipe our eyes, loving the music. She said, 'It made me think of Dad. That jealousy of nothing.' Oysters at the quay. On the bus we were quiet, gazing out the window at the city, this spectacle. 'Everything is older, here,' she said. 'I wish I didn't have to leave.' At Via Veneto we ran into L and the Cretan. The Greeks were charming and funny, behaved towards Mum with gentle respect, shook her hand upon leaving.

'Your mother strikes me,' says R's son, 'as as someone who doesn't often enjoy herself. She seemed to be surprised whenever she laughed.'

————

Etty Hillesum's diary. Her father visits. All our good intentions, she thinks, are *as nothing* before the huge negative force of our feelings towards our parents. The best that's possible is intense self-control.

————

'I lied,' said V.

————

We talked at dinner about fights where plates were thrown. I said I'd loved the machine in *The Rake's Progress* that turned broken crockery into bread: 'I wish I'd had one of those when I was married to F.' 'Oh!' said Z. 'Did you smash things? I've always dreamt of that. I've only ever been close to people who sulked.' 'There's a wonderful moment,' I said, 'when you hear the *sound* of the smash, but it's very short, and then you have to clean up the mess. You have to get down on your knees.'

————

On the spare bed at R's in the afternoon I try to sleep, counting my breathing, but wide awake. Something's gone. I know what it is: the necessity for stoicism. A hard jacket's been taken off me. At first what I notice about its absence is a kind of blank surprise—then a fencelessness. My thoughts no longer run up against the monolith. I lie under the cheap quilt, calm, empty, complete, as if at the end of some trial. 'The monolith.' That smashed thing. Full of holes. Air and light now pass through its breached walls. Who's responsible?

————

A novelist gives a boring, shallow lecture. Why don't people say what they have learnt about life and what they believe in? I don't think artists should presume to speak unless they are prepared to say something serious—even if they're obliged to slip it in among the fluffed-up egg-whites like a bitter pill.

————

'One thing your wife's done for you all these years is to create around you a cushion of comfort and attention. Hasn't she.' Staggered to see he has no idea he is dependent on this. Men who will not stoop to teach themselves the domestic skills and talents that women possess (or have had to cultivate): they live in a mess, without attractive comforts, waiting for some woman to arrive in a fluster bearing gifts, ready to set the place to rights.

———

I cooked spinach with butter and garlic. He made no comment and ate it without apparent relish. Perhaps he is going to be discontented and hard to please.

———

It feels like spring, and the shops are full of linen clothes not very well cut.

———

What causes stupidity? And what *is* it?

———

Going along the quay I saw the Opera House sails against a perfectly pure sky at sunset: they were *mauve*, the most delicate colour—such beauty, and soon I might be living in the city where it can occur.

———

A man on the building site sings aloud with a joyful shout—a falling and rising riff, like a warrior singing about battle.

———

R said enthusiastically that Emerson had 'anticipated certain concepts in depth psychology'. V's face lost all expression, like a blackboard just wiped. 'Projection, for example,' R continued, soldiering on. 'The idea that we project on to others what is inside us.' He had no word to say. I laughed and went out into the kitchen.

———

I'm tired. My life's in limbo because he has not told the whole truth.

———

Visited a class at Glebe High School. The usual scornful, bored, closed faces one would expect in fourth-formers but the teacher used his imagination, and we got somewhere. The girls were very retiring. The bell went and the boys scattered; then the girls gathered in a tight group around me and the teacher. A Chinese girl asked, 'Do artists have—strange moods?' Another, packing her books, said over her shoulder to the teacher, 'But teaching's an art, sir, I reckon.' I don't know if it's an art, but I remember that it's hard labour: the cold modern building, the inarticulate kids—I take off my hat to teachers.

———

'You said I was emotionally naïve,' said V. 'What did you mean?'

'I don't think you know much about the fluctuations of emotions that people go through in their relations with each other.'

'But I've been married. And as an artist I've observed.'

'Yes, but your life hasn't depended on it.'

———

I walked a mile along streets near the dilapidated Canberra motel, looking for something to eat. I passed sad, neglected-looking buildings, cheap home units with blankets hooked over their windows. Yards of beaten earth. Arrangements of chicken wire and boxes near the gates—cages, but with no animals in them.

———

Her anxiety, at the meeting. Her super-willingness to grasp my points. Her eager face, the poised pen, the notebook.

———

R says that now is the time when I should consider what giving up my separateness could mean, that if I live with him I will of necessity become 'cook and bottle-washer'. Painfully I consider these propositions. But how could I not live with him? Could I fight him about the housework? Could I make demands and hold out for them?

———

In the cafe R and I agreed that we were probably rather androgynous and that we liked this. I said I felt I was physically made of a dryer, harder substance than some more feminine women. She said she wished in fantasy to be an opera singer, but that she could 'never bear that burden of flesh'. The paradoxical, or contradictory, idea that in order to produce an ethereal, heavenly or superhuman sound one must be even *more* fleshly than ordinary humans.

_____

Two sparrows fuck on a twig outside the window. He hops on to her back and off, she flutters her wings very fast against her body, he hops on again—they do this five times within two minutes.

_____

The empty apartment, a shell of fantasy, not a single stick of furniture, a long space full of light.

_____

The sick man died, at last. By now he will be only a pile of hot ash and crumbled bones. The part of him that suffered has been consumed. But his wife. What will she do with all the love?

_____

'At our little girl's funeral,' said the woman, 'I fell over.'
  'Do you mean you fainted?'
  'No, I didn't faint.'
  'Did you trip?'
  'No. I couldn't stand. I fell down.'

_____

After the service we walked on the beach. E was very vivid and pretty in her black crepe skirt and jacket and her pink blouse with black spots. The escarpment looms over the road and the town. By four the day is ended.

_____

In Bar Italia he looked narrower, paler, with darker eyes. I couldn't look at him enough, the sight of him was so precious to me.

_____

U's Englishman went back to Cambridge, where she was meant to join him; but somehow she just never went. I imagine returning to

Melbourne and quietly sinking back into my previous life—as if
these recent upheavals had occurred in some opium trance. I know
this is a kind of death wish, a slide into inertia. But these fantasies
have occurred.

———

The child is doing her homework, making a list of twenty-six things
(A–Z) that Captain Cook would have taken on his journey: 'N?'
    H: 'Nibs.'
    Her older brother: 'They would have had quills, not nibs.'
    H: 'I bet they had nibs.'
    Brother: (*smoothly*) 'They didn't invent nibs till 1830.'
    H: 'You just made that up.'
    Brother: 'No I didn't. I read it in a history of calligraphy that
came with my italic nib set.'

———

We will learn a great deal about each other now.

———

Fear makes people literal-minded.

———

Dreamt I bought a pair of black high-heeled shoes and wore them
with socks. Pleased with my appearance. But when I met my sister
in a cafe and asked her if she liked them, she said, 'No. You look
about fifty in them.' She hadn't waited for me, had already ordered
her breakfast. I crept away wounded, with hunched shoulders.

———

To P's show. I looked out the gallery window through the rain to
Government House with its little flag, took a breath, and began.
I realised that each picture contains hidden things: a sheep on a
globe, two little yachts: you could look at them for a long time and
be always finding her secret messages. And best of all is the way she
puts on the paint: nothing lumpy or bumpy; nothing *thick*. A svelte
surface, sometimes with a golden note or a glimmer in it, seeming
to have been built up out of many very fine layers.

'V's aged a great deal,' said his friend, 'over the last few years. He's an old-fashioned Australian country man who's passionately interested in modern European culture.' 'He's always struck me,' I said, 'as someone the modern world has passed by. It's as if he hasn't even *noticed* it.'

My nun's long, detailed story of arriving at the decision to leave the Little Sisters of Jesus. Of choosing life above a promise. 'I don't know what I've missed and what I haven't missed.' I listened with full attention, fascinated, watching her face as she spoke: her smooth skin, her bones, her curly grey hair in its pretty crop.

In the newspaper a list of 'the suits men buy: navy 60%, charcoal-grey 25%, mid-grey 12%, brown 2%, other 1%'.

V inveighs against the 'tribal' urge of women to 'rush in' and support each other when one of them's 'discarded'. What the hell does he expect women to do? I hold my tongue, remembering having to lie on the floor with the pain of being 'discarded'.

I ask, 'How are you?'

He replies, levelly and vaguely, 'Oh...all right.'

I feel foolish, reproached for having asked. Maybe he expects me to *probe*, since he is not forthcoming. I start to see what I could be in for.

Wonderful spring day, little perfumed gusts of daphne, freesias, the very beginning of pittosporum. Windows rattle in the balmy wind. What a dry city Melbourne is: its winds come in off dry, grassy plains, while Sydney's come off water. I wrote several extremely long sentences, the labour of which afforded me the most exquisite pleasure and satisfaction.

At the kitchen table with a pot of tea and a packet of Venetian biscuits I recommence *A la Recherche du temps perdu* (in English). My life now is likely to be filled with change, upheavals, departures, lies, white lies, damned lies, and a host of anxieties and sorrows. I need a large-structured element in which to rest and which I can step in and out of without fear of having lost the thread.

———

A puppy yapping in someone's yard woke me at 1 am and I couldn't fall asleep for ages. Why are night thoughts always so much more pessimistic, sorrowful and panicky than thoughts on the same topics in daylight?

———

The old woman showed me her Kakadu photos. 'See? That thing there's a crocodile. They're brown, and they're scaly, and we've intruded on to their territory.'

———

F calls to ask me a language question. Now it's over I remember how much I *like* him. He must never have had my full attention. I could begin to torture myself about this. Walking to church rehearsing my cruelty, selfishness, neglect, I wondered if there's a way to free oneself of guilt, of finally squaring it with oneself so that the load drops off. The first hymn we sang mentioned 'cancelled crimes'.

———

New kitchen doors and windows are in. Chaos but room full of light. I sit at the table eating my breakfast and gazing out at SKY. Royalties $3000. Can I spin this out for four months?

———

Crazy about the way Proust uses physical objects to keep his huge, billowing sentences grounded.

———

In my freshly painted kitchen I turn on the heating, spread out my papers on the tablecloth, and entertain a treacherous fantasy: a fantasy to protect me from *the fear of failure* which is, I think, what I am 'suffering from': I *wish* for failure so that once again I will be free to spread out my papers on this tablecloth. 'I'd like to retire there and do *nothing,*/or nothing much, forever, in two bare rooms.' —Elizabeth Bishop, 'The End of March'

———

A doona that's been folded, but flat, so it resembles a worn-out asparagus drooping sadly rather than 'a wafer' or a small clean cloud.

———

I am a woman. I (i) long to be of service (ii) like domestic order (iii) am socially quite skilful—at organising lists of appointments etc (iv) can do basic cooking (v) feel an urge to fill gaps where otherwise chaos, awkwardness, discomfort (physical, emotional, social) might occur (vi) like to make practical demonstrations of love. All I need to attend to is that I keep enough of myself free for my work and the hours of private mental time this requires. I mean that my attention to him and his needs should not outweigh my attention to myself for work. '*All* I need'! This terribly hard thing, for a woman.

———

The perfume of pittosporum cuts the air, sharp as lemons. The form of its foliage—puffed, rounded flounces, each lying on the next layer down—in heavy cascades. The leaves are shiny and the flowers fan out in waxy sprays.

———

'I don't even *like* women. It's terrible to say this but women drive most blokes crazy.'

'I'm a woman too, you know.'

'Ah, no. You're different.'

———

Dreamt I said to the hairdresser, 'I want my hair to be purple, and curly.' She gave me a doubtful, ironic look and I said, disgruntled, 'Oh, all right then, just take off a bit over the ears.'

———

The French woman is sixty but looks twenty-five years younger. Her youthful bounce, her round face. I liked her for having on under her red and yellow dress a grubby old white T-shirt. The spectacle of the grim Anglo-Saxon man softened by Gallic flirtatiousness is comical, he is so unselfconsciously *keen* on her, so impressed by her unAustralian, unmasculine quality. 'She's got a marvellous *spirit*,' he raves later, then pulls himself up and his voice fades: 'Oh, so have you—I've always liked *your*, um, spirit…' 'Oh, for God's sake!' I burst out, in a spasm of embarrassment. 'You don't have to talk about me! *I* liked her, too!' How on earth is it possible to behave with grace in this bombed-out minefield between men and women?

———

I must stop being *passive*. I must work out exactly what I need, and start arranging things so I can *have* it.

———

Backyard ravaged, rubbish gone, my essentials halfway to Sydney. Very shaky inside, afraid, sad, guilty.

———

My brother and his wife say goodbye to me in Lygon Street: their baby in his adventurous blue cap with earflaps; this adorable, reticent child. Whenever he smiles he turns his face away, as if to hide his merriment.

———

My sisters packed my car for me: their brisk, cheerful practicality. It was soon done and I had this neat vehicle layered with a weird selection of my worldly possessions. They spread the tartan rug over the lot 'to prevent distracting glare if the sun shines in'.

———

5 am. Viscount Motel, Albury. Somewhere birds are singing madly—showers and blasts of trills. In the night mother-guilt fell on me like a ton of bricks, memories of M's early childhood, its upheavals. I lay here tired and disoriented. Thought of 'cancelled

sins', of 'absolution', 'forgiveness'. All these manifestations of grace that I long for.

———

At Goulburn stopped for food. A 'Lilac Festival' in a park with no lilacs in evidence. A sign outside a tent, its gist: 'Don't get the idea that to get into heaven you only have to lead a good life, go to church etc—you also MUST BELIEVE that Christ died for you personally.' Sorry but nobody's going to tell me what I MUST BELIEVE. How can anyone MUST BELIEVE anything?

———

E's pretty, English-seeming house in Enmore—the heavy old blue-and-white crockery, the white-framed doors opening on to a narrow back garden full of trees. A good piano, and she too is a beginner. I take courage. Very much at ease with her, felt liked and treated with affection. She has offered me the upstairs front room. Two French windows that face east (or is it north?) and let in the noise of distant trains. I have brought two lamps, two kitchen dishes, my enamel saucepan, some rubber gloves, the filing cabinet and my white Ikea clothes rack.

———

He made some ravioli with sauce out of a jar. It was delicious.

———

Swam ten laps at 6 am. Now I feel my stomach muscles. Read some Hemingway, then Carver again. Carver's middle period. Large respect for him, the jagged voices, the catastrophes, the spare language and the striving for spare imagery. In such a landscape of struggle, panic, despair, the old images he uses have a deep and emblematic power. *The hem of the garment.* The simple becomes tremendous.

———

F: 'You seem to have a very powerful influence on people and they tend to find it necessary to break away from you and more often than not they do it the hard way.'

I said I did not know the skills of sharing a life with someone. V said I'd be okay as long as I did not 'behave briskly—with brisk independence'. I felt chastened, as if *taught*. 'I'm not a tyrant, am I?' he said. 'I think you're probably the kind of tyrant,' I said, 'who simply assumes things will be done the way he likes them, and if they're not he's surprised and rather hurt.'

Thick emotions in conflict. There is always the shadow side of our happiness. The private thought of his wife alone in their house. He speaks of her, but not of it. Perhaps all happiness has its shadow, or has to be supported by the sorrow of someone else. Sometimes the longing to see my girl is *sharp*. I feel it 'in my breast', as poets say. My heart and lungs are obliged to toil at their work instead of behaving with natural rhythm.

I went to Grace Bros and bought some cream paint. Stood waiting to cross Broadway and thought vaguely, 'This is Sydney and I live here now.'

V's friend W came to his place for dinner. She was tall and handsome in a shapeless, burnt-orange cotton dress pulled in with a leather belt. Bare legs, orange Chinese slippers. In his presence I notice her mannerisms of mouth and face, her persona which is 'open', 'good-tempered', 'intelligent', 'funny' etc. We watched the Ellis–Harkin fight on TV. Two young, smooth-bodied fellows battering at each other's heads. When a boxer drops his head and puts up his big stupid gloves to protect it I feel the kind of rage and pity I'd feel if I saw a child having to ward off a blow.

In E's balcony room I slept for eleven hours. Light and air of a clarity so perfect that a gum-tree branch outside my window looks transparent: light coming at it from every side.

'Our desires cut across one another, and in this confused existence it is rare for happiness to coincide with the desire that clamoured for it.' —Proust, *Within a Budding Grove*

In the unfinished house high above the ocean the new widow served three of us a large and delicious meal. She was composed, friendly, ready to laugh; but her face, Z said on the way home, was 'tired, and full of sorrow'. We were all writers. Z talked about the way one can't believe, looking back on a book, that in order to write it one went through gruesome stages of uncertainty, fear, ignorance—because the published book looks like the result of certain smoothly taken decisions, the product of a mind functioning *consciously*. Relieved that this happens even to someone as famous as Z.

Dreamt that V's wife drove up to my house in a car packed with her belongings; it had been arranged that she could store them all at my place. I offered to give her a hand. The house lacked storage space but I saw I could pile her things up against a wall in my bedroom, which was enormous, bare, dim and pleasant, with floorboards and a shuttered window; they wouldn't be in the way, and I could keep an eye on them for her.

V showed me some drawings by a painter with a very big reputation. 'He had a problem with facility. He was lazy. He didn't fight it so it all looks too easy.' 'What's your facility?' 'In writing? I haven't got one. But I have to fight my habit of putting in little jokes that nobody but me will understand for fifty years.'

In Chippendale, a man in thick-rimmed glasses was pulling down the charred remains of a back fence, shed and dunny. He worked grimly, alone and in silence, and his whole face, front and forearms were stained black with ash, like a figure in a vision of hell.

———

I try to write a letter like someone in a Don DeLillo novel: 'I am doing my best here to dress and groom, by mending things from earlier days, but in my closet there's a chaos that's enormous. I lost my little grey suitcase, how come, which I'm permanently sad and disappointed. This is for the present time goodbye, believe me, your poor sister…'

———

I thought today that I would like to write a novel in which physical violence would occur.

———

Walked with V along the cliff path to Bronte. We sat on the grass and surveyed the outrageous beauty of the scene. I began to see why he's spent twenty years inside a house. The ocean was *chirping* with light.

———

R tells me she is thinking of training as a Jungian analyst. Thinking of this extremely suitable proposition, and after reading a severe article about German literature, I feel ignorant, lacking in intellectual power or organising ability. I'm not and never will be a real intellectual. It's not my nature. I forget things, and am distracted by surface sparkle. I will probably never write anything large, lasting, solid or influential. Is this a proper life I am leading? It is a kind of half-life—living secretly in a strange city, asking people to lie for me and cover my tracks.

———

I never knew before the difference between sadness and sorrow. Sadness is general, broad, heavy, passive. Sorrow is sharper, more focused, more active, working hard. I could even say labouring. Labouring with sorrow. When I think of his wife's unhappiness, my own 'indignities' almost vanish—because the reason he gives for requiring them is to save her from further pain. He does not see that this is unlikely to work, in the long run.

———

The 'civilised' world is full of wounded people. I don't know what could alter this.

———

V showed me a couple of American short stories he likes: Irwin Shaw, 'The Girls in Their Summer Dresses' and 'Mixed Doubles' and then one by Cheever, 'The Enormous Radio'. They brought me up once more against the hopelessness of men and women, the vast chasms between them—the death of sexual love, wandering attention, physical degeneration, men's wide-ranging sexual fantasies and greed. At the market we had a stupid quarrel about a melon. In the car he wouldn't meet my eye, and down I plummeted. I longed to say, 'What happened? What's gone wrong?' but I was scared he'd say, 'Nothing! You're neurotic! You're imagining it!'

———

R is the only person I know who can make comments on people's behaviour and character—very sharp and accurate comments—without descending into judgment. She is like a scientist.

———

Peter Carey wins the Booker for *Oscar and Lucinda*. We confess to each other, with shameful laughs, a small sinking sensation. 'He and I started out at about the same time,' says V, 'but he threw it into overdrive and now all I can see of him is his tail-lights.' I realise how differently we think about our work in the world: I see that he is able to imagine his work in that league, while to me it is not even thinkable—it never crosses my mind.

———

G comes over. V becomes attentive but oddly passive. G drinks vodka with beer chasers and is soon slumping loosely: 'Am I slurring my words?' H: 'Yes, but you're making perfect sense.' He reports that Jane Campion's new movie has a sequence in which a woman goes out into the desert with her father. I feel relieved, as if my film won't need to be made after all. We watch him get into his Merc, reverse down the street at sixty kph and disappear.

———

Hot weather a bit alarming due to news reports of THE GREENHOUSE EFFECT: it's only the end of October but yesterday it was thirty-six degrees, exactly like a day of high summer in Melbourne—gusty winds, dry air, gasping sun, white sky.

———

My lovely bed at E's. Clean, comfortable, welcoming. In the morning, she suggests laps at the Enmore pool. We swim separately, without speaking, wrapped in our separate thoughts.

———

G calls and relates an extraordinary tale, like something by Beaumarchais or from a French movie, about going with M-C to a fitting of her wedding dress, pretending to be 'a gay hairdresser, picking up her hair and saying, "What are you going to do with this?" I saw a little silk slip, you know, really short, and I said, "I'll give you this as a wedding present, you can wear it on your wedding night!"' All the while, telling me this in a melancholy, sighing voice, he is dragging on a cigarette or a joint, breathing in, breathing out.

———

When I reported this to V, he launched a leisurely disquisition on women, beauty, clothes, their responsibilities in this regard. I lost my temper, argued wildly about the injustice of women's position as *regarded creatures* who are constantly obliged to think carefully about their self-presentation—the neurotic obsession with one's appearance that results from this. I tried to examine my physical sensations in order to grasp what was going on—a heaviness and sense of turmoil under the ribcage. V seemed puzzled and surprised by how 'cranky' I got, and as I calmed down I felt ashamed of my intemperance—but I wonder if in the end he was trying to argue me round to the point at which *women can't be artists*. If we reached this point, it would mean either (1) that I am barking up the wrong tree in my life or (2) that I am something *other than a woman*. After this we watched 'Murphy's Law' on TV. Quite horrible how one sits there with one's beloved's legs across one's lap and watches people kill, bash, stab, rape and insult each other on a nasty little flickering screen.

———

Venetian paintings at the gallery, with R. A small Adam and Eve being driven out of the garden by an angel whose wings are a blur of gold; an Annunciation—angel in flight, in a crushed blue garment, holding a single tall and perfect lily; a Virgin whose cloak, of a profound and mouth-watering crimson, is knotted over her belly in the dead centre of the picture.

———

V said he needed to buy 'a strong kitchen chair'. I said, with a quick vision of my kitchen in Melbourne, 'I've got a pretty set of four...' and suddenly my heart thumped to the floor. I said, 'I'm homesick.' He laughed. On my way back to E's I thought, 'Tomorrow I will be forty-six. And for a while there I lived in a house which was MINE.' Oh, shut up.

———

Last time I visited R her son was bumptious with me and we squabbled. Today he was subdued and sweet. He complimented me on my white backpack and said it matched a white hat I'd had on the other day. I accepted his atonement with relief.

———

V said to me that I had 'an extraordinary mind—you think things right through, by prisming them through yourself. Your mind is ten times as good as mine.' What? Doesn't he see my laziness? My disinclination to *think*?

———

I turn up at his place on the evening of my birthday, an hour early, wearing heels and a long skirt, thinking he had invited me to dinner. He has no food: 'I didn't know whether you were going to bring it.' He returns to the typewriter. I am completely without resources, standing at the bench in my inappropriate clothes, nothing to do, a non-guest, a non-person. So I leave without further discussion and drive back to E's, and here I am in a *room which is mine*, in comfortable clothes, having abandoned all sense of occasion. I sit here missing my family. I am forty-six and *I exist*. I *do*.

———

A letter from Dad. 'Thank you for the pencil sharpener. I have sharpened every pencil I ever had and the little drawer is nearly full of shavings.'

———

A growing affection for E. Her seriousness and self-discipline. My spirits rise in her house, with its tall windows and slanting light. She says things like this: 'I was the only one in the pool this morning. Sun was crinkling along the bottom.' We like to talk about everything. She says she has femocrat friends who earn up to $70,000. 'What do they *spend* it on?' 'They take taxis. They haven't got time to cook so they eat out four nights a week. They have to look good—they spend a lot on elegant clothes.' She told me she'd met a man at a party who was a psychologist at Silverwater prison. He said that the people in jail who are most 'like oneself', most likely to examine themselves and change, are the murderers.

———

'I'm becoming fussily pedantic in supermarkets or whatever you call 'em.'

   'What you call "being fussily pedantic" other people call "shopping".'

———

We quarrel over his demand for furtiveness. I find it humiliating. He says I've over-reacted to a minor event. I say he doesn't know how minor or major this incident is *to me*. Our wills clash. I feel the toughness and irony in him and I display my own. He says, 'I've suffered horribly through all this, these last few months.' 'I know you have. But you don't *show* it.' 'You only had to *look* at me, to see it.' I begin to be ashamed of myself. 'I love you,' he says, 'without pride.' 'I know you do,' I say humbly; '*I* love *you*, but proudly.' I return to E's, a sobered woman. This terrible pride. Through it I begin to understand the imagery of Christianity—the longing to be washed, to have chains struck from me.

––––––

Still raining. The air all over Sydney is filled with a deep hiss.

––––––

Dreamt I was in a play but had not learnt my lines. Another character spoke to me expectantly and my mind was blank. I feigned a collapse, fell to the ground and lay there for a long time. Nobody came to see how I was. I looked up and everyone had gone.

––––––

Y comes up from Melbourne: a wonderful day of talk at E's kitchen table. Nourished by the company of women.

––––––

A writer announces in a powerful voice that his new novel is the most important book that's been written in Australia in the last decade, that it must be published in hardback, and that if this means other writers have to forfeit their publishing subsidy to cover this, he does not care. E and I appalled by this, but when I report it to V he approves: a writer should do everything in his power to get his book well published and noticed. Echo of Stendhal: 'Neglect nothing that can make you great', a sentiment that V quotes with fiery approval but that makes me shudder with embarrassment. Women artists, I think, are more modest, but also more passive. Did Stendhal become the Good/Great Writer he's acknowledged to be today because he forced himself into the limelight, or because he wrote good books?

––––––

At the photo shop a brown and bouncing Greek girl said to me, 'I got a new neighbour yesterday! And they like the same music I do!

This morning they put on a really old record that I love—I can't wait to get home and make friends!'

———

I want to write things that push down deeper roots into *the archetypal*. Things whose separate parts have multiple connections with their own structure. Dawning awareness of the point of art, and the limits of my work so far. I can't learn *anything* through my intellect alone. I do it first, or it happens to me, and the mind catches up later. This is why I could never be argued into becoming a Christian. *Do* some people join up because of an argument? Pascal's bet?

———

V reports evening calls from various interested women who have heard he's left his marriage. What have I done? Opened him up and now all the women in the world push past me and rush in. One phones to tell him she loves him, that she always has, and that she expects a letter from him within two weeks. Another turns up and stays till midnight—I remember meeting her outside a gallery a year ago: in her thirties, very good-looking, an aggrieved vibe, something *un-light* about her, a little cross face, unsmiling, expecting the worst from the world. I ought to step back on to my own turf and let whatever happens happen. If I were in Melbourne I'd go up to Primrose Gully and stay there.

———

At E's place she and I watched a doco about Jung in which some old analysts were interviewed. One of them said, 'You have to be *lonely*, in order to experience the unconscious.'

———

Reread my screenplay. The last section is dreadful—a post-mortem feeling. R came over to E's for tea. Her light presence. We talked about standards in art, what it means that her mother likes Pro Hart, whether aesthetics is separate (as a study) from ordinary life. Whenever she's with me I feel cheerful, curious, hopeful. In the evening I wrote out a series of system cards for the screenplay, one for each little scene. Gloom rolled away. I called F and we spoke affectionately of this and that. Woken at 6 am in my balcony room by crackling thunder and a steady flood of rain.

———

'One completely overcomes only what one assimilates.' —André Gide, *Journals*

Thus I must assimilate my jealousy. By what process is this to be achieved? What a cold writer, what a cold *man* Gide is, for all his talk of passions—trembling while reading Shakespeare and so on. In his thin-lipped French way he tries to find and tell the truth, but he has no humour, no sense of laughter. I go cold all over, reading him.

———

Melvyn Bragg interviews Saul Bellow on TV about *The Dean's December*. Bellow grandly puts shit on sociologists, psychologists and criminologists for their failure to cure what's wrong with society. V gives an admiring cheer. I am disappointed and say little. 'I think,' says V, 'you weren't very interested in what he was talking about.' I realise I am withholding so as not to rock V's boat. So I say, 'I'll tell you what I really think. I think he's a windbag.' To my surprise when we discuss this V comes a long way towards my point of view. So we are not dug in. Our egos are not in charge of our ideas. We try to list writers who became windy. Hemingway. Henry James. Faulkner? (I haven't read him). We agree that windy-ness is a male failing on the whole, and that women's failing tends to be wetness. 'Your mate Carver,' he says, 'is not windy at all.' Is windy-ness to do with ambition? Is it also an American failing? Chekhov, we agree, is never windy. We decide to go away for the weekend. To have 'an adventure'.

———

At E's I opened the balcony door. A wind rushed in and blew my screenplay system cards all over the floor. I saw at once that this was *a sign*: that having used the cards to show me the order of the (hopeless) third draft, I had been allowing that order to dominate my rewrite.

R says that the topics and language of social discourse, with men and women, are set by men. We tailor ourselves to their demands. It would be absurd, she said, to make crude demands: 'Okay, now it's our turn.' We start to laugh, imagining them sitting there biting their lips until 'we' had had 'our' go. Maybe, I say, we're behaving wisely in conducting our discourse among ourselves where it can develop its own organic freedoms. R jumps on this: 'But that's an argument for separatism. Aren't there witty, steady, womanly women who succeed in altering the discourse, when men and women are talking together?' 'But aren't those "witty women",' I said, 'the ones who've absorbed the male modes, and who are competitive with men on *their* terms? Have you ever seen it happen?'

Dreamt I stood at a fence and looked at a house. One corner of it crumbled and collapsed. Out of the rubble were brought four dead babies: very small, homunculi, in fact. They were laid in a line across the garden, half under a tarp. A man and I looked at them. Was there a form of verbal rite we had to perform? Later I came back and found that rats had chewed their faces away. The emotional tone of this I have forgotten.

V is reading Robert Craft's biography of Stravinsky. Driving up the highway he tells me in an awe-struck tone that Stravinsky used to come in to lunch with his wife and children and forbid them to speak not only to him but to each other. I said that this was egotistical and unreasonable. V admitted it was 'tyrannical', but claimed it was justified by Stravinsky's need to maintain in his mind, while eating his lunch, the architecture of sounds that he'd been creating all morning and would return to in the afternoon. I kept my temper by imagining beautiful *napery*, a tall window with closed shutters and a hot day outside, a tiled floor, thick glasses. Clean hands.

I notice hard, square calluses on the backs of V's heels: 'Look. As if you'd once had wings but they've been surgically removed.' 'Mercury treatment,' he says, without missing a beat.

The smile a man gets when he's about to come out with something he wants to say but feels he shouldn't: a smile of *daring*—the look that accompanies an act of irreverence, disloyalty, insolence, cheek.

'His mother and his aunt were seated opposite one another on two brightly painted chairs...They had bought the chairs that very morning and were consequently feeling light-hearted and festive. When the children arrived they were singing a little song together.'
—Jane Bowles, 'A Guatemalan Idyll'

My beautiful old Mont Blanc shorthand pen rolled off the table. I caught it but its nib stabbed right into the meat of my middle finger and left a blue mark like a tiny jail tattoo. I had the pen repaired but it's lost its silky, flexible quality. Its strokes are not *inky* any more.

The end of the movie. Who can *help* me with this? I groaned all day and then at 5 pm something happened. Strange power and freedom I experience, when I start to invent. It has its own logic. I feel my way along some kind of dark thread.

During dinner at R's place a colossal storm burst above the house: sky white with lightning, a crackling so violent that we feared to be roasted where we sat. Rain fell in steady floods, even entering the house at certain points. At the storm's height came a great knocking at the front door. We exchanged looks of Shakespearean apprehension. The boy ran to open. It was not a panting messenger or fleeing princess but his sodden schoolfriend bringing a Comedy Company record he had won in a raffle.

———

V showed me the first eight pages of the notebooks he is going to publish. He went on at such length about its severity that I was afraid I wouldn't like it, but half a page in I was riveted—his sharp eye, everything fresh, tough and surprising—and the ideas for his weird stories forming in the gaps. Felt impressed, respectful. When I tell him this he writhes and looks away, begins again to criticise them and make little of them.

———

A movie actress in an interview speaks about 'the important daily obligation of endearing yourself to someone, the daily confirmation of love'. This is where I have always failed, in the past.

———

I went to dinner at my agent's. The other guests were Patrick White, in savage mood, and Manoly Lascaris. 'Patrick, we should perhaps send Manning some flowers in hospital,' says Manoly. 'I don't *want* to,' snarled Patrick. '*I've* had artery problems, *I've* had a clot. When the Writers Against Nuclear Arms people invited me to Canberra I said I couldn't, that I'd been told I mustn't go—and Manning said, "*I've* got a clot, and *I'm* going."' I cried on my way home. With terror, and shock at his trembling thinness. I couldn't fall asleep till after midnight, then dreamt I had written a poem about the evening's events and wanted to type it on V's typewriter.

———

An old man on an escalator, with six small children clustered round him. The youngest one is holding his hand. At the bottom she pulls away and he leaves his hand stretched after her, it stays in the air as a large gesture of farewell. Intercut the escalator scene with the action. Each time there is one child fewer. And each time it's darker, and the child's dress is whiter; and when the last one darts away, he is waving to her from the gathering darkness.

———

E says she has vivid and blissful memories of being a child, with her mother. She urges me to read Alice Miller's *The Drama of the Gifted Child*. I do, and begin to see why I have no memory of ever being held by Mum, and no memory of the birth of any of the younger kids except one, and that one only because when we were taken to see Mum and the new baby a nesting magpie swooped me in the hospital grounds.

———

I scrambled to the end of the movie. Now I daren't even open the folder.

———

Christmas Eve in Melbourne. P's new house: it suits her. Shoes off and on to a rack inside the front door. Little furniture, very orderly—everything light and white. A meditation room. Her new housemate resembles, in a softer way, her former husband: a kind, intelligent face, with none of her ex's blunt, laughing masculinity.

———

M's father called to tell me that his old friend had killed herself. Yesterday morning. A drug overdose. I started shaking. Tried to speak and only babbled. Opened the back door of my empty house (the 'tenants' have gone home for Christmas) and saw a forest of weeds higher than my head—only recent rains can have saved the roses and the lilac bush—dry blue rags dangled from the jacaranda. Thick mats of creeping weed had grown right across the hose, up the wall of the shed and along the clothesline. I threw myself at it bare-handed, tore it out root and branch, hacked around the lavender bushes, then with a mattock wrenched up great coarse thistles and dandelions, all the while sobbing and raging—how can she be dead—the time we drove across the Nullarbor and up to Exmouth with the Maoists, starting each morning with the tape of 'Mr Bojangles', stayed in remote caravan parks, she thought stealing was politically justified, she stole a battery from outside a service station and it was a dud, then the drugs and how she sort of disappeared, when I'd knock at her front door she wouldn't

come out, her junkie boyfriend would stand with one arm across
the doorway meaning *Don't come in*. A long, slow process of self-
destruction. How men were drawn to it, to her intent. Intent upon
dying. Her pale skin, thick hair and delicate fingers, her slender
little body and heavy breasts, her laughter, her *cleverness*. In an
hour my hands were wrecked. Huge weeping blisters had broken
on both my palms.

———

V made a big effort with my father, who returned the courtesy
though at first he was aggressive and competitive: 'I dunno if you've
ever ridden a motorbike; *I* have.' Wilcannia is mentioned. 'Been to
Wilcannia? *I* have, and…' V held his own in a relaxed but energetic
manner, and the two men became the main event. My brother's
toddler, his busy crawling, head down, like the dog in V's notebooks:
'on a specific errand'.

———

At Primrose Gully too there is neglect and disrepair. Heavy rains
have filled the tanks but caused the mud-brick veranda to collapse,
and the chicken-wire back gate is barely holding out of the garden a
flood of sand. I see now that it's irresponsible to *lend* a place to someone
and expect them to care for it. Low clouds filled the sky, covering
a good moon. The dog clawed at fleas. Frogs struck loud, ringing
notes in the bottom dam all night long. A beautiful, chill morning,
and very still, after the rats' night scampering. Kookaburras, frogs,
crickets. A pure sky. Two koalas, five kangaroos, crimson rosellas,
several rabbits. I suppose I'll have to sell it. 'It's served its purpose,'
says V, 'but it's over.'

———

His manly dreams. 'I dreamed I was bowling to Don Bradman. I
dreamed I shot a policeman.'

———

Back in Sydney I feel uprooted all over again. I tell V I want to rent
myself a place up here, a flat of my own, an office with a bed in it.

He thinks this is a terrible idea—I would be paving the way for 'bolting'.

———

I squabble with O about rigor mortis, how long it lasts. I say it goes on forever. He disputes this, due to what he has seen in fish. To settle it I call an undertaker. He says that it 'drops out' after three or four days: 'Limbs can be straightened with a little bit of pressure.' O as always is gracious in victory.

———

Do people burn in hell for telling lies? Do they burn in hell for hurting people to whom they have made unkeepable promises? Do they burn in hell for breaking promises?

———

Summer evening at Bondi. The curved scoop of beach and bay is filled with a light haze which as darkness comes turns into a mist and wets the grass, flips the ends of my hair into pagodas.

———

All these women coming out of the woodwork. I feel like a dusty old piece of carpet. There must be some childhood chasm of disappointment and rejection that is the paradigm. I am terrified that he will lie to me. That I will have handed myself over to him and he will betray me. 'If we fuck this up, if we spoil it,' he says, 'we're not worthy to be on this *earth*.'

———

I do not want to sell Primrose Gully. That's where I taught myself to be a self-respecting woman. A lesson that has to be relearnt every day.

———

G invited V to see *Tosca* at the Opera House, and afterwards took him to 'some damn bar in Darlinghurst where there was a tableful of very young, very good-looking, very well-dressed people who all knew him. The girls were models, I think, maybe they were photographers' models. They were very *sweet*, rather like children.

And completely empty. Two of the girls came and sat with us. They were both wearing very short skirts, one with a torn-off edge—do you know what I mean?'

———

Dreamt I was dancing with my mother.

1989

New Year's resolution: to read about something in a very orderly and purposeful way; to know about something other than myself.

———

A visit to Darling Point, a high apartment with a staggering view of the harbour. I rush to the windows. Ships gliding behind a headland then their upper parts reappearing fleetingly between houses and pine trees: unsettling conjunction of vessel and vegetation. Changing light, the bridge, the Opera House, between whose eggshell sails light slid delicately sideways. Way, way down, the carefully shaven lawns, clipped shrubbery, a pool in which a young woman in a V-striped costume swam alone, suspended in aqua jelly, her limbs working like a frog's.

———

South African movie, *A World Apart*. The tortured man's face, bruised, caked, aghast. He gulps and gulps, staring straight into the camera with wild eyes, while the police take the wet whips out of the bucket.

———

They like my screenplay. A lot. Maybe they always flatter the writer at the beginning?

———

I try to tell V about the visits of the Mighty Force. I suppose he's embarrassed. He closes it down. 'Did you turn around?' 'No.'

'Because if you had, there probably wouldn't have been anything there.'

———

Elizabeth Jolley's new novel *My Father's Moon*. She re-uses and reworks images from her earlier work, brings forth experiences that she'd often hinted at but never fully expressed. I can learn from this. I used to think that if I'd said something once I could never say it again, but in her book I see how rich a simple thing can be when you turn it this way and that and show it again and again in different contexts.

———

I'm so sick of lies. The lying is making me sick.

———

Read in the *Times Literary Supplement* a review of Mallarmé's letters. The account of his life, personality and thought caused in me an eruption of powerful disgust—to the point of philistinism. I wanted to fart or belch, to yell crudely, 'Oh, come off it. Go to the shop and buy some butter, or a lolly, you exquisite thing.' The first line of one of his poems, '*Ses purs ongles*', made me feel quite frenzied. Fingernails that have never scratched, dug, become grubby, broken.

———

'The stars glitter with the same rhythm as the grasshoppers' chirp.'
—Camus, *Carnets*

———

The woman who's typing E's manuscript for her rushes into the kitchen with a hanky over her face, crying over the death of the mother's lover. E is delighted. We stand grinning while the typist blows her reddened nose. We agree it's the best review she'll ever get.

———

Ayatollah Khomeini announces a reward of seven million dollars to any Muslim who murders Salman Rushdie, and two million to a citizen of any other kind. V (who is personally acquainted with

Rushdie): 'I reckon he's a dead man.' I can't compute it. If I think about it long enough I get a crazed feeling, a spasm of mad laughter. These *men*. They think they can make a law to stop words they don't like being said, and when that doesn't work they say, 'I'll *kill* you.'

———

Three women and V argue at the dinner table about the Stravinsky's lunch phenomenon. E and I take a firm stand against domestic tyranny. V 'trusts' that Stravinsky needed what he said he needed. As in any forceful argument, at a certain point I was obliged to ask myself, 'What am I actually saying, here?' I realised I was saying that *I* would not have tolerated being told to shut up at the lunch table by my father or my husband, no matter what mighty thoughts he was entertaining, or hatching, or endeavouring to keep unsullied in his head. Why didn't the maid take him a tray, in his studio?

———

V announces that two well-known journalist friends of his, a man and a woman, are coming to his place after work for a drink. Plainly I am not invited and it is assumed that I will make myself scarce for the evening. Keeping a rein on myself I say vaguely that I might call L and see if he wants to go out to eat. V pretends to be outraged. Later, when I laugh at some witticism of his, he says, 'Does L ever say anything really witty?' Our crude manoeuvrings. I hate this. All the resolutions I make. They cause an extreme sense of strain; as if I had a rubber band stretched across the inside of my chest cavity. Next day I hear that the journalists didn't turn up.

———

I write a letter to the Iranian ambassador. 'Your Excellency: as I am (no doubt like you, Sir, and like many other sincere Muslims and Christians trying to live on this earth together) a believer in a God of mercy who does not require us to murder each other in his name, I beg you most urgently to use your influence with your government to reverse the call to Muslims to put to death on account of his book the writer Salman Rushdie. Yours respectfully.' I show it to four friends. They ask me to change 'I' to 'we', and we all sign it.

———

Autumn, suddenly, is here. Angle of light more oblique, air dryer and gentler.

———

He does what he calls 'old man things': before the start of a TV show we're going to watch, he sets out the teacups with milk and biscuits. I am not used to this and find it endearing.

———

I think I might burn all these diaries. What if I died and people got hold of them and read them? Their endless self-obsession, anecdotes, self-excuses, rationalisations. Meanness about others.

———

A visit from Mum. Terrific strain I'm under, when she and I are with other people. When we're alone I can submit to this vast, slow, stunning stream of monologue and apply as little of my concentration to it as I need to (about fifteen per cent) in order to remain calm. Yesterday she talked so much—on the drive in from the airport, meeting E, shopping at Leichhardt, having coffee at Via Veneto, driving to Manly, walking on the beach—that by bedtime she was hoarse. She never asks a question, or listens. She starts every anecdote days, months or even years before its proper starting point. Her only liveliness in speech comes when she can criticise: idiot skateboard riders, lunatics on motorbikes, men unloading trucks in narrow streets, stupid dills who drop rubbish or leave security doors ajar. A film of the world as she sees it would be always swelling, blurring, lurching, swivelling—sparkling and looming *with danger*. At moments, while she drones on, there comes over me a painful tenderness. This 'tenderness', which if I told the truth I would have to call pity, has to do with my dread of becoming like her. V asks her straight out which of my books she likes the best. She says, shyly, *'The Children's Bach.'* I am embarrassed and don't know where to look. I always give them copies, with a loving message written in the front, but she has never told me whether she's read any of them. *And I've never asked.*

———

V tells me he's going to work at 'having more goodness'.

'What do you mean?'

'I want to be kinder. More open. Less selfish, less severe.'

'What makes you want to change?'

'These notebooks I'm publishing. This dreadful person who wrote them: severe, pompous, humourless.'

He says he thinks of 'getting a job at the hospital, as a porter'.

———

Z and I enrol in a German conversation course at the Goethe-Institut. We're surprised to be put in Intermediate. We'd thought lower. Since I left school I've suffered colossal loss of German vocabulary, though sentence structure is still burnt into my memory. Others in the class are miles worse. Z says on our way home that he wanted the teacher, a gentle, pretty girl, to correct every mistake he made, in speaking. He thinks she's 'too soft'.

———

S's husband tells me that since his father died, last week, he feels 'as if blood's oozing through my skin—no pain, but energy's draining away, downwards'.

———

Dreamt I looked at myself in a mirror and saw the face of a good-looking, smiling young man of mixed race: light-brown skin, brown eyes, black curly hair just washed and flopping in wet, heavy locks, large mouth, perfect teeth, pink gums. At first I was thrown off balance by this new reflection of 'myself', but soon I rather took to it and began to examine it with a happy admiration. I moved the lips, showed the teeth, practised different expressions (mostly smiles), and said aloud, 'So *this* is what it's like to have a big mouth!' Later, R was very impressed by this. 'What a wonderful image of integration!'

———

V presses me to read a symposium in *Salmagundi* magazine called 'Art and Intellect in America'. He is sombrely impressed by the contribution of George Steiner, who makes a slashing attack on any American pretensions to a culture able to hold a candle to that of Europe. My hackles go up. Where does Steiner get off? Hasn't he heard of jazz? Contemporary art and literature produced under any but totalitarian regimes, he says, are 'an embarrassment'. All right—the horror of the Holocaust is unanswerable. *But we are still here.* What about the losses, griefs and sacrifices, the small heroisms that occur each day, often unnoticed, in people's relations with each other? What about death, and cruelty, and fear, and children, and love? People suffer. Don't we still have to find the meaning in our lives that only art offers? I try to put these thoughts to V: 'Where does this leave us—you? If you agree with him, how come you haven't given up trying to write novels? That'd be the only action consistent with his argument, wouldn't it?' I had a weird feeling that V was seeing the argument only distantly, as a brilliant performance by a man he admires for maintaining excoriating standards—'taking it right up to the Yanks'.

———

There's a big a cappella gospel choir singing tonight at the Paddington RSL. I long to go. But can't think of one single person I know in the whole city who'd go with me.

———

Doing my German homework it dawns on me that this is how it must feel to be a 'dumb' kid at school. I keep coming up against words I don't know, hitting and re-hitting a brick wall; dense darkness in front of me; stomach pains, restlessness; a blocked sensation, shame, irritation, boredom, fear. And physical rage—I want to jump up and start smashing things.

———

Dreamt I went back to our empty family house in Geelong. It

was in beautiful condition, polished, swept, orderly. M was with me and I needed to find a room for her to live in. But in the first bedroom I entered stood two small alarm clocks, both ticking like mad. Couldn't sleep here, with such a racket going on. The second room was locked. I found the key. Its floor was heaped with rubbish, garbage, shit from some animal. But plenty of light was coming in through the window. Just inside the door, on the floor, stood a second pair of little alarm clocks, ticking fast and wildly, making an almost hysterical noise: sharp, small, crazily fast. I was amazed that they'd kept going in there, all those years.

———

On the Hume Highway, a ute containing four black sheepdogs and one very subdued sheep.

———

Things I had forgotten about Melbourne: 1. Cold autumn nights. 2. The way the air in shadow, even mid-afternoon, is chilled while the sunny air is warm to hot. 3. Condensation on a car by 10 pm. 4. How casually excellent a quite ordinary restaurant can be. 5. The clarity of the air. 6. A dewy stillness in the morning: air still capable of biting, though the sky shows a warm day coming.

———

Alice Munro is deceptively naturalistic. All that present tense, detail of clothes, household matters, then two or three pages in there's a gear change and everything gets deeper and more wildly resonant. She doesn't answer the questions she makes you ask. She wants you to walk away *anxious*.

———

V reports Z's 'outburst' against 'women's writing' with its 'domestic nuances' which he dislikes and is not interested in. V tries to get me to pick up my lip but without success since he doesn't hide the fact that he agrees with Z. Later R says, 'To me it's an absolute rule, psychologically, that if someone frequently inveighs against something in another, it's to do with something they hate in themselves.'

———

The director calls to say how much she liked my screenplay. But she can't do it, because she's about to start a year's work on a three-part television series, and after that a movie of her own in New Zealand. I say, 'We can't think of another director who could do it.' 'Oh,' she says with a light laugh, 'I think it's pretty director-proof.' But it's not. Nothing is.

———

These terrible long sentences, in my unfinished story. How could I have gone so far off the track? They have no natural rhythm or inner syntactic logic. Ugly, clumsy, a stupid grid.

———

I'm sitting on the floor in my room at E's, reading old dreams in a diary, when she comes in and gives me four new 3B pencils.

———

If I report a dream to V, the comments he makes are aesthetic rather than psychological.

———

The old artist in his huge, damp-smelling house on the harbour. Broken venetians, dark outside, only thing visible on the water a lit-up tourist boat. Once he addressed me by V's wife's name; no one seemed to notice. V pointed out a spot of foxing on the edge of a faded old painting: 'What's this?' 'Oh, I don't know how that got there. Must've come through from the back. Oh, it doesn't matter. Let it change.' That's when I started to like him. He talked about the way his ex-wives dispose of his early works carelessly: his current companion went to visit one of them in New York: 'She'd let one of my things slip down behind a radiator.' A wicked laugh. He drank quite a large glass of neat gin, to fight a cold he thought was coming on. The folded-paper parcel of Chinese herbs he takes for 'general health': strange twigs, roots, stems, flattened hunks of dark rubbery or waxy substances. These he boils up in a ceramic pot with a spout, into an evil-looking black decoction with a taste like cough medicine. We enjoyed remembering old commercials for cough cures: Buckley's Canadiol, Bonnington's Irish Moss 'with pectoral oxymel of carrageen'. His companion is a sculptor, very likeable, strong and energetic, and graceful, with narrow feet and calves—maroon shoes with low heels, AA fitting (I asked her).

————

R says she sees in V's face 'signs of nervous suffering'.

————

V speaks about his wife with sorrow: 'She's completely gone from my life.' 'What do you miss most, about her?' 'Her cheerfulness. Her generosity.' I'm sad for him, for her. And I thought painfully of F, his merriments, our games and laughter, our outings with dogs to the Maribyrnong—how the removal of daily French, with its possibilities of hilarity, verbal invention, mimicry, was like a door shut in my face.

————

I've put the bloody story away. A vast and sweet relief. Into my head at all hours flood ideas (or are they fantasies?) for a novel. I madly make notes. No anxiety about it—only excitement, optimism, a sense of boundlessness. Whenever one of the characters gets too close to my family I get a faint reluctance, a tinge of emotional nausea, feeling the tug of that maelstrom.

————

Z says that what writers need most of all is patience. We have to learn to wait till we're ready.

————

Royalties came yesterday. I got $1206. V owes money. So gloomy that we can't help laughing. Queensland sends me five tiny violets taped to a sheet of paper: 'So small. So early. Too delicate to pick and yet I did on my way back from the chooks. A harsh, unsympathetic, ruthless wind.' Her letters are long, rambling streams of consciousness, never demanding a reply, but I pick out the eyes, paste them in my diary, and answer them on a postcard.

At the Cat Protection Society op shop near E's I find a New Testament in Modern English, translated by J. B. Phillips. It reads like a great yarn, with good cross-headings: 'His strange words to the fig-tree.' 'Jesus puts an unanswerable question.' Memory of the terrifying dinner with Patrick and Manoly. I wish I'd had the nerve to say, 'How can you sit there talking like that about other people with that great big cross hanging round your neck?'

Dreamt that someone gave birth to a baby that had muscly little feathered wings high up on its back. It lay there on its belly, naked, while we looked at it—with admiration, but also a slight anxiety, as if at something that had been allowed to *go too far*.

'I sometimes think the world is divided into people who survive from their own inner strength and those who have to latch on to others to survive.' —Elizabeth Jolley, interview in *Good Weekend*

Reading Luke's Gospel I see why Steiner is so terribly wrong when he says that only people living under totalitarian regimes can produce art worthy of the name. *We all live under the totalitarian regime of the world's evil.* And it's in the terms in which our own culture manifests it that we have to express our struggle against it, or our longing for glimpses of *good*.

Driving to town with a big bag of field mushrooms on the back seat, we saw an astonishing sunset. It secretly reminded me of a long orgasm: pulsing, wide, vivid, generous—the whole sky filled with clouds of every kind—wide slivers of gilt and blazing orange, then delicate grey scooped veils, then tiny bright scallops high up—to the north a tender, apricot-pink, melting wash. For a while we drove towards it, along a curving up-and-down road, and at each new rise or corner a further splendour presented itself—we gasped and cried out. The clouds would lose vividness and become pearly, dappled with pink scales—then we'd sweep round a bend that gave us a view lower down towards the horizon where a whole new band of blazing brass and orange would have been lying in wait. I looked over my shoulder, and the entire sky, as far as the eastern horizon, was stained, tipped, scaled, looped, and daubed. It seemed to go on forever.

———

At the boring literary dinner the famous writer's wife takes a quail from a platter and offers me one. When I look doubtfully at them she picks hers up and makes it trot across the plate on tiny legs, saying 'Hello Helen!' in a squeaky voice. I think we will get on. Late in the speechifying a man in his fifties cries, 'None of the young women are speaking. Why don't the women speak?' I ran my eye round the room and saw that the women were slumped, glassy with boredom, humouring the men in their game of being intellectuals of wit and style—their lumbering playfulness. Another bloke sings out, '*Young* women? I don't see any young women here!' An older man calls, 'You get *very* poor marks—for ungallantry.' It was sad, and yet I was free of it, a stranger dropped in from another planet.

———

'The man who raped me,' says my nun, 'nearly killed me, but because I went to a Catholic doctor four hours afterwards instead of three, he wouldn't wash me out.' '*What*?' 'According to Catholic law, to wash someone out more than three hours after a rape counts as an abortion.' 'Where's *that* written?' 'Oh, in some Catholic bullshit somewhere.'

———

Start with the dog. The only member of the household who can't accept its demise.

———

To R and O's for dinner. A sweet evening. I mended a rip in their boy's primary-school shorts, which (to V's dismay) he removed in the dining room and handed to me, then asked if he could put on an old record he'd found in an op shop. He lowered the needle. It was 'Shine On, You Crazy Diamond'. Even the adults stopped talking. His younger sister, who was lying on the couch beside me reading, laid her bare feet across my lap and I stitched away on top of them, full of nameless emotion.

———

Feel a strong urge to go out and buy a chain and cross to put around my neck—to make a declaration, to spend the rest of my life on my knees. Something! *Anything!*

———

Someone has stolen my good denim jacket and both my street directories, Sydney and Melbourne, out of the car.

———

On the plane to Melbourne I sat next to a Catholic bishop on his way home from a policy-making conference. Thin bloke in his fifties with well-formed features, one of those hard, serviceable faces that his generation of Australian men have: dry, tough, gives nothing away unless you can shock it into a reaction. I longed to ask him about spiritual things but was too shy—felt it would not be his area. I asked him about his work, his diocese, what he did when he visited a parish. His answers gave me a picture of the church as a vast bureaucratic edifice. At the baggage carrousel he wished me well and said (as I had hoped), 'God bless.'

———

E at the lunch table, telling me about a friend's collapsing marriage, got upset and shouted, 'She handed him a loaded gun! So he *shot* her! Why do women *do* this to themselves?'

———

To church at Pentecost. The Holy Spirit is the only part of Christianity I've got any actual personal experience of. I don't understand 'God' or even 'Jesus', but the Holy Spirit has stood behind me on many different days, even though for a long time I was too frightened to acknowledge it or 'call out to it'. It has visited me and comforted me and become part of me. We sang 'Come Down, O Love Divine' and tears ran down my nose, I had to keep blowing it. When the server put the little cube of bread on my palm I saw it, in huge close-up, expand back to its full shape after the pressure of his fingertip and thumb was removed from it; and yet it consisted only of holes, or of porousnesses, of pale brown threads of matter existing only to keep the porousnesses apart. The vicar said, 'The blood of Christ which was shed for you...' and handed me the cup. I drank from it.

———

I've sold my books. I've let my house. I've agreed to sell Primrose Gully. I've changed cities. I've got no home. I am not to answer the phone at V's, or be present when certain visitors come, or leave my stuff lying around. I am forty-six-and-a-half and I am humiliated. V is unable to resolve the thing by telling his wife the truth. I say to Z that I wish V would deliver the coup de grâce. 'The trouble is,' says Z, 'that to do that, which I agree he must do, he'll have to admit, to himself as much as to her, that his leaving her had something to do with you. He seems to need to keep the two things separate in his mind. He's still *saying* they're separate—as late as yesterday he was saying it. What I think he should do is tell her that your existence hastened the end, but that he'd felt it was over for quite some time already.' 'And did you tell him that?' 'Oh *no*.' 'Why not?' 'Oh, I couldn't do *that*. That would be to deny the whole way he sees himself and his situation.' 'But Z. You're his *friend*. It's the responsibility, the *duty* of friends to help each other see what they're doing. How else can we find out what we're like?' Z seemed very surprised and put off by this definition of friendship.

———

M phones. Our dog. 'I got home from work at midnight and called her. She didn't come. I went out into the yard and saw her against the fence. Her head was up high on a funny angle and the rest of her was sort of collapsed. Her collar was caught on the back gate.

She must have been trying to get out. I knew straight away she was dead. I rushed back inside, I panicked, I couldn't go near her or touch her or anything. I shut myself in, I thought someone was out there, someone had killed her. I rang up F and he came straight over. He was terrific, he did everything. He unhooked her and dug a big hole and buried her, and then we both cried a lot. I wanted to bury her with her ball but she lost it yesterday.' Her boyfriend (an ex-Catholic sceptic) also came, and said a prayer: 'God, please take this dog's soul...'

The unusual colour of her fur—a silvery grey that almost shone in the dark. I got out my photo albums and looked for her. Not many where she was the star, but often a corner of her was visible in a picture of something else: a nose, a paw, a length of silvery back. Cried for her terrible faithfulness, her loneliness and confusion when our household broke up, how she would escape and trot the five kms to F's, missing death on the roads. And the way she used to flick up her hind legs in a gay little gambol when she set out with us on a walk.

I love it here at E's. Every morning I sit at my table and plough forward in the Old Testament. Stories in Judges full of savagery and horror—then suddenly comes Ruth, a tale of gentle fidelity, courtesy, correctness, generosity, happiness. After reading this book I will never be the same.

Work offers come and I take them. I don't want to go over to V's. What if his wife comes visiting and I'm there? Maybe a terrible explosion of truth is exactly what's needed. I said, 'She needs you to tell her the truth. Somewhere in herself she knows you haven't told her everything.' He will not accept this screamingly obvious fact. He decides to invite two friends to dinner, and casually assumes that I'll cook. I say I won't: he can't expect me to turn on wifely service and then when it suits him pretend I'm only a casual acquaintance. He's furious. We slug it out. He says he objects to the way I make flat pronouncements. I say he makes assumptions that aren't even acknowledged by him as assumptions until I challenge them. I can't see he's got a leg to stand on here. We reach a truce, the passionate kind still available to lovers. But there's a reserve between us. We both feel it.

———

Reread my movie. I think it's good. I think it will be made. I can stop worrying about money.

———

Evening at E's in Enmore, already dark at half past five, sound of trains, sky clouded, a chill. Memory of being a wife, of being the one who's in the house when the man comes home.

———

In the gallery V and I run into two people he knows. One, a sagging-faced, white-haired fellow with a glass of red in his hand, tells me he had sat next to a man on a flight to Hong Kong, who saw him reading *Postcards from Surfers* and said he was my father. 'What did he look like?' 'Oh, I don't remember. But he told me some very interesting things about you.' 'What did he tell you?' 'I can't recall, but I wrote them down in my notebook.' Next, his companion, a woman in her fifties, begins to question me: am I living up here now? 'Yes,' I say, feeling relaxed, smooth, and rather dangerous. 'I've still got my house in North Fitzroy, but I'm staying with a woman friend over in Enmore.' Her greenish-yellow eyes give a cold flash: 'And how long have you been up here?' 'A couple of months, now.' I feel so calm and powerful that I know I can deal with anything she says or does. Put a foot wrong, my good woman, and I will splatter you all over the map.

———

I walk into V's. He hugs me and I smell perfume on the neck of his jumper. Cigarette ash on the carpet. Over his shoulder I count with my eyes the number of dishes waiting to be washed. I keep my mouth shut. He drives me back to E's and remarks that I become livelier as we approach her house.

———

Imagine not crediting the Apocrypha when Tobit contains a line like 'The boy left with the angel, and the dog followed behind.'

———

The army has entered Tiananmen Square and machine-gunned students. 'A tiny girl with a plait hanging down her back' whose body 'comes apart'. The boy whose 'guts are fanned out like a crushed cat's'. Stupefied. Only later do I 'feel' anything. It comes in small, dull punches. This, and the scenes of maddened crowds of men swarming up on to Khomeini's throne and kissing it, jumping up and down, howling and beating at their foreheads with their palms—I want more and more to believe in God, though I don't know why. It's certainly not for comfort, specially while reading the Old Testament, whose violence is as shocking as anything I read of in the papers or see on TV.

———

'When I come to Sydney, Helen,' says M on the phone, 'will you cook me hot meals?'

———

A friend of V's has left his wife. Tells V he's had 'lizards crawling in his stomach for seven years'; that she was 'a very, very difficult person'. Foolishly I ask if I am 'a difficult person'. Yes, he says, I am 'the most hypersensitive person, in moods,' that he has 'ever known'. I retort that he is a difficult person too—that his tendency to resist even minor change (e.g. suggestions to buy something, to ring someone up) means I'm always having to drag him out of his rigid negativity. Both of us are ruffled by this, but allow our feathers to settle, and turn on the TV.

———

I ask R if she minds my having used something she once said to me in an essay I'm writing. 'It's not even an issue,' she says. 'The way *we* talk, where everything that's said leads on to the next thing, how can any lines be drawn between what I thought and what you thought? Or where one idea ended and the next began?'

———

Dinner in a restaurant with V and a bunch of other writers. Everyone laughing and at ease. The door opens to admit the solitary figure of G, white and thin-faced from work, looking for a place to eat and read on in Anthony Powell. He joins us and all is merry. He murmurs to me, 'I'm terribly happy, except when I look at my wife.' I report this to V later. He groans and says, 'Oh, is *that* how he feels. He's a goner.'

———

I'm only really afraid of one thing, namely, that something should happen to hurt M.

———

A movie on TV about John Waters. I laughed till I was weak and grateful—I've been missing that angle of life—shit and fart jokes, the utter refusal to be in any way serious, intellectual or polite—and what *is* the quality Divine has, that 'puts everybody in a good mood all the time'? I said to V, 'There's never any little *treats* in your fridge. And there's not enough light and fresh air.' He hates light and likes to keep the windows closed against the cold, though the place is a box in which he smokes cigars. He won't ever stay a night with me over at E's: 'If I've slept somewhere else I find it really hard to get started on my work the next morning.' I say briskly, 'I used to be like that in primary school. But I got over it.' He is delaying to infinity the duty of levelling with his wife. He is permanently lying doggo: 'I don't know why I have to tell her.' Dumbfounded, I say, 'You're thinking of *not* telling her?' 'I don't see why I should have to,' he says, in a lightly defensive tone. I let it pass, in sheer astonishment. As if he thinks of himself as having simply walked out of her life.

———

From Queensland come two lines of Richard Lovelace's poem 'The Grasse-hopper': 'Oh thou that swing'st upon the waving haire/ Of some well-filled Oaten Beard.'

———

G's smashed marriage. His white face, racked, its deep vertical lines, in the coffee shop at 9 am, Victoria Street. 'Last night I stayed in a cheap hotel in Darling Point. $28 a night. So cold. The coverlet was so thin'—he separates thumb and forefinger—'that I didn't get warm enough to sleep till 8 am.' His long, detailed story of betrayal, lies, lust and helpless love. Driving home I saw a couple on a zebra crossing, in their sixties, grey hair, in comfortable, well-worn clothes, holding hands, their faces lit by a gentle happiness. Up the stone steps to the museum they went, smiling, not looking at each other—going out to enjoy the world together.

———

Dreamt Dad handed me a cheque for $1000. In a box on it, to show the purpose of the cheque, he had written, 'For music and lost friendships.'

———

The little aloofness that beauty needs.

———

Magpies are warbling. A pink sunrise.

———

Late in the evening at Mum's seventieth birthday Dad asked me to dance with him and I said no. 'Want to have a dance, miss?' 'I'm double-parked, Dad.'

———

'It's mad,' said Z, 'to think that only what lasts matters. How can that *be*? If we lose *everything*? It *can't* be. And we *all* lose everything. Everything.' I asked if he found the ephemeral enough; I said that so far I thought I did. He said yes. I said that what he'd been saying reminded me of the end of Ecclesiastes. '"In the day when the keepers of the house shall tremble...And those that look out of the

windows be darkened, and the grasshopper shall be a burden..."'
He went very still, looking right at me. 'That passage,' he said, 'is
the centre of my book.'

———

This morning when I was sitting on E's outside lavatory, two small
birds flipped, perched, whirred right in front of me on the wisteria
twigs. Fat little ones with pale brown bellies, darker wings patterned
like their heads with rows of evenly-spaced round white dots, as
perfect as an Aboriginal painting; and on their backs, under their
wings, just above their stumpy tail feathers, a flash of red. Their
movements never fluid. A bird moves sharply from one posture to
the next, holds it briefly, then shifts to another—snap, snap, snap.

———

A slow peace comes from just lying in each other's arms.

———

In my admiring essay for *Scripsi* about Elizabeth Jolley's *My
Father's Moon* I said that Stendhal's book *On Love* was 'charming if
somewhat juvenile'. V hit the roof. How dare I make this 'tossed-off,
impertinent' remark? Glumly I contemplate replacing 'juvenile'
with 'unhelpful'.

———

I saw a little gold cross in a pawnshop window and bought it for $39.
With chain. I wore it for two days under my T-shirt. I imagined that
when I was asked what it meant I would reply, 'It reminds me of a
possibility.' This morning I took it off. It seemed a burden somehow,
or too clear a statement of something I am unsure about. Relief of
putting it into the little wooden box with M's baby teeth and my
second wedding ring. Another day I will take it out and think again.

———

I am too narrow. Always turning over the same ground. (Morandi.
Patiently turned and turned.)

———

Search for the feeling that came *before* the anger and deal with that:

it's usually hurt, fear, embarrassment.

———

'Herbert alone can say, *My Lord*.' —Peter Porter, 'A Clumsy Catechism'

———

Out walking, I'm cheerfully telling him about something that happened today and he changes the subject, cuts right across me mid-sentence. I protest. He digs in. I go over the top. Oh, how I hate to be told that it's 'not worth having all these feelings', that we 'shouldn't have to talk about this rubbish'—as if the real, proper, reasonable behaviour is always his, and mine is aberrant, my protest a stupid, hysterical temper tantrum that 'at nearly fifty' he was 'too old to have to deal with'.

———

'The love problem is part of mankind's heavy toll of suffering, and nobody should be ashamed of having to pay his tribute.' —Jung, 'The Development of Personality'

———

To dinner at Antipodes with G and his new girlfriend, M-C. G had had a haircut that made him look harrowed and old, like George Orwell. The girlfriend engaged V in conversation. When she turned away he leaned over and whispered to me, 'It won't last. She as much as told me so.'

———

V took me (with, as cover, the adventurous beauty, who's just published her first novel) up the coast to visit his and his wife's friend, the widow of a famous painter. On the drive he kept telling us what a 'great reader' she was. I was prepared for a little old librarian in a tweed skirt. I thought maybe we'd get on. She turned out to be a grandly beautiful old woman with a helmet of silver hair, a high-class accent and a carefree, laughing manner. I had to suppress an urge to address her as Ma'am, a word I've never in my life thought of using. The wall of windows overlooked air and bush, and the huge

room was lined, packed, strewn with books. The table was so close
to the shelves that when a point was disputed during lunch she could
reach an arm behind her and produce Fowler's *English Usage*. She
treated me and the beauty with charming courtesy, but had trouble
meeting my eye. Several times she summoned up all her grit and
praised my work, but around her head crackled a static of muffled
anger. I went mousy and quiet. I could see from their playful teasing
that she and V adored each other, so, since he could do no wrong,
she bounced her anger about me off the adventurous beauty and
her new book (which she had already read). Under her intelligent,
benevolent, lightly bullying critique, the adventurer floundered.
After a while I took her over to the fireplace and brushed her hair.
She submitted with bowed head. Her hair was fair and springy, a
wonderful thick mass of it. I worked away with the brush until she
recovered her equilibrium.

When we got home, V went for me. It took me a moment to
grasp that he must have been trying to conduct the visit according
to some secret timetable of revelation, and that I, having failed to
read his mind, had thrown a spanner in the works. Why the hell,
he shouted, had the beauty and I been so ridiculously hypersensitive and unsociable? He was upset, not making sense: 'As I've said
before, she loves to talk, and she's generous. I know her fifty times
better than you do, and I—' 'Of course you do! I don't know her at
all!' Under his stream of reproaches I started to flag. Finally he ran
out of steam. We sat on the couch. In a little while he said, humbly,
'Did you like her, much?' 'Yes,' I said, with aching heart, 'yes, I did.
Of course I did. She's fabulous. I've never met anyone remotely
like her. But it couldn't have been anything but difficult, the first
time.' I did like her very much. I wonder if she might come to like
me. Anyway I sent her a thank you note. The following morning
he gets a phone call from W, also an intimate of the great reader.
Turns out the great reader had been under the impression that *I*
was pressuring *him* not to tell his wife the truth. I explode. 'I hope

someone straightened her out on *that*!'

———

Just as I'm wondering how I can get someone to tell me about building sites, one of the old junkies calls up for a chat and tells me he's working as a builder's labourer. This story is growing, in spite of me. I couldn't stop it now, even if I tried: I'm only a channel for its unformed mass. I come at it in small darts and larger rushes. 'I put on once more with joy the hateful harness.'

———

In Ariel bookshop V shows me Tess Gallagher's tribute to Raymond Carver. A quiet, modest testament to their happiness.

———

Close to midnight in the little street behind V's building a phalanx of Aboriginal boys emerges from the dark behind us—their soft, spread-out advance. I hear one murmur, 'We'll take *that* one.' I hunch against the grab for my backpack but they part around us as if we weren't there and cluster round the driver's door of a parked white Impreza—a sharp thump—V raises one arm in protest—the car starts with a roar, its lights blaze and it surges away from the kerb.

———

Writing has become a pleasure that I nevertheless postpone, for some reason. Connections make themselves of their own volition.

———

Three days of Lit Board assessment. The usual blood on the walls but, also as usual, I left feeling justice had been done, if by a process too organic and fluid to be described as logical.

———

A card (one of her husband's photos) comes from the great reader. 'I am telling you the naked truth when I say I am your devoted fan. You are wise and diplomatic and will be good for our *thick* mutual friend.'

———

V goes out to dinner with some art-world friends and returns scowling darkly: the wife of one of the painters had stated with confidence that Scott Fitzgerald is a better writer than Proust.

Repeatedly struck by his old-fashionedness. He's never heard of anything. He didn't know, till I happened to mention it, that women's shirts button right over left. 'How on earth did you manage it? To stay buried for a whole generation?' His friend the old sculptor, too, has been dug up out of some remote bog. An endearing man of fine aesthetic sensibility who seems never to have found it necessary to examine himself. Measures all human behaviour (in which he is hardly interested at all) from a point of view of innocent self-interest—is surprised that other people (especially women) should exhibit needs, thoughts or emotions which don't fit in with his daily work and thought patterns. And yet a strange, almost child-like attentiveness: he notices that the light in the room is bothering my eyes—limps out and returns with a red eye-shade, which I wear for the duration of the visit. He wears one himself, plus sunglasses, while working, he says. V loves to quote the sculptor's dictum: 'When the chips are down, women don't give a fuck about art.' I laugh, but privately expand the word 'art' to mean 'what blokes need in order to go on producing art without tedious emotional interruptions'.

The opening pages of what I'm writing feel false and stiff. I've gone in at the wrong point. I want either (a) to get myself right out of this book, as in *The Children's Bach*, or (b) to write everything from an innermost point of myself that I have not yet discovered.

What I love on my desk is the notebooks I've typed up, their freshness, their *un-public* tone, their glancing quality and high sensuous awareness. Nothing 'serious' I write can ever match these—exactly as my accounts of dreams, scribbled before I'm completely awake, contain more blunt truth of feeling or observation than I can ever produce when I'm sitting up at my desk telling myself I am 'writing a novel'.

———

I was throwing the I Ching. It told me to pay attention to 'the shadowy'. V, pretending scornful reluctance, asks it a silent question. It replies: 'Even with slender means, the sentiments of the heart can be expressed.' 'What did you ask it?' 'Whether I was a bad person.'

———

I need to free myself from the hierarchy with the novel on top. I need to devise a form that is flexible and open enough to contain all my details, all my small things. If only I could *blow out realism* while at the same time sinking deeply into what is most real.

———

The old professor, after we'd been to dinner with him at R and O's place: 'How pleasant it was. There was no master of ceremonies.'

———

My publishers, both women, are fighting for their lives in a brutal economic climate. I heard Y being interviewed on the radio. The broadcaster lectured her very slowly, restating what she had already said as if she had not said it. He pointed out that their company was probably about to be squeezed out of business by the multinationals. 'Why,' he said, 'don't you just lie back? And take it?'

———

Work stalls. I reproach myself for not 'thinking', 'studying', 'reading' about this state of drift while I am in it. But the point is to *be* in it, not to examine it.

———

Dreamt I saw a photo of myself sitting alone in a cinema, asleep, with my head resting on my bent arm. I wake, spring up and look around. I am young, wearing a beautiful pale-pink dress in a material both light and heavy: like muslin stitched with pinkish-white sequins. It falls gracefully against my body when I move. I step forward and walk with purpose out of the photo. As I leave the frame I see that I am wearing, with this dress pink to the point of shimmering into silver-white, a pair of *red shoes*.

———

Country motel. For hours, from the next room, we heard the cries of a woman being fucked. Repeated bouts of it, for twenty minutes at a time, the head of the bed thudding against the wall. The man was totally silent throughout, and there seemed to be, for her at least, no orgasm, no release or rest, just these rhythmic, bestial cries. Once she said, 'Oh, sorry.' Later, 'No—no, please.' Later again, in a cross, warning voice: 'Get off me. I said get *off* me, Kevin.'

———

Dreamt V and I were in a flotilla of dinghies. To our right, as high as an apartment block, a vast wave was forming, a colossal wall of water, and on its very summit the first frill of breaking foam.

———

R has deeply offended V by telling him she doesn't think much of the work of a certain New Zealand painter he admires. He comes home in a towering rage. Everything she'd said was 'crass' and 'banal', she 'has no credentials'. I argue for her right to have an opinion. He calls her on the phone and says he's sorry if he's 'upset' her. She replies that she hadn't been at all upset—that he must have been projecting. He renews his attack. She stands up to him, she won't bite, so he drops her and swings it around into a tremendous rolling argument between him and me. It goes on for three days and nights. He can't seem to put it down. His incredible, obsessive stamina—as if he's fighting for his life. It seems to be about the ownership of the culture, about who shall speak. I get him on the ropes about this, so he narrows and narrows his attack until it becomes about R's 'tone', in a conversation at which I was not present—and I should not, he says, discuss the matter any further with her. When we fall out like this I am painfully aware that the apartment belongs to him. I get an urge to hide in a corner, and find myself standing in the doorway of the tiny laundry, without turning

on the light. He roams about, stands with hands in pockets between
lounge room and veranda. When he turns and sees me he laughs:
'You look as if you're standing in a punishment cell.' He claims to
have had to 'correct' me when, the night before last, I'd raised my
voice and spoken 'harshly' as we argued. '*Correct* me? You objected.
I corrected myself.' He accuses me of having 'cross-examined' him.
I point out that he's starting to use courtroom terms, as if I were at
fault and not simply disagreeing with him. He clicks his tongue
irritably: 'Oh, don't pick me up on individual words—just listen
to the general flow!' I begin to think less of him and this hurts me,
but I'm not stopping now. 'You accuse R of demolition,' I say, 'but
what about your demolition of *her* work? Poetry? You've swept it
away—you've declared that what means the most to her is beneath
your notice. And when you make a running joke of it, she goes
along with it, because as a woman she's used to having this done to
her—she's used to having to back off and conduct her most intense
interests in secret.' 'Yes,' he says, 'that was awful, I shouldn't have
done that, even if it was just a joke. But...I often talk to her...
about poetry...' His voice slows down and becomes magisterial.
'Yes, I often speak to R...about poetry...I give her books, I show her
articles...' 'Yes, but you don't *listen* to her about poetry. You don't
want to hear what *she's* got to say—what she *knows*.'

Night after night he wheeled in the heavy artillery, and I dug in.
Each bout lasted hours. 'It says here,' he said, 'that Graham Greene
prays. Do you pray?' 'Yes, but not to ask for things.' 'What do you
pray for?' 'I try to submit myself to something, so I can stop being
angry, or frightened.' '*I*,' he said, in a mocking tone, 'don't have to
pray in order not to be angry.' He accuses me of disloyalty because
I wouldn't 'give him the benefit of the doubt' about the disgraceful
nature of R's tone, this toe-hold of territory I had driven him on to
and that he would not abandon. I became stunned, slowed-down,
capable only of careful physical movements. But I stuck to my guns.
Finally I ask him, 'What is it you *want* from me, that I can't seem

to give?' '*Nothing*,' he says savagely. 'I want *nothing*.' I get up from the table and put on my backpack. 'Are you leaving? I wouldn't advise you to.' He stands in front of me, barefoot, shirt unbuttoned, waistband of boxer shorts showing over his trousers. I go into the laundry, he goes into the bathroom. I stand there in the dark with my forehead against the dryer.

I begin to wash the dishes. I'm so tired I'm hallucinating. I can't sense where in the tiny flat he is: I see a shape dart in the corner of my left eye, and think he's crouching in the dark to jump out and frighten me. I put down the dishcloth and step sideways to check. Nothing there. He has gone into the bedroom. I lie on the couch. 'Are you coming to bed?' The married person's question. 'In a little while.' I wash my feet, put on my nightie, get into bed. 'I'm aching like a bastard,' he says. 'It's those bloody typhoid and yellow fever shots. I feel hollow behind the eyes and in the chest—as if hot winds were blowing all through me, down my arms and legs.' I say nothing. He lays down his book (*African Discovery*) and turns to me: 'Forgive me, if I've made you unhappy and angry.' I'm amazed that after all that madness he can lay his weapons down. H: 'I'm sorry too.' V: 'You haven't done anything to be sorry for.' We lie side by side, wrung out. 'It's astonishing,' he says, 'and I'm mortified by it—how I wanted to go on and *on* with it, even when I could see it was making you more and more unhappy. I never got bored with it. I wanted to *keep going*.' He was speaking almost wonderingly, as if about something he'd never experienced before. I said, 'We had to get to the end of it.' He said, 'I love you more, for your toughness and your seriousness.' I don't remember now what I said.

———

The old leftie academic told me that her ancient mother's need for constant care was showing up quarrel-points between her and her sisters. 'Yes,' I said with sympathy, 'caring for old parents— I'm not looking forward to that, much.' 'Yours,' she said, with a narrow, sidelong look, 'might be so rich that everything will work out harmoniously.' I'm always rocked by these sideswipes she seems driven to make. After her first visit to my place: 'Of course, my house isn't nearly as big and beautiful as yours.'

———

A letter from a young woman university student: do I try to write with a female voice? Do I consider myself a feminist writer? Hard to answer but I come up with this: 'Whenever I'm writing badly I almost always realise, after weeks of pointless struggle, that I've been trying unconsciously to write like a man, i.e. at too great a distance from myself. So I stop telling myself "I am writing a novel" and I sit quietly and wait for images to present themselves, and then I follow. I stop trying to be ringmaster and whip everything into shape by cleverness and willpower. I *am* "clever", and I *have* got "will". But these attributes invariably lead me down the wrong track.'

———

V leaves for Africa via Toronto. I cook, I eat, I iron, I watch Buster Keaton on TV and laugh till tears come to my eyes. W calls, suggests we go to a Japanese movie she says is described as 'a breathtaking puzzling thriller about a psychotic nightmarish maze of delusions'. We're going to be friends, I can tell.

———

R comes over to V's. While we're talking she looks past my head at a painting on the wall. 'Gosh,' she says, 'that McCahon really *is* something, isn't it.' I stare at her: 'You mean to say I had to go through all that for *nothing*?' She shrugs, and goes on gazing at it. 'I saw it at night. I never noticed the elephant's-breath grey of the sky before.'

———

Wrote another page of 'Recording Angel'. And another. When I look into my folder I find whole passages dashed off that I have forgotten writing. And as soon as I start a story, images come to mind and there is a place for them. This mystery. A novelist in the *TLS* says his writing consists of 'small acts of war'. I don't get that.

For me it's confrontation, then reconciliation, then integration, then release.

———

Air tonight very still, and smelling strongly of warmth, of air itself. Began *Beloved*. Full of wonder and respect.

———

In California an earthquake. A freeway has collapsed. 'Throughout the long evening, a heavy silence was occasionally pierced by a cry.'

———

To church with R. From the sunny garden, voices of children at play while the quiet rituals are observed.

———

The Mahabharata on TV. I watch with eyes out on stalks. 'What? Those stinking bogs? Those gruesome forests?'

———

I have to swear an affidavit for F's and my divorce. I went to the university bank and asked if they had a JP. A shy young man with gold-rimmed spectacles dug out from his glassed cubicle a tiny, battered, green New Testament. There we stood at the open counter, in full view of customers and tellers. I wanted to say, 'This is for a divorce. It's rather personal. Can we do it in your cubicle?' But I thought I should discipline myself to do things wherever I am presented with them. I kept my palm flat on the little green book and he asked me to swear. I swore, and read out the highlighted words: 'So help me God.' The solemn moment of the oath rushed past me, like the moment of communion at the altar rail. I didn't prepare myself. Is that why it flowed past me without ceremony?

———

Three good reviews of V's book. I experience a mixture of pleasure and pride, and a tiny lemon-drop of envy.

———

At church a baby girl was baptised. She lay quietly in the vicar's arms, absorbed in contemplation of things around her, her eyes very wide and bright, her hands spread like stars. During communion a man played a long and beautiful piece on the piano. I asked him later what it was: Beethoven. He played correctly, and with feeling, but he is not 'a good pianist' and that's why I enjoyed it so much, because it was hard come by and humbly offered.

———

G's stories about his girlfriend. She sounds like a version of what I used to be: an anima figure on the loose, rolling wildly across the deck.

———

V must be in Mali by now. I think of him with affection, as he is in our common life here—drying himself, reading—his well-shaped legs and high arches, his scowl. His loosening neck skin that reminds me deliciously of my grandfather.

———

Swam. The pink light that swarms on the surface of a green pool.

———

Dad talking about a bloke from Hopetoun called Parsey Trewin: 'He was terribly agile and strong. People said he was the best wheat-lumper in the country.' 'How big were the bags?' 'Three bushels of wheat per bag, and a bushel weighs sixty pounds.'

———

Dreamt of a guy in a band who was youthful, vigorous, cheeky, healthy. Feel bored even at the *thought* of dreaming about him.

———

E is editing the introduction to a famous Australian novel that's being reissued: 'I need a *crowbar* to get some air and light into his sentences—huge, clonking great subordinate clauses back to back.'

———

A wind blows along the street under the balcony. Dead leaves hiss, sirens whoop in a choir on Parramatta Road.

———

Ran home to catch the Melbourne Cup on TV. I'd forgotten how excited I always am by the race—the tension, how *long* it seems, and the marvellous beauty of the horses—all mythology seems to be packed into those profile shots of their stretched necks, powerful bodies—I could *cast myself* before gods so tremendous! I remembered standing at the rail at Flemington and hearing the roar come rolling round the track, keeping pace with the horses as they ran—the colossal creatures when they surge by, unimaginably tall and alive—then the weeping jockey with the microphone shoved in his face—pausing and pausing, turning away his eyes to control his sobs of joy—the stupid questions, his rush of words—'and then, and then I—I knew I was on the right horse...'

———

I love Thea Astley. Today she said to me, 'I just want to write like Raymond Carver. That's all I want, and it'll never happen.'

———

Got to get this angel story finished before V gets back. At least a draft to a possible full stop. I can't work any faster or smoother because I don't 'know' what I want it to 'say'. I'm finding out as I go.

———

Lunch with G at the Bayswater Brasserie. I am spectacularly plain with greasy hair hooked off my neck with a pink plastic clip, while he is wearing a suit and elegant tortoise-shell glasses. He asks if we can change tables: I'd chosen one in a comfortably dim corner, clearly unfashionable. He explains that he was being stared at, in a way that made his back 'prickle', by a very successful TV producer who had been 'hanging round' his wife since he left her, visiting her and offering her expensive presents: 'A mantel clock' (a brand I'd never heard of), 'an Italian writing set, made of wood. Things he brings back from his trips.'

H: 'What was the payoff?'

G: (*offended perhaps by the naïve crudity of the question*) 'Payoff?'

H: 'I mean what did he want? Blokes don't give presents like that without a reason, do they?'

G: 'Well, he's a suitor, I guess. He told her she ought to divorce me for a lot of money and use it to set up a gallery.'

———

Have stopped wearing my watch. Enormous reduction in pointless anxiety level.

———

R lends me George Herbert's poems. O and I dig out archaic spellings—'grones', 'choak'd'—and become quite hilarious.

———

Y calls. They have had to sell the publishing house to Penguin. Her voice is quiet, as if weakened. They've been wrecked by high interest rates. 'It's like losing a child,' she says. She spoke for a long time. I felt shaken by the news. This must be how kids feel when they're told their parents are getting a divorce: the shock of it shows how little you know, how much you've taken for granted, and how strenuously and with what generous self-command you have been protected.

———

To lunch yesterday at the great reader's. E and Y came too. The great reader is very taken with both of them, and everybody sparkles. Y tells us that very late one night before *The Children's Bach* came out, the biographer had called her and told her the book 'must be stopped—Helen must be *stopped from publishing it.*' I was so jolted by this that I instantly forgot it. For twenty-four hours. It came back just now, bringing with it a (short-lived) spasm of amazed anger. During the lunch I began to see what's lively, energetic, iconoclastic, experienced i.e. *lovable* about the great reader. I've met her too late—she's old, she'll die, I'll be *sad* when she dies.

———

People are sitting on top of the Berlin Wall. They're chipping chunks out of it with chisels, for souvenirs.

———

Eyes troubling me, rolling bars of blur. Thunder is tearing the air into strips outside the balcony, rain is pouring down, making the air silver.

———

Talking with R about original sin, which she doesn't believe in and I do (I think), I realised that my mind is troubled by much darker and more gruesome thoughts than hers is. 'What sort of stuff do you mean?' 'Oh,' I said, 'fantasies of murder, blood-letting…When I look at Peter Booth's paintings I don't see things there that are unfamiliar. The very bottom layers of my mind, the real vile murk of it, are like his paintings.' And saying this to her I thought, 'I need to get this stuff into my work, and *I will*.'

———

Lunch with the Cretan. I tell him about my pointless struggles to work my stuff into the shape of a novel, and my determination to write only what it's personally urgent for me to write. As I speak he leans forward smiling, smiling, and his eyes shine so brightly that I think they're about to overflow with tears. I pause, and he says with joy, 'I can't tell you how good it is to hear you say these things. I've been through exactly the same process. I had this story to tell, but I thought about theory, I thought, "I have to have a multi-vocal narration" and so on—and it became *impossible*—till I realised that all it needed was to be told simply.'

———

Raymond Carver's impersonal 'I'.

———

Two junkies in Andiamo, at the table next to ours. Girl on the nod, her head falling in a slow vertical arc, her face dull, a lump of meat under tangled hair. I long to feast my eyes on her depravity. The attraction of the disgusting, of a public loss of self-control.

———

V returns. Our reunion. He has brought home a book of Morandi paintings. So beautiful, so quiet. We sit close together on the couch and turn the pages, not needing to speak.

Immediately his presence here is normal. I can hardly remember
his absence. He quietly reverses minor changes I'd made: moves the
fruit bowl back to its former position, takes the pink cleaning cloth
out of the bathroom and drops it in the laundry. This place is very,
very small. He is worried about *where we will eat in winter*, since
I suggested (where does one write a letter, or one's diary?) that I
might use as my private spot a corner of the indoor table. His desk,
which was mine for five weeks, is the airy one near the north-facing
window. In London a famous agent took him on; he can't wait to get
started. I have moved my daytime operations across the big road into
the Fisher Library. I can work there all right, as long as I don't need
to type anything. Somehow, without a word having been spoken, I
seem to have accepted that my presence in the flat is superfluous to
requirements during his working hours. In the mornings I feel him
waiting for me to leave.

I gave 'Recording Angel' to E and am anxious that she will find me
somehow monstrous. A monstrous detachment. But this morning
she said, 'I think it's fabulous. Keep it quiet till you've got a whole
collection done. It's going to depend on what sits around it, and on
how you pick up the ends that are hanging. It's brave.'

H: (*uncomfortably*) 'I think it's *brutal*.'

E: 'I thought it was brutal the first time I read it, but then I read
it again.'

I'm wondering whether perhaps I am a monster. Not whether
people will *think* I'm a monster, but whether I *am* one. She speaks
further about it, though, and I lose my panic and feel an optimistic
technical interest in the challenges it presents.

V to someone on the phone: 'Since I've been alone...'

E's balcony room is still free. I can walk there in forty minutes, across the university. The possibility of tea, of a salad for lunch with a hard-boiled egg and a potato, somewhere to wander around without disturbing anyone—me and E working away all day in our little factory, a women's world to balance against the rest of our lives where men and their demands make it hard to avoid becoming objects to their subjects.

———

Maybe we could sell everything and move to the country. An Elders man at Berry shows us a house in a beautiful valley. V in full flight (cricket on the radio) as we drive home. We begin to fantasise an isolated life. (I'm scared.)

———

Ate at the Brasserie with G who spoke of his work so interestingly that V was impressed and later remarked on his 'intelligence and experience'. The bill was $94.50. I seized it before V could see it, and whacked down $65 in cash, which he didn't notice. Felt proud of G as he spoke of these musical matters we know nothing of.

———

Terror stabs me at the idea of country life. What am I afraid of?

———

I've been deceiving myself into third-person writing again. Yesterday I picked up Naipaul's *Enigma of Arrival* and read the opening sentences: 'For the first four days it rained. I hardly knew where I was.' A quiet and dignified first-person voice: instant calm. The struggle went out of me.

———

A friend of V's calls him, wanting to hear about Timbuktu. 'I've ruined the dream of it,' says V, 'now that I've experienced it.'

———

After the service a little boy of four or so sidled out of the church alone, his hands clasped at the waist. He went up to a bored, crabby-looking bigger girl, and asked in a tone of suppressed panic, 'Have you seen my dad? Or my mum?' 'No,' says the girl, and skips away. I took him in charge. I was careful not to rush it; didn't offer my hand till we'd been searching a good five minutes. We found his parents at a meeting in the hall. I led him back into the church garden. 'Have you been drinking a cold drink?' 'Yes,' he whispered. 'What did you have?' 'I had some cordial.' 'Do you know how I knew you had a drink?' 'No.' 'Because you've got a little bit of orange on your top lip.' For the first and only time he looked up, with a crooked smile, and met my eye. 'It wasn't orange,' he said. 'It was red.' He plodded beside me on his square feet in square sandals, holding my hand. 'It was the same colour as—' He pointed at the reddish-brown gravel we were walking on.

———

V went on so long about the 'appalling' and 'mediocre' ABC books program he was interviewed on that I told him to stop grumbling or shut up. He's the first bloke I've been able to argue with to the shouting stage and still feel solid underneath—moments later we're walking arm in arm, pretending to sulk, asking each other for a kiss. Each evening we watch TV in silence, struck with awe at what's happening in East Germany. These millions of people who have *had enough*. The top party members who not only lived in luxurious guarded apartments but were creaming off money and stashing it in Swiss bank accounts.

———

In the middle of the night, hearing the rain still steadily pouring, V mumbled, 'There's definitely something strange happening to the climate.' In the morning he flew away to Christchurch with two art guys to look at the McCahons. Being alone here is very pleasant. Lately I've been snappy, easily angered, bossy. V continues to be loving to me, in a puzzled way, trying to steer round my incomprehensible moods.

———

A letter from the Polish philosopher: 'Now the sky is filled with clouds of delicate colour, and the land below is an outline of human lodgings.'

I wrote another page of whatever it is I'm writing. Trying to flatten the boy's affect: hard to write in a way that gets his dead quality but at the same time creates the sensual world he is dead to, while also giving hints of something untapped in him which will painfully grow, much later.

A perfect, calm summer night in Melbourne: dry air still warm from the day, music from cars with windows rolled down, groups of people in loose clothes walking along the dry, warm, flat streets to places where they will dance. Alone in my borrowed car I feel *the loss of youth*—the stiffening of my spine, the over-sensitivity of my ears, the disappearance of whatever looks I once had. I remember the hours of dancing, the cheap clothes we wore with style, the laughter and the sweat. Thought of Sydney with indifference, even dislike.

At M's I lie on her bed while she sews and irons, muttering instructions and comments to herself. Her astonishing, rewarding beauty. I gaze at her, mystified. Often I see her father's face surfacing in hers—his jawline, his fine nose; but never my own.

A cool, grey day at Primrose Gully. On the murky pond, two brown ducks that F bought at the market are peacefully cruising. Little finches everywhere. Vegetation around the house is all overgrown and out of control. I start to snip off aggressive shoots and runners, then see it is pointless and no longer my business. How wildly birds twitter, up here. A small eucalypt in front of the house has grown three feet and sprouted new, brightly gleaming, reddish-brown leaves. The movements of its foliage are relaxed and slow, like loose sleeves. By nightfall, when I stand outside, I can hear a soft, persistent, ubiquitous whirring, a light nervous tapping made by thousands of insects working among the leaves of the trees within earshot. Did I really spend all those nights up here on my own? Over the back ridge, in a sky not yet quite dark, the evening star.

———

At Y's. V still asleep. I'm noticing an obscure feeling of shame, as if at dinner last night I'd done something gross or hurtful, though I'm pretty sure I didn't. Y is always courteous and hostly, but sometimes her glances unnerve me: distant, or preoccupied, even hostile. It's easy to be here with V, though. Open expressions of affection are possible, even in public. A sense that we're in league together, socially. Relief and pleasure of this, after more than a year of dissembling.

———

Last night I was sorting ironed clothes on the stereo, with the iron and board still set up behind me. As I worked I gradually became aware that I was moving my mouth sympathetically with my hands, in the manner of an old person; and when I glanced up I found that V had been watching me, obviously noticing my 'old' expression too for instead of smiling at me as he normally does when caught in contemplation he flicked his eyes away, almost furtively, then looked back. I smiled broadly. I said nothing. Nor did he.

———

V is reading *The Double Helix*, by James Watson, the DNA guy. He relates with relish how the American Pauling, 'a giant in chemistry', was also working in that field, and how Pauling's son came into Watson and Crick's lab with a letter from his father that contained his discoveries about the structure. 'They grabbed it eagerly,' said V, 'and read it, and within a few minutes they both realised that he'd made a blinding, fundamental chemical error. He'd already sent his paper to a magazine and it was to be published in six weeks. They saw that the roof was going to fall in on him. They could have told him in time for him to withdraw it, but they didn't. Because it would give them more time. Instead they went down to the pub and toasted his failure.' 'How awful!' I said. 'I thought people were supposed to work together to understand our world.' 'Bugger that! If you're on the brink of a major discovery you don't let some poor bastard from *America* get in first! It's a competition!'

―――――

Dreamt I was going to let my house. A man I'd never heard of applied. I was about to let it to him, but when I asked M and her friends who he was, they said he was horrible, a real creep and dickhead, and not the sort of person I should let my house to.

1990

When I pulled the cloth cover off my typewriter a moth flew out.

———

The light entering the painter's studio through its sawtooth roof windows was very even, so that nothing seemed to cast shadow, and when I sat at the table watching people talking to each other in groups, I wished I had brought my camera (though I would have been too shy to use it in this company), because of the smooth, agreeable definition given to people's features by this light that did not seem to have a source but existed in the room evenly, calmly, without favouring one object, one surface above another: there was light in front of people, beside them, behind them; they seemed to float evenly in light.

———

The fireworks I liked best were the big blossoming ones that seemed to move towards you, giving the impression that you were travelling fast into an exploding area of deep space—heading into a galaxy. Also those that blew out into a puffball, then each atom of the explosion drooped like a lily.

———

Artists' wives who have a gritty ambition, who manage their husbands' affairs. V, I notice, will always, while criticising them for their 'stupidity' and 'greed', maintain the need for them to exist and function as they do. Over and over I see that he is used to being cossetted. He is helpless, bereft-looking, when I don't swing automatically into a maternal role. He does not possess a wallet, but keeps a few notes screwed up in his pocket. 'Have you got—? I've left my card at home.' If there is a task to be done that he sees I don't particularly want to do and that he has no desire to do either, he will say 'I can do it'—not 'I will' but 'I can'. He likes to put things back in order, but does not notice dirt.

———

Back at E's, all morning contentedly alone in her house. Not ready to open my folder. I've been reading too many literary reviews. The paralysis they provoke in me, a brick wall in front of my face, blankness where previously I saw corridors of narrative possibility opening out on to landscapes of what I know, remember or can invent.

———

'The immense beatitude of loving and being loved.' —Anthony Burgess in a BBC interview

———

The letter I wrote V in Mali, confessing envy of how seriously his work is taken in the British literary world, never reached him. And I never told him about it. Why should he have to carry this sour little load for me? When I do touch on the matter of envy, at dinner with him and E—very lightly, making mock of myself—his mood darkens. When men refuse to admit what they are feeling, women must either dance attendance or devise a neutral mode—or withdraw into our private thoughts till the coast is clear.

———

Further hours of struggle. Apparently I had seemed 'sceptical' when he brought home his report of the painter's 'idiotic' wife who'd claimed that Scott Fitzgerald was a greater writer than Proust. Well, I said, it *was* hard to believe that anyone could really think such a thing. But *why wouldn't I take his word for it?* Because he has a tendency to caricature people he disagrees with: he never remembers the name of a 'stupid woman' who has made an offending remark. When I ask 'What was she like?' or 'What does she do?' he can only say that she had a very pointy nose or wore too much lipstick. On this basis, even if I agree that her remark is silly, I don't think I'm being disloyal to him if I don't agree that she is a moron. This sends him into orbit. When I raise my voice he snaps, 'Oh, behave yourself! I shouldn't allow—I mean, it shouldn't be allowed that we speak sharply to each other.'

––––––

After the ridiculous argument I carried downstairs to the rubbish bin, wrapped in several layers of newspaper, the remains of the Christmas ham, which had gone slimy and begun to stink. It was roughly the size and weight of a new-born baby.

––––––

Later I thought that I should destroy my description of our fight. Our *naked struggle for supremacy*. But that would be…destructive. So I went to work. I was alarmed by what I was writing. I hardly knew from what squalid dream world it was issuing.

––––––

Constantly surprised by strands and echoes of other stories that return—as if the thing were knitting itself and I were no more than the dummy holding the needles.

––––––

At Neilsen Park we sat peacefully together looking at the ships, the green water, the grey sky with high strips of pink that ended in complex boiling curls—like Maori carvings, V said.

––––––

Dreamt of watching M, at twelve or so, in her little bathers, diving and frolicking neatly in a huge brown African river.

––––––

A boat with forty-nine people on board, capacity twenty, sinks off Port Stephens. Five small children drown. The parents, in the water, see them through the cabin windows: they'd been 'resting' in there when it sank.

Sick for my house. With many windows and rooms of my own. How have I allowed this narrowing to happen to me? If I want to be truthful and clear I must always be ready to be alone. What are the compromises I will not make?

With V to the great reader's. Hours of quiet, each of us with a book, then eating, drinking, laughing and comparing notes. Her style and stride in conversation. Pale spreads of lightning for hours, and the occasional fork that stabs the horizon. A wild-eyed, rearing, strutting, thieving raven. A magpie which utters, from the ground, a light, liquid gush of song as casually as—a god, perhaps.

At E's a little blonde English girl of ten, with a London accent. We were magnetically drawn to each other: we gossiped, provoked, confided, teased. I was besotted with her. 'Do you learn music?' 'Well...I've got a recorder I can play. And a trumpet.' 'A trumpet! Can you get a note out of it?' 'I wouldn't call it exactly a *note*. But a *sound*.' We laughed so terribly that tears ran down our cheeks. Each time my paroxysms would subside she would turn her pink, sunburnt face full on to me and utter a bursting gush of giggles that would set me off again. I'd forgotten about girls' giggling—that orgasmic collapse of all inner resistance. My life here lacks certain dimensions: kids, dancing, noise in the house, loud music.

Our moving to the country fantasy has been nipped in the bud. By Dad. I learn the hard way that the North Fitzroy house they 'helped me to buy' does not belong to me at all. Even with one's parents one ought to read the fine print. Dad writes V a letter of such brutally blokey insults that I throw myself on the bed and bawl loudly for ten minutes. V is amazed and disgusted. By everything. And I don't blame him. Secretly, though, I know it was a dumb fantasy. I toil for days to boil my rage down into a letter of eight terse lines to Dad.

V: 'Good on you, sweetheart. It's a little masterpiece. It shows you think he's being an idiot, and yet it's *jolly*. Well done.'

_____

The luxury of rewriting. There is always something there, forgotten, waiting for your attention.

_____

J is here from Western Australia to do publicity. I introduce him to V and they get on. Great bursts of talk in the noisy cafe with rain pouring down outside. 'When I first read your short stories,' says J, 'I thought, now, if I can just get past *this* bastard—' We all laugh. Watching V's pleasure at the younger man's compliment I try to think whether I have ever looked at an older writer of either gender and *pitted myself.* Perhaps if I had…

_____

Read *The Aspern Papers* with joy. Its beauty, its drive, its seriousness but its lightness of touch. It didn't frighten me into dropping the pen forever, as Proust was doing several months ago.

_____

Whenever I have pace or verb problems I get out *Kidnapped*. The intense *practicality* of Stevenson's prose. Nothing there but 'muscle and blood and skin and bone'. And he shifts it along using semi-colons. Forward movement in smooth surges rather than the staccato effect of full stops.

_____

Tristan und Isolde with V. We took a little picnic for the intervals and ate it sitting on the steps with O and R. All of us excited and thrilled. At last the penny dropped about Wagner. Swept away by the music—in Act 3 I realised, sitting forward open-mouthed, that for long stretches of time I had not even glanced at the surtitles. I was completely *listening*.

_____

W has gone away and lent me her house, on Pittwater, for a couple of days. Not only did I leave my watch at home but the power is off. I'm here alone with no stove, no fridge, no radio. Somewhere a crow, *hark, hark.* From time to time a great NUT crashes on to the roof and bounces once or twice. I lie on the bed reading Walter Benjamin's *Moscow Diary*, his record of the so-called love between him and Asja Lacis who sounds a frightful piece of work. Relief when I read of hopeless love-journeys made by others: I am not the only one. During *Tristan* last weekend, when the king discovers the lovers' treachery, great waves of shame went lurching through me, betrayals I had perpetrated, especially of F: I must have had the glazed eyes of someone possessed.

———

Mum writes: 'Dad thought he had cancer and they'd just stitched him up and nobody was game to tell him. It was a twisted small intestine, which the doc just disentangled. He has lost a lot of weight and don't tell anyone I said so, but he really looks his age and a bit more.'

———

When V went to the toilet in the restaurant I said to Z, very fast, 'Z— my father's been sick. He was in hospital. I thought he was going to die, but then he got better, and I felt awful—almost disappointed.' 'When they do die,' said Z, 'you'll probably have all sorts of feelings you could never have foreseen.' I saw V approaching and changed the subject. He's heard enough about my father to sink a ship.

———

Since I've been 'happy', my openness to what my senses can observe has lessened. Beauties of nature are less piercing. They strike me less *personally*, I mean with less meaning that's personal to *me*.

———

On the ferry this morning, when I sat on the top deck with M and her boyfriend and the boat moved off towards the next stop, a strange sensation came over me, to do with the blue and sparkling water, the clear sky, hot sunshine and a fresh breeze moving in steadily from the open sea: a memory of a happiness from so long ago that I couldn't even locate it in time. Maybe this is my first day of being old.

———

After they had gone on up the coast with their friends, V grumbled at length about the 'terminal informality' of 'young people in Australia'—apparently the boyfriend had *played his guitar* while V was speaking on the phone. 'They could've stayed in a motel. They're on holiday, aren't they?' He doesn't seem to remember that when you're young you don't have any money. 'You don't really understand, do you,' I said to him, 'that if I haven't got a place for my kid to stay when she visits me, there's something wrong? In my life?' 'Is it me,' he asks, quietly, 'or is it the apartment?' We talk about how hard it is to show each other the deepest parts of our separate lives—e.g. the first visit to the great reader. We try to work it out. Because we love and respect each other.

———

William Styron in *Darkness Visible*—how hearing Brahms' 'Alto Rhapsody' had hauled him back from suicide. A day when I'd been struggling with V and was dully washing up: the radio was on, and they played a Brahms string quartet. For the first time I knew what the word 'grace' meant. It came dropping gently on my head, through the music. My anger and sadness flowed out of me and were gone.

———

'...stretched out his hand. She pricked it, and he did begin to laugh, and she laughed too, and drove the pin quite deep, and kept glancing into his eyes, which ran helplessly in every direction.' —Turgenev, *First Love*

All those *ands*. I should worry less.

———

The famous British writers at the Wellington festival. We've read them, we're drawn to them, they interest us. V is confident and gets a response, but I sidle up to them so self-effacingly that they don't notice me. James Fenton describes to me how to make stuffing for a chicken, but doesn't meet my eye. Ian McEwan and I talk about piano lessons, we've both tried to learn Bartók's *Mikrokosmos*, but we don't make any real contact. What *is* contact, anyway, and why do I need it?

––––––

Last night at sunset, the incredible purity and emptiness of the pink sky, the bony flanks of the hills—how close we are here to the bottom of the earth. Something terrifying about such clarity. Is this what McCahon's on about?

––––––

Jan Morris was at the dinner. When she entered the room the world was a warmer place. Thick, dry, wavy, grey hair, a face both mannish and feminine, cheeks of a rosy ivory above the faint shadow as it were of five o'clock. A sweetness of expression—attentive, intelligent, warm—a terrific listener. At 10 pm, in a pause, she straightened up and said in a firm, cheerful tone, 'Well. I must go home to bed.' I felt melted by her, somehow, and blessed by her company.

––––––

When we got home from New Zealand, V looked for a place to hang a tiny orange McCahon he had bought in Wellington. The only possible place was already occupied by a picture I'd brought with me from Melbourne, a pastel drawing by T of a road at night; after he came back from Africa and didn't like where I'd put it, I'd moved it to a spot over my corner of the table. Now he took down T's picture from that spot and replaced it with the orange McCahon, which looked very good and right there, and I said so, but I was sad, not knowing where I would be allowed to hang T's picture with its meaning personal to me. I went into the laundry and started to do some handwashing. He came in after me and said, affectionately, 'What's going on in here? Is something wrong?' I said, 'Oh, I feel a bit sad about my picture.' He burst out: 'Oh, I'm not going to put up with this! You're sulking in here as if I'd taken your picture down without asking you! I *said* we were only trying it *out* in that spot, that if you didn't like it there we could put the other one back!' I said, 'I'm not sulking. I came in here to do the washing. I didn't want to parade in front of you the fact that I felt sad.' 'Yes but you *showed* it.' 'Do you mean I have to pretend not to feel sad so you won't be uncomfortable?' 'Of *course* I don't mean that!' He rushed out of the laundry, whisked the McCahon off the wall, put the T back, and whirled out of the flat, slamming the door behind him.

There is of course a highly developed aesthetic behind all this, against which my sentimental tastes can gain no purchase. It's not worth stating them. I haven't got the stamina to face the blowback.

Later I took down T's night road. Later still he put the McCahon back up.

———

He said that I was very 'touchy'. I said that this was true. He asked what he did, or was, that made him hard to live with. After a lot of thought I said it was his tendency to enjoy stressing the negative in everything that came up; that it made me very tired, as if I were dragging behind me a heavy bundle, 'the vibe'. I notice that since this conversation he's stopped snarling, whenever the phone rings, 'Oh, who the *fuck* can this be?'

———

Shakespeare's fabulous verbs: 'If you hide the crown, even in your hearts, there will he *rake* for it.'

———

I propose to V that I should have the bedroom walls as my picture territory. He agrees at once. When his friend the painter comes to visit I overhear V telling him all about it, with comic grimaces, conspiratorial glances, apprehensive shrugs and so on. I resolve not to bite.

———

The great reader's had a heart attack. I keep suggesting V should get his arse to the hospital but he grumbles and fulminates about 'all the bloody women' who are 'flapping around like headless chooks' and 'speaking in dark and sombre tones'. I suppose he is scared of seeing his wife. She ranks me and of course I can't go, but I long to say to the great reader, 'I've only just had the good fortune to meet you. Don't you go and die on me.'

A good day's work. My mind moved freely, as if all its windows were open and air could blow through. While I was writing and rewriting, with intense curiosity and pleasure, the dream Maxine has of 'the tiny sad monarch with his orb and sceptre', my old dream title from years ago, 'Cosmo Cosmolino', came back and strode into place as the title for this story but also perhaps for the whole book.

R called to me across King Street: 'How fortuitous! I've just been working out my whole position on life with the help of a dream I had that you were in.'

Letter from T: 'Some pastels are drawing themselves as I hesitantly run along behind.'

I sent 'A Vigil' to J. He wrote back that he didn't like it. It's 'too awful and unrelieved. Am I missing something?' I saw at once that he's right; and that the angelic nature of the two men at the crematorium has remained, through my cowardice, hidden inside my head. Had to lie on the couch for fifteen minutes in my desolated pride. But lying there I began to see ways to shine light beams into the unrelieved mass of misery: only the bird shrieks, not the boy; cut out references to shit...

Fish and chips on the grassy slope at Bondi last night with V, R and O. Happy foolery and merriment. Admired once again the way O never bears a grudge: his extraordinary clarity of soul. Driving home down William Street we saw a 6'2" creature striding along

in nothing but a G-string and minimal bra—stiff blond wig—
wonderfully creamy white skin—skilful make-up—and carrying
a very long, very slender whip.

———

'I was taught as a child,' said J, 'always to be polite to strangers, in
case they were angels.'

———

V's gone to New Zealand again, about the *catalogue raisonné* they
want him to do. Bereft without him at the end of the day but kept
working. Later he called to say he had food poisoning, sick and
wretched, alone except for a guy who brought him three bananas.

———

Flipped through the old typescript of *The Children's Bach*. The
extreme simplicity and shortness of the sentences. My work is very
minor. It will never be noticed by the world at large. But this does
not excuse me from the responsibilities of any artist.

———

V is home, and sick again—bad headache, nausea, the shits. I tiptoe
about. 'Can I get you anything? Would you like a herbal tea?' He
rolls away with a groan: 'Aw, I'm not drinking *that* bloody muck.'
Later, when I sit on the bed next to him, he says, 'What are you gonna
do about your hair? Didn't you say you were gonna do something
with it?' 'Why?' I say, alarmed. 'Does it look awful or something?'
'No, but it's getting a bit sort of *thick*, isn't it?'

———

My sister and her friend and I met at the Caffe Troppo the other
night. The waiter brought us some bread and my sister said to me,
'When I left the church you wrote to me, "Doesn't he say *Whenever
two or three are gathered together in my name?*"' She held up her
piece of bread and said, 'This is the body of Christ.' Her friend did
the same, and I did too. Then we ate the bread and drank a whole
bottle of wine.

———

V and I walked round Glebe late in the afternoon. Still warm enough for a T-shirt. Beautiful houses. Dark gardens, each with its solitary cricket.

———

At the Balkan, tired after a day's work, I told V I was going to have a coffee tomorrow with W. He was surprised and disapproving: 'What are you seeing *her* for? We're already seeing her at the weekend.' He talked about Bloomsbury Publishing, who have signed my book (at his instigation, through their publisher, whom he knows). He said Nadine Gordimer had recently moved to Bloomsbury: 'They need people. Their list is *hopeless*. They've got almost nobody.' Stung, I foolishly said, 'What about me?' 'What *about* you.' 'Not that I'm suggesting I'm...' 'What *are* you suggesting?' The rest of the meal passed in awkward small talk. Back at his building, I followed him along the hall. What am I doing here? Cheek by jowl in a narrow flat with a man who scowls when I say I want to go out with a friend?

———

Dreamt I was in a courtroom. The great reader was to give evidence about the value of one of her late husband's paintings, and V was an expert witness. The great reader began to address the court in a wildly agitated manner: 'I'm scared! I've no idea *why* I'm so scared, but I am! I'm scared!'

———

A weekend with V and W up at the great reader's. She is thinner, more subdued; has given up smoking entirely: 'There's nothing like suddenly not being able to breathe, darling bird, to make one see reason.' Sometimes while the rest of us chattered and laughed she sat at the table looking quietly into the distance. The sharpness of the air, up there, its cleanness. The high gum trees streaming in the wind. W and I dyed a T-shirt pink and then washed and waxed the cars. While the great reader rested, V and W and I went down to the beach and picked up beer cans, stubbies and other rubbish. In half an hour each of us was hauling a couple of bulging white plastic bags, and our self-righteousness had given way to a simple hunting spirit: we no longer conversed but progressed bent double along the beach, fossicking in piles of driftwood and dry seaweed. Two little girls ran after us to join in. All this on a cold, clear afternoon with a wind blowing.

———

Today I wrote a page and a half about someone called Janet—name chosen for its briskness, dryness, lack of feminine grace or charm. I am probably cranky and distant lately. It's to do with the blank, contemplative state I'm in when work goes well. Uh oh. The Stravinsky's lunch syndrome. When the piece of work exists, I can almost live in it. V is patient and continues to express love for me. I am ashamed of my absentness, and determine to be sweeter to him.

———

I filled out a questionnaire. Under 'Who (known or unknown, living or dead) has had the greatest influence on you intellectually?' I wrote R's name. But I didn't tell anybody.

———

I keep waking earlier than V. The second or third time, I realise this is a way of achieving a short period of privacy, the way I did when I was a mother.

———

We saw de Kooning on TV wearing two tartan shirts at once. This morning I stopped at the Cat Protection op shop and found a beauty: blurry pinks, greys, blues, greens, yellows. Fifty cents.

———

I think of my characters now as actual people. Their 'paltry experiences' have actually happened. I long to continue the slow, deliberate hacking of stone which will allow me to know their futures.

———

Pentecost. As the service progressed I became aware that all the imagery of the invocation and action of the Holy Spirit is in my

story. Light, fire, wind, breath. I leaned forward with my head on
my arms and whispered, 'Help. Help. Help.' (Is that praying?) I
need help to *keep it up*. And if I can, the book itself will take me
where it wants to go.

———

Once they find the clock in the locked room I was at a bit of a loss.
Then I wrote about the way the twig cradle sweetened the room,
and about the season of winds, but I don't know how to fit it into
the narrative, which must keep moving forward, in its looping way.
I have forty-two pages in my folder.

———

Ran into the old leftie academic on my way back to V's. She asked
if I ever got homesick. I said I did. And then she asked me in a
very delicate way whether V had ever considered moving down to
Melbourne to live. At that moment, a fantasy of our living in my
house got hold of me, and I can't shake it off. Today, washing my
knickers in a bucket, I said to V that I was homesick and homeless: 'Why don't we live in my house?' Pause. 'There's something
about Melbourne,' he said, 'that I find—I find that in Melbourne
I get really depressed. And don't forget that in Melbourne you'd
get tangled up with your family again.' I went on washing, and he
became very interested in a stray piece of metal that was lying on
the laundry floor. He walked away with it, and began to try it out
on various parts of the fridge.

———

The book rolls forward at its own rate, acting as a black hole that
sucks into it everything I think, witness, overhear and see on TV.
Today, instead of trying to perfect each paragraph before I moved
forward, I thought, 'Fuck this! I'll keep barrelling on.' Hours passed
in big bursts and I ended up with seven pages of stuff I could never
have foreseen or invented. Reeled back to V's with sore eyes and
an empty head. This must be how it's done—take your foot off the
brake, unpurse the lips and see where it takes you.

'I think I've got a mother problem,' says my sister, 'rather than a father problem.'

Me: (*astonished*) 'How do you mean?'

Her: 'I *never* have any good moments with Mum. With Dad at least you can have a laugh occasionally, but Mum's so boring.'

Me: 'But don't you find a lot of Dad's horrible characteristics in yourself? A tendency to bully, and to be impatient and angry? *I* do.'

Her: 'It's better to be him, to have those characteristics, which you can learn to channel, or to rein in, than to be like Mum—a bloody *doormat*.'

Steel-grey Melbourne skies, a cloud at 5 pm the colour of gabardine behind the bare elm branches in North Fitzroy. Ground dark and damp. Can't think how I could have left this city.

To St Kilda marina with T who has bought a small yacht. A new version of the eternal dilemma: the bloke she lives with has a captain's ticket and so, according to the law of the sea, on board her own boat he is master. Her aggrieved account is split by wild laughter. We talk with our usual brutal frankness. The yacht: its ingenious layout, the clever storage and sleeping arrangements, but I was scared of its masts and stays, their tension, a hard professionalism. I'll never go to sea. Not even with her.

After dinner in their new 'townhouse' in Kew, Dad offers to play me something from a CD he's just bought—Pavarotti singing 'Caruso' from *The Fortunate Pilgrim*. That voice comes pouring into the room. We listen to the end without looking at each other. Dad: (*shyly*) 'What do you think of it?' Me: (*sincerely*) 'It's beautiful, Dad. It's a really lovely song. The arrangement's brilliant. And his voice is magnificent.' Gratification all round, hostilities forgotten, oiled by a very large scotch he had poured for me, but also by the fact that earlier, snooping upstairs, I'd discovered that my photo was not among the display of family pictures enshrined on a bureau near his desk, but was in his bedroom, on the dressing table, alongside his photos of Mum and his father. I want to say but don't dare, 'Dad, don't you want me to be happy? I am, with V, for the first time in many years. Can't you stop being jealous, and let me be happy?'

———

Gave a copy of my story to Y, and to the Polish philosopher.

———

This is what I miss in Sydney: messing around at somebody's house on a winter afternoon, sharing a bottle of crap pink champagne, working through the ukulele songbook ('Melancholy Baby', 'On Moonlight Bay'), reminding ourselves of stories from the past. Somebody knocks up a batch of drop scones. M plays the piano. We even sing a round. I miss V down here, especially at night. But the singing would have been too much for him.

———

In the *TLS* someone quotes Virginia Woolf's dismissal of R. L. Stevenson's 'dapper little adjectives'. Ooh I was furious! She's a goddess, but at that moment I wanted to kick her flabby Bloomsbury arse. Into the heather.

———

Dreamt I was with a bunch of men who were about to be put in prison. All the women had gathered for the parting. Music was played. The women had to dance, and we did, merrily and with great springiness, leaping high into the air. But when the music stopped and we turned around, the men had been rounded up and hustled away by brutish guards. Men and guards moved across a rainy paddock.

———

V was looking glum. I tried to pester it out of him with teasing and affection, but all he'd say was, 'I'm changing. I've changed. I've lost my edge. I'm not as sharply defined, when I'm with people, as I used to be.'

———

I've always thought that Glenn Gould was my all-time favourite and best, but last night I heard a CD of Sviatoslav Richter playing Beethoven's Piano Sonata No. 17, 'The Tempest'. When he laid down the opening arpeggio, as gently and self-effacingly as if only checking that the piano was in tune, I wanted to prostrate myself.

———

V woke and related an astonishing dream, teeming with imagery— a sleeping woman, a bull, 'two pelicans waddling down a road, black and white, like bloated magpies'. I sat there with popping eyes. It was like some fabulous painting—a Picasso—I don't know. And then he says, 'Now, I defy *anyone* to make any sense out of that.' I bit my lip and remembered what Jung used to say to himself before he approached anyone's dream: '*I do not understand this dream.*' But I felt so tenderly for him, showered with these treasures that he doesn't know what to do with. I wanted to reassure him, and encourage him, but I didn't know how.

———

The sky-blue shirt! I could never have planned it! It came from wonderful nowhere-land, like a brilliant blue tile, an Isfahan mosque tile. I couldn't believe I'd written it! I feel as if I'm a reader too, only more hard-working than the rest.

———

Me: 'I've got no idea what that "Uncompleted" story of yours is about. Not the faintest idea.'

V: 'Yes, but hasn't it got a sort of *austere beauty*?'

We shouted with laughter; and I thought, I must read it again.

———

The writer from America told me she was 'involved with a married man'. We spoke warmly about the difficulties of this. 'Why is it,' she said, 'that when you love someone you always want *more*?

You think, "Once a week will be enough", but it never is.' Later I thought I should have said, 'It's because you want to get past "being in love" and through to an ordinary peaceful life on the other side, if you can.'

———

Out to eat with G and his four younger brothers, all guitarists. I got there early and had a vodka while reading on in Ratushinskaya's prison-camp book. G told me the producer hopes to cast Bruno Ganz in my movie; and he is interested. Having written this I stare at the words in silence.

———

My sister is in charge of our parents' credit card account while they're travelling in Europe. 'In one month,' she tells me on the phone, 'they spent $500 on lunches. And the awful book they gave me for my birthday cost *fifteen bucks*. I also noticed they donated $25 to the Guide Dogs.'

———

The producer told me Bruno Ganz was eager to get the part. 'Eager' was the word she used. In my euphoria I pretended to bite the table edge.

———

I think the point of my story has come to me. I don't dare to write it down in case I scare it away. As usual it presented itself 'twixt sleep and waking'.

———

The blunt candour R and I are capable of, in conversation. There is nothing that may not be said.

———

Dreamt I was in charge of quite a small baby. I carried it about with me, holding it in my arms, wherever I went.

———

After *Lulu* at the Town Hall, we went to eat at Antipodes. Some of the cast were drinking there. A waiter brought out a slice of cake with a sparkler stuck in it, the group broke into 'Happy Birthday', and in the last few notes Lulu and die Gräfin Geschwitz let rip in harmony, at full operatic strength. Plates and glasses jostled on the tables.

————

The whole time I'm writing I'm nearly exploding with the tension of making myself sit still.

————

V, puzzled, shows me a photo in *Women's Weekly*. 'Look. That's not a very good baby, is it? It looks like an old man.' 'It doesn't always look like that, I imagine. It's probably just got a little expression on its face.'

————

I got to the end of *Cosmo*. Where is this stuff coming from? The weird state I'm in. I have to apply my intellect but at the same time keep my instincts wide open. I need to hover between these levels.

————

The Aboriginal activist at dinner. Her tales about clashes with politicians had a swashbuckling quality that made us laugh but I felt slightly cowed by her. Late in the evening, though, she talked about Aboriginal beliefs—death, the return of spirits—in a way I could have listened to all night. Her face softened and lit up: she spoke with loving reverence.

————

Y sat down with me and talked about my stories. As always she was able, with her extraordinary delicacy and skill, to point out the potential in what was still sketchy and clumsy. So grateful, so relieved. 'You don't have to publish a whole *lot* of stories, you know,' she said, 'just to prove you've been working.' I showed her my possible epigraph, from Mother Julian of Norwich: 'After all this, I became more serious.' We laughed. Her husband passed through the room and told me I should 'marry V. He's terrific.'

————

At E's book launch everyone was happy. The young editor was wearing stockings with little golden fleur-de-lys on them.

———

M's twenty-first. A rocking party in a Fitzroy pub. F's speech brought the house down—perfect comic timing, full of hilarious wit and affection. M stood listening at the front of the dense crowd: her face was a vision of wild delight, almost unbearable to look at, she was so illuminated and joyful. I felt humble before her, irrelevant, shaken by the ending of this twenty-one-year stage of my life. I begin to understand my mother.

———

V brings in the *Herald*: Patrick White is dead. Stunned, and vague. Our agent wept on the phone, telling me how when she was putting his wooden cross in his pocket, in the coffin, she'd found they'd put a tissue in there: 'We took *that* out!' I said, 'You'd think at *least* a linen handkerchief.'

———

Things have turned rocky between me and R. An awful feeling that I've used up her affection, that it's drained away. She must be fed up with me and my neediness. I'm always turning up at their place and squabbling with O and bashing their ears. Am I inflated, when I walk in? They both seem to want to puncture me. V takes a certain grim pleasure in the spectacle. 'It's much better this way. It's more *realistic*. You used to talk about her as if she was the Virgin Mary. Touching the hem of her garment.'

———

The difficulty of being in a couple, the long haul, the struggles for freedom within it, the demands for support and love, the disappointments, surprises, angers, the secret contempts. I used to feel things better. When I was on my own, in spite of my sometimes bitter loneliness, I used to notice things intensely. My senses were sharp. Now I'm dulled and ordinary. I plod from day to day.

———

V turns to me upon waking and says, 'We wouldn't have a *destructive* love, would we?' I laugh. There's something weirdly virginal about him. He can't have read Yeats: 'All true love must die/ Alter at the best/ Into some lesser thing./ Prove that I lie.' I say, 'I find living with someone very hard, sometimes.' 'Yes,' he says, 'you *have* got something hard, or indifferent, in you. A hard centre, an indifferent spot in the middle of you—very small, but hard.'

———

To *Lohengrin* with a very musical woman who'd never seen Wagner before. At interval she turns to me and says, 'This is *weird*.' The strange metallic rigidity of the knights in their forest, the inhuman quality of the characters and their dilemmas. The *swan*. We try to stifle our laughter, but soon become absorbed, and at the end agree that it was somehow marvellous.

———

Dreamt that V and I walked past a rubbish bin out of which stuck the hindquarters of a brown dog that was foraging in it. V tried to take hold of the dog to help it out, but it turned on him and sank its teeth into his left forearm. V, though he must have been in pain, kept an expressionless face, and staggered away from the bin with the snarling beast dangling from his arm.

———

At W's fiftieth birthday party I got talking with a very clever four-year-old boy. He asked if he could tell me a fairy story. Away he went, with gusto: 'And so...she skipped along at the huntsman's side...and the stepmother was *ac*-tually FYOUrious!' He bared his teeth and rolled his eyes and clenched his tiny fists.

———

I tell V, trying not to sound 'hard', that we can't go on living in this tiny flat. We need to live in a place where I can have my own room to work in: a room with a desk, and also a bed. He is not happy about this. He replies that I've 'got a problem'; that 'independence is all very well, but deep independence is a dangerous bore'.

I delivered the screenplay again, after reworking two scenes that the producer came and collected from me at E's. When she'd left I lay on the bed. In a while I turned on the radio, and into the room flowed a saxophone and a piano, very melodious and quiet. I lay there on my back, hearing the patterns of the music, the way the instruments moved with and against each other. I thought that I had been behaving like a 'creedless puritan', driving myself in work until the feeling side of me had almost died.

Just as I'm heading out the door to work, V says, 'Listen—do you want to go back to Melbourne?' 'Don't tease me, sweetheart.' 'No— really—if you did feel you'd be much happier there, we could…' I had to rush out, but as I drove past Central I began to notice something tight inside me loosening. I thought of my bike. My kitchen. The *area* of the place. The loosening of things I hadn't known I was holding so tight.

Dreamt I marched into a bottle shop and announced in a grand, resolute voice, 'Stand back. I'm going to BUY something.'

At E's today R told me what's wrong. My whole nature is 'too sensitive, hypersensitive'. She wonders why I'm not exhausted all the time, from being 'so aware, and alert'. She says I bend over backwards too far, with V, in an attempt to get it right; that I ought to learn to switch off and let things past me. I asked in a small voice if she could explain to me more exactly *how* I was 'hypersensitive'— I hoped that at last somebody might be going to tell me something useful about myself, that I could get a handle on, and apply. But she became vague, declining, I suppose, to get further involved. I tried to be light about it: 'I guess I'll have to change my whole nature.' She laughed: 'I don't think so.' On the doorstep she said, 'Gosh, you look exhausted! I wish I'd kept my mouth shut!' I closed the door and looked at myself in the mirror. I looked white, and older, with dark rings under my eyes.

———

'Do you think people can change, at our age?' I said to V in bed. 'Oh…no, not really. Only round the edges. Why? What happened at lunch?' R must have spoken to him on the phone. I burst into tears and gave an account. He made it clear he agreed with R's opinion. But after a while he said, 'Does it help that somebody loves you?'

———

Dreamt that a tiny little girl came up to me in a dark, cyclone-fenced concrete enclosure and asked me in a trembling whisper, 'Excuse me—how many pairs of pants do I need to wear, to go and do wee, in here?' I picked her up and carried her on my arm, saying, 'Only one—and do you want me to help you? It *is* a bit spooky in here, if you're on your own.' She relaxed against me with a sigh, and as I carried her in towards the lavatory I could hear her whispering to herself, 'Safe. *Safe.*'

———

V keeps saying that Sydney is more 'exciting' than Melbourne, that Melbourne is 'suburban'—what if 'suburbanism' gets into his writing? I'm remembering the freshness of the air there, the chill of even a summer morning, how delicious its water is. I think about my house with a delirious daring. I see myself walking from room to room: an act of indescribable luxury.

———

'On some days,' wrote the Polish philosopher, 'any contact with others makes me feel afterwards depleted, as if I lost a chunk of myself, spoke too much or not enough—some mismanagement of self and energy…Panic, panic, it can be a little thing, a sudden heaviness that accompanies a reluctance to look up a word in the dictionary, a little death.'

———

It's as if I'd been totally and uncritically in love with R for ten years, and now she's driving me to back off and return her to her status as another person and not a glorious icon of perfection and omniscience. 'It's a good thing, I suppose,' I said, 'but I miss the way we were.' '*I* don't,' she said. 'That kind of intimacy is very seductive, but I think it's rather dangerous.' Fantasies of sharp retorts, of escape from all intimacy: a bare room, a table.

———

Up at the great reader's V and I saw a marvellous bird. It sprang up from behind some rocks and perched on a branch, staring at us with fierce, yellow, large, almost-human eyes. An owl? Not square enough. Must be a hawk. A small eagle? Got feathered legs. But the eyes are so big. Don't owls sleep all day? V was fascinated by it, moved: 'It's not scared of us at all. It's absolutely fearless.' I notice how deeply he responds to nature. He becomes fully absorbed, while I experience it as a background to my private thoughts.

———

At Christmas dinner Mum isolates me in a corner and behaves in a very emotional manner, holding my hand, hugging and kissing me many times, saying how glad she is that I'm 'coming home'. Dad can't meet V's eye or shake his hand but tells a couple of very funny stories. Later V said, 'He's clever. He really knows how to tell a story—how to show the awful part of a story.'

———

A perfect, pure summer's night in Melbourne. At sunset, a long pink cloud, ridged as neat and fine as salmon flesh. People in another garden talking quietly. Every now and then a burst of laughter. The sky very clear, as if the air were finer and clearer than in Sydney where it's always thickened by moisture, perfume, a great warmth remaining from the day's sun. Out the front, now, beside the plane tree, a small three-quarter moon.

1991

C has let me the room above her office on Brunswick Street, a small, pretty space overlooking foliage. Relief of this *immense*. I set it up, and worked smoothly and productively for hours on the screenplay rewrite.

———

V: 'I feel as if I'm not really here, as if I don't know *where* I am.' Meanwhile I know exactly where *I* am—back in town: I've lent one sister $5400 to pay her Visa bill, and another bit me for $600 'till the end of March'.

———

I bought an old piano. I have forgotten almost everything. Except Small Prelude No. 1 and Prelude No. 1 of the 48. I stagger and limp through them.

———

Easter, and E came to stay. She and I spent a day and a night up at Primrose Gully. Terribly dry, the ground cracking. The farmland beyond the valley has a short silver hide on it. Birds sang. Koalas in the trees. A full moon shone all night. We walked over to the opposite ridge. Vast skies streaked and webbed with cloud, tiny wrens wherever we looked.

———

At dinner people talked about sex with strangers on planes. For once I was entirely innocent. One man said that his work colleague claimed he 'always got a fuck on an international flight. But he says you never have anything to do with the person sitting next to you, otherwise over the remaining hours of the flight you have to develop a *relationship*.'

———

Dew-soaked, glittering mornings, long warm dry days. Gardened all afternoon with V. We dug with mattock and spade, we shifted soil about in a barrow, planted a solanum rantonnetii, chives, parsley and thyme. We are now very slowed down and feeling our muscles. And reckless enough to say we are happy, though he refused point-blank even to consider coming out to hear my sister's band.

———

I realise that Dad will forever see everything bad that's happened to me as *my fault*.

———

In a Chinese restaurant in Kew V breaks open his fortune cookie: 'The world is always ready to receive talent with open arms.' He shows it to the waiter, who laughs scornfully and says in a loud, firm voice, 'Bullshit!'

———

Rajiv Gandhi has been assassinated by a bomb in a bunch of flowers.

———

Cold morning and I was up before six. Light comes as a brick-pinkness on the plane leaves, which are still only half down. Out the back the broad beans we planted have popped up like rows of tiny soldiers. Someone's rooster crows; then I hear the magpies. Standing in my own yard I feel almost relieved that my friendship with R is over. Maybe she's right: 'Opposite types threaten each other simply by existing.' V comes to the back door. We walk together to the shop to buy the paper, talking and laughing all the way.

———

The old professor has died. At home, in the afternoon, 'in his wife's arms'. One thing you could be sure of, if you died in *her* arms, is that nothing you did would disgust or dismay her.

———

I have so nearly finished this book that I can hardly make myself leave my office at the end of the day.

———

I call a married couple to invite them to dinner. The husband answers: 'Well, that would be very nice, but there's a problem—we've split up. She's left.' Thunderstruck silence. I ask what happened. He outlines his bewilderment in such a steady, bright, laughing voice that I also begin to feel bright and gay, as if we were discussing the odd behaviour of some other species.

———

The born-again and I meet at the gallery. He says he would like to marry, but because he works only with men, building the Harbour Tunnel, he never meets any women, and doesn't know how to.

———

I saw a fine cut of *Chez Nous* today. *Cosmo* had driven it right out of my head, so that as the plot unfolded I got shock after shock of narrative pleasure—at the *deepening* of the narrative. I kept thinking, 'Oh yes! There's this! And this! And this!' I snivelled a bit and shouted with immoderate laughter. I was shameless about laughing uncontrollably at things that others present found only mildly amusing.

———

I dyed two pairs of white trousers from Esprit, one a beautiful dark green, the other a dusky rose pink. Dyeing is wonderful. One feels original, and satisfied with oneself for being frugal, and resourceful. Waiting for the dye shop to open, I skimmed a few pages of V's first novel. His colloquial tone, so funny and controlled; the powerful visual images; and his splintering of sentences by the use of colloquialism—I felt by comparison a prim classicist. Tonight he's gone out with my sister to see Lester Ellis fight Attila the Hun or some such. Home alone I cook spinach and receive faxes from the

Chez Nous people demanding further dialogue for post-synching. I feel put-upon, but ultimately competent. The director says she asked Bruno Ganz, on the way to the airport for his flight home, if he thought he'd ever come back to Australia. He replied (she *said*), 'If there is another script as good as this one, then I will come.'

———

I delivered the *Cosmo* manuscript to Y on Borsari's corner as she zoomed through Carlton on her way to Footscray. I opened the door, slung the fat photocopy on to the seat beside her, and slammed it shut. On the plane to Sydney now I'm still listing useful words I come across, with notes as to where they might beef up some passage or other. A 'brooding' sound passes from Patrick White's pine trees to the extra cello in 'Recording Angel'.

———

V rings me at E's: a 'bitumen-coloured dog' ran at him as he pedalled my bike home from the bread shop. He crashed to the ground and broke three ribs. In casualty they gave him a hit of pethidine and wanted to keep him in—'over-servicing, as usual'—*of course* he said no and came straight home. And no, he does *not* need anybody to look after him. I take this at face value and go about my Sydney business. Next evening I call him. He's been lying down all day because it hurts so much. At 5 pm he drove himself to the hospital and asked for another jab. No, he *hasn't* taken his clothes off and got into bed with a hot water bottle. No, he *hasn't* had anything to eat, or called anybody—who on earth could he ask for help, during the daytime? He doesn't *know* anybody in Melbourne! He doesn't want any bloody women coming round making a fuss! No, *of course* he doesn't need me to come home! I lose my temper and shout at him. Then I call my sister and she says she'll rush round there and make sure he's all right. Oh, I could bloody *strangle* him.

———

Y's editing as always tough, thorough yet somehow painless. In fact, exhilarating. We laughed a lot over the thing. Vast relief.

In the pew sheet at church they had a Leunig cartoon. 'There was once a man who could no longer believe things that were said. All he could trust was sighing, sobbing, swearing, screaming and singing. If you asked him why he no longer believed he would sigh…He would sob…He would scream and swear…And then he would start to sing like a bird.' I suppose he too was told he was hypersensitive.

We heard 'Death and the Maiden' played twice in one evening. Some Canadians played first, a very melodious interpretation, free, sweet and large; but then the Russians threw themselves fiercely into the drama of it, burning and brooding away, a tight ensemble, always leaning in. The tall cellist swayed so much in the second movement that he was almost dancing. I loved both versions but V wouldn't have a bar of the Canadians: too young, he declared, too ignorant of Europe.

'Last night the stars keenly glittered and sparkled with frost till the sky was all ablaze with them, and the night was strangely light, almost as bright as if there had been a moon. There seemed to be something that we did not know of giving light.' —*The Diary of the Rev Francis Kilvert*

V's gone to New Zealand. I miss him and his stern naval haircut.

I've reviewed David Marr's mighty biography of Patrick White. My parents read the review in the paper. Dad said to me, 'I think the writer of that book will be…*enchanted* by what you said about it.' Watching him struggle for the word I felt like bawling.

Labour of rewriting *Cosmo*. I see its hideous overwrittenness, its laughable clogging with adjectives. Strained, self-conscious, affected, over-ambitious, too complicated. By 4 pm I lost heart completely and rode home in the cold. Ate carrots, mayonnaise. Could have devoured the whole *house*, furniture and all, in my discomfiture.

———

Dinner with some painter friends of V's. A lot of roaring about art critics, how terrible they are, how nothing can be done about them and in the end they don't matter. Someone asked me if I had ever had a bad review. I said, 'Of course!' He looked incredulous. I did not pursue the matter. As we were all leaving, he said to me, 'I'm reading *Monkey Grip*. I'd never read it before. I'm enjoying it.' I smiled and said, 'Thanks.' His expression stiffened: 'I'll leave comments till I've finished.'

———

Out walking as it was getting light, V and I passed a blackbird singing on a wire. A very beautiful song, melodic, generously paced, sweet. V laughed: 'I build good nests. I find many worms.'

———

Y's become a grandmother. 'My women friends,' she said, 'have divided into two distinct groups: those who think it's simply wonderful news, and those who ask me carefully how I "feel" about it, as if I mightn't like it. But I find it doesn't touch on the area of vanity, or anxiety about age, at all.'

———

I'm scared that with *Cosmo* I will come a cropper.

———

The pregnant woman showed us a tiny singlet. I asked: 'Is it double 0?' 'Triple.' Even V laughed at its ridiculous smallness.

———

J interviewed on TV. I notice that his chin is high, all the time, as if nerving himself to do it, or defying something.

———

When V says he's finding it very hard to work in Melbourne, the novelist from New York makes some trenchant remarks. What happens, he says, traditionally—that is primitively, or in our instincts—when a man and a woman decide to marry or live together, is that the man takes the woman on to *his* turf. He proceeds to detach her from her family and her friends, and they continue to live, together, in the area of life he's carved out for himself. V, though, has left his own territory and come entirely on to mine. He has no family and no kids, he's estranged from his wife of twenty-four years, he has sold his piece of property, and he's here.

———

In the company of my parents V is generous to a degree rarely seen. Dad is courteous to him but still can't seem to meet his eye, and yet V goes on *working*, socially, with grace and ease. When he feels it's right, V will always go the extra mile, and more.

———

We planted two climbing roses near the front veranda. Cold wind, grey sky. Scrabbled in the dirt, panting. Brought buckets of good soil from the backyard; dug; clawed with both hands. Erased signs of struggle. Rain fell, heavily but briefly. Now the sun is out, among torn and fast-moving clouds. Rose stubs are standing up to all this, quivering a little. The reddish tinge of their stems.

———

Sometimes I wonder if this whole part of my life—including the book—is menopausal. A kind of lament for the children I didn't have.

———

I can't space out the last section. It *won't space out*. After an hour of struggle I got on my bike, rode up to Carlton, bought myself a white raincoat, and came home to bed. Lay there with a hot water bottle and let my mind roam destructively over the book. Saw nothing but its faults: puffy, hollow, false, affected. Thought of giving back the advance and crawling into a hole. Longed for the cold comfort of minimalism, the bone and sinew where no fat clings.

———

'Mount Pinatubo sunsets' every evening. People say it's dust from the distant eruptions—the sky a bizarre, alarming, metallic, brownish-pink behind wild, ragged clouds.

———

The visiting conductor's patience with our daggy suburban *Messiah* choir, a brilliant teacher, people sprang to obey and to learn. He put the tenors in the front row. One bloke, whenever he went for a high note, visibly clenched his buttock muscles. When the sopranos sang, one lone voice, very thin and feeble and hopelessly off-key, tried to take part. The conductor's eyes contracted, then he carried on as if it weren't happening.

———

Dreamt that in a seaside town I was standing with a man on a pontoon under which the ocean heaved. As we gripped the rail, two immense dark-green glistening swells rose and passed under us, tilting the pontoon like a matchbox.

———

The ousting of Gorbachev, tanks rolling on the streets of Moscow. The failed coup. Young soldiers' funerals, great posters of their faces, weeping crowds, a Jewish violinist playing at a grave, Orthodox priests in golden vestments swinging censers. A toppled statue of Lenin, dangling from a crane, sweeps through the air horizontal, a huge black angel. These colossal events unroll before our eyes. We sit gaping, silent. A head-shot of Yeltsin, sour-faced and squinting, one fist clenched high. 'I think it's terrific,' says V, 'how they don't *smile*. Behind that face there's a lot of deep, hard experience.' V has a tremendous respect and admiration for power.

———

At dinner a woman talks about how her mother had recently tried to confide in her about her past sexual experiences, or affairs. The daughter had been unable to accept it, and had turned away: 'I felt it as a fault in me, that I couldn't let her confide in me.' 'I don't see why that's a fault,' said V. 'Why should you be expected to listen to that kind of thing?' Pause, while everyone registers this. 'I'm her daughter,' says the woman, quietly and patiently. 'She needed to confide in me. She needed to tell me some things about her life.' 'I don't think,' says V, leaning back with his hands folded behind his neck, 'that you should feel that as a failure.'

———

My sister reports that her disagreeable mother-in-law had said to her, 'Goodness—you're looking more and more like Helen!' When the mother-in-law had gone home, my sister's husband said to her, 'She didn't mean that as a compliment, you know. I was impressed by the way you handled it.' Driving home, V and I become quite weak with laughter, though actually it's rather sobering.

———

No matter how I kick against them, all the things that Y told me I'd have to do to this bloody book I've ended up having to do. Or rather they end up doing themselves, because she was right. Every day I think it's still the day before. I'm exhausted. I conk out at 3 pm, my neck and shoulders ache, my fingers are clumsy and sticky. I look around and see that the room is dirty. I turn off the typewriter, the lights, the radiator. I put on my coat, walk down the stairs, wheel out my bike, and ride home. I'm so tired that I can't tell how far away things are. Thoughts about the outside world arrive thickly and are unsubtle.

———

A short, light, friendly letter from R: 'I regret the gracelessness.'

———

Y and I sat by her fire and worked through the remaining problems. She had an idea that in one stroke untied a knot that had been driving me insane for a week. It was such a brilliant inspiration that my mind went blank and I sat there with my mouth hanging open.

———

I ran into the law student at Notturno. We talked about *Thelma and Louise*, which for obvious reasons I had liked more than he had. I said, 'I felt gratified by it, as a fantasy.' 'What, of going on the road?'

'No. Of killing someone.' His eyes snapped into focus: 'Oh! I see what you mean!'

———

Alone in the house in the early evening. It's getting dark. Cars passing are already lit up. Only a bit of pale sky showing between the bare plane branches. A dog is barking. A bird sings sweetly and tunefully. Sounds like spring. My cramped spirit starts to relax and spread through the rooms.

———

While V's at the fight I watch a fabulous doco about Mstislav Rostropovich. His terrifying, diamond-dripping diva of a wife, his daughter in a huge fur hat that brilliantly suits her. In a hush between movements a woman's voice rings out in the packed auditorium: 'Slava is Zeus!' Cut to the green room. Slava staggers in, someone strips off his jacket, his white shirt is soaked with sweat, they fuss around him, mopping and dabbing. He collapses on to a couch, holding his head. In whirls the daughter, shining bright in a silver-plated evening gown, and flings herself on to the couch beside him: 'My sweet daddy! That bitch will not leave this place alive!' The wife strides in and announces in a tone of blood-chilling calm: 'They *caught* her.'

———

I desperately miss sleeping alone. I long for it, I crave it. I don't think I'm a very nice person. Not cut out for this.

———

'In every work of genius we recognise our own rejected thoughts: they come back to us with a certain alienated majesty.' —Emerson, 'Self-Reliance'

———

V called and called to me from the backyard but I was busy cooking and would not come. 'Hel. Come out. It's serious.' At last I stamped out there, scowling. He pointed to the broad bean plants, which are chin-high. I leaned over, expecting a pest, and saw that the flowers had begun to turn into *actual beans.*

———

Hot flushes, several times a day, and sometimes in the night.

———

The great reader in the bar. 'A good hostess,' she says, 'should kill the guest.' I adore the way she speaks, I can't resist pulling out my notebook. 'His attention span to women, darling bird, was so short that it made me *haiku* everything.' Seeing me writing she laughs, takes a swig of wine and cries, '*Beeeee mai Boswell!*'

———

At the third dinner for V's fiftieth birthday one of the painters began again his diatribe against domesticity and its adverse effects on men, especially artists. 'We've got to be *very, very careful.* We have to express our *dark* selves.' The women laughed scornfully, and the hostess fell asleep in her chair. On and on the men ranted, about the dreariness of the *Age*, the ugliness of Melbourne's architecture, the hopelessness of its galleries and theatres. I 'went to the toilet' and slid into a room where one of the children was watching *Animal House* on TV. I leaned on a cushion, 'just for a moment', and next thing V was shaking me, saying in a shocked voice, 'Come on! You can't go to sleep *here*!' I dragged myself up, put my shoes back on and reported for further social duty. The hostess was still out like a light, sitting upright at the table.

———

After the cast and crew screening of *Chez Nous* in Sydney, a woman I once worked with came up to me and said, with a strange, slow urgency, 'Helen, I'm in *pain*. What did she do wrong?' People who think about behaviour in terms of innocence, crime and punish-ment, instead of as a constantly changing swarm of almost chemical events. I loved lots of things about the movie, felt doubtful about others, and am still numb about the rest.

———

R came to E's for lunch. She looked exactly the same. I was nervous beforehand but her company was as always: lively, quick, gentle, intelligent, funny. When she was leaving she said, 'I've missed you.' I said, 'Me too.' I could have let out a sob, but didn't, and the moment passed.

———

Before I left for Sydney V asked with elaborate casualness where my *Cosmo* proofs were so he could read it while I was away. In a similar tone I pointed them out to him on the shelf. The infant in me secretly longed for a phone call at E's saying, 'I've read it! It's wonderful!' Instead I obliged myself to behave as if he weren't reading it and I didn't care. He met my plane, greeted me affectionately as always, but did not mention the book. I too avoided the topic till the following morning. H: (*with hard-working breeziness*) 'Did you manage to have a look at *Cosmo* while I was away?' V: (*driving along beside the river to the Botanic Gardens*) 'Yes, I did. I was planning not to talk about it till tomorrow.' H: (*heart sinks. Why the delay? Did he find it too awful?*) 'Oh. Do you feel like telling me now?' V: (*pulls up at intersection; without looking at me puts hand on my knee*) 'It's very good, sweetheart. I'm proud of you. It's beautifully written, in places. Yes, it's very good.' I was so keyed up for criticism that I was at a loss. Everything he went on to say about it was technical, intelligent and to the point. A couple of minor things 'needed attention'. At home he showed them to me. His suggestions were subtle and good, and I knew I could use them.

———

Very warm day. I lay on the kitchen couch dozing and reading old copies of the *TLS*. Late in the afternoon V came and sat in a chair and told me about an idea he's got, based on something the great reader's husband told him years ago—about an Australian man who lived in the south of France, and planted a stand of eucalypts. Each tree bore a metal plaque naming its type. But during the war the Germans came and commandeered the plaques for scrap metal, and he lost his classification. Ever afterwards he hung about the village cafe waiting for Australian tourists to pass through, and asking them to come and identify the trees. 'So I thought,' he went on, 'I'd make him have a marriageable daughter...'

I sat up. He had a sudden urge to rearrange the furniture in his work room. He wanted his table to face a bare brick wall. We pushed and shoved, I vacuumed dramatically. He was so casually blank, or 'level', as he would say—'level' is his desired state of being—that I didn't know how to express my excitement, or where to put it. So I swallowed it.

———

Our friends' ultrasound. The recognisable shape of skull and nose, the tiny raised hand. We all gazed at it in wonder. V's face was soft. 'Isn't it miraculous!'

———

Dreamt I searched the piano in vain for the key of S. My teacher instructed me to play a gold ring that one of us was wearing.

———

'Once we lose our sense of grievance, everything, including physical pain, becomes easier to bear.' —Germaine Greer, *The Change*

———

Breakfast at Marios for my birthday. Y came. We discussed the drowning of Robert Maxwell, and the appearance on TV of Kerry Packer who is making a bid for the Fairfax empire. I said I had found Packer repellent, a huge toad-like bully. Y said, 'I fell in love with him on TV. I fell in love with his *power*.' And V spoke with a shining face about Maxwell: 'Just imagine him, striding the world!'

———

In his car O said, 'I've heard that in your new book there's a brain tumour story, and that Y wanted you to change it.' H: 'It's true that there's a brain tumour in it. It's not true that Y asked me to change it.' He started the motor, and said in a calm, pleasant voice, 'Well, I'll just have to be patient, and wait.'

A heaviness, around the heart. A heaviness in breathing. I keep running through details of the story, trying to 'be him' and 'see it through his eyes'. Is it a vengeful story? Not as far as I can tell, in my present state of awareness. Does it give a *complex* picture of my relationship with O? Yes. Very. It goes through the worst of both of us, and the best of him. It was necessary for me to write this story. I remember asking Raymond Carver if there was any line he drew round parts of his life, or people he's been engaged with, across which he would not go. He thought for a moment, very carefully, and said, 'It's my job to write down life as I see it.' Pause. 'It's a jungle out there.' Patrick White's savagery. His utter ruthlessness. Chekhov, the women in *The Darling* and *The Butterfly*: do people imagine that he made up these terrible characters, from thin air?

I gardened, on my own. Spitting with rain. Sang to myself and thought.

V is seriously getting started on his book. From the door I see the plans spread out all over his desk. He really means business. Strange how differently we approach writing. I blunder in blindly and scrub-bash my way through a trackless forest, but he stays well back until he has laid out the route, created a fundamental map. He has an *aim* in mind.

J is taking his young son to Paris because he's writing a book about 'a bloke travelling with his son'. I thought about M and me, our travels, how I put her on trains alone, sent her to a *colonie de vacances* in Brittany that I'd never even heard of, let alone seen.

Now that it's V's turn to start a big piece of work I sense an obliga-tion to remove myself from the premises during the day. How did this come about? By an osmotic process. Something in the air. That

I instinctively obey. I rode around on my bike, looking for a place to be. The library was closed. V has not mentioned any aspect of my book or remarked on it at all, since the proofs went back. I have no idea whether it affected him, whether any of its ideas interested him. I don't expect him ever to say, and I don't dare to ask. I'm scared his face would go blank.

———

As soon as we had ordered our food at Toki, V said, 'Right. Now. *Insurance.*' Couldn't I see I was squandering money? That insurance companies calculated the odds and then slugged people exactly where their deepest anxieties lay? I flailed away about fire and flood. Next he said I had been intractable about his suggestion of a row of pittosporum trees in the garden. I said they would have made a wall of darkness, and that anyway he dominated the house's interior aesthetic, even in my own room. What, he asked, did I want aesthetically that I didn't have? I said curtains on the big kitchen windows and a little bit of caneite above the phone to pin things on. *Caneite?* He poured out a diatribe against people who stick things on fridge doors or kitchen walls—it was 'unconvincing'—it would be fifty times better to have the little black McCahon on the wall beside the fridge. I fired up and said that a kitchen was the working heart of the house, an organic room where things constantly changed, rather than a space for art to be contemplated. He got sarcastic, using words like 'art gallery' and 'museum' and 'mausoleum'. I said I hadn't used any of these words. He said I'd spoken 'with contempt'. I said I felt dispossessed and did not think it was fair that I had to go out all day—why didn't we make the shed out the back into a studio so he could work there without the house having to be kept empty all around him? I said I needed somewhere to *be* during the day when I wasn't working. He said I was neurotic: that I'd come home yesterday miserable because a *library* was closed.

———

In the morning I thought that if I couldn't stay home I could take a mattress to my office so I could be comfortable there all day and read. This is awful, and boring. If I could argue calmly, without losing my temper or acting out a victim role, I would have a…better life. Is it my manner that's the problem? Or is it the content of my demands?

———

I think he fights for ART and its HIGHER VALUE because, having no children and never having wanted any, he resents the high moral tone I apparently take when I assert the value of what one learns from domestic and family life, and from the company of children. 'I don't know,' he says, 'how people who aren't artists can keep going, not making a shape of themselves. I s'pose they do it through children.' He really sees them as alternatives.

———

Y came to Marios bringing bound proofs of *Cosmo*. I think it's all right. Even quite good. But I also noticed its anxious perfectness. I made up my mind, next time, to blast that aspect of my writing to kingdom come.

———

'Dear R and O, I had planned to give you a copy of this book next January when the hardbacks will be printed, but since rumours have already begun to circulate about its contents, I am sending you the first holdable copy that has reached me. With love always, no matter how hard it gets.'

———

I'm trying to become a more practised questioner, to listen patiently with full attention and real curiosity, and to stop using people's answers as triggers for a monologue about *me*. I ask, and I keep my mouth shut and my eyes on the other person's face. In this I'm copying V, who is brilliant at it.

———

V invites my father to come with him to see some paintings that are to be auctioned. Dad accepts, but says to me, 'I don't know anything about paintings. I'm only going for one reason—to see what a bunch of ster-youpid bloody pricks they were.'

———

Driving back from Primrose Gully we hit an animal. It was a very solid, lethal thump and V kept going, but the other man called out, 'Hey-hey!' V pulled over and they walked back. It was a rabbit. V delivered the death-chop with the side of his hand. 'Ooh, ooh,' whimpered the pregnant woman. They put the rabbit into the salad bowl in the boot and we drove on, comparing notes on how to cook rabbits. V skinned it skilfully over the sink. He called me to watch while he slit open its belly: the tightly packed, beautifully designed guts neatly filling their cavity. I put the pieces into a marinade of red wine and onions, and we went to bed. I said, 'When I saw how perfectly its guts were arranged I thought, "All that brilliant evolution, just to be slit open and eaten."' 'You could say that about the wine in the marinade, too,' he said. 'All those grapes.'

———

Dreamt that O stepped out of a hallway into a lobby where I was waiting, and approached me with his arms wide open, and a big smile. He looked young, healthy, cheerful; dressed in light-coloured clothes. He took me in his arms and said, 'That's a very, very beautiful story.' I told the dream to the Polish philosopher. I said, 'I don't want to hurt him. I want him to see that I needed to show our friendship in the most complex way I could. I don't want him to take it as an attack.' 'But it's not an attack. You've shown the friendship on a deep level. Look—could you perhaps consider the dream as his actual response, I mean his *eventual* response, even if it doesn't happen immediately? Even if you have to wait quite a long time?' Her delicacy of manner. Like Y, she knows how to couch a challenge in language that seduces, relaxes and exhilarates.

———

G and M-C, have come to stay. Suddenly he and V are like a pair of schoolboys, cackling with hysterical laughter at the breakfast table. Sometimes I feel like kicking them, two giggling ninnies putting on Pommy accents, a copy of Wisden always at the ready, but when M-C and I join in it becomes fun for us too. I think G is *good* for V, dragging him back to some neglected stage of himself, before he became harsh and solemn.

———

Dreamt I looked at myself in a wall mirror and I had another woman's face. It was me, but I looked like someone else. Movements of 'my' muscles produced expressions on this face that were unfamiliar and did not correspond with 'me'.

———

R writes that I have been 'punitive' to O in my story. The word keeps appearing in my thoughts. Is it true? I snap at V. He takes it quietly, and stoically. I get down on my knees in the dirt. Plant beans, capsicum and basil. Grey sky, cool wind. Hear myself panting and grunting. As the light fades the sky takes on a lurid tinge. A faint pinkish gold glimmers on the undersides of leaves. 'Punitive' floats in and out. I keep on working.

———

I was about to buy a washed-out denim jacket in Chapel Street when V came in and pointed out, correctly, that the darker one the salesgirl was wearing was a more attractive colour. She took it off and sold it to me. Later I found in its pocket a used tissue with lipstick on it and many drops of dried blood, as if from an insect bite or a pimple. I didn't mention this to V, who was already alarmed at my having donned a garment still warm from a stranger's body.

———

Now Paul Keating is PM. He says, 'I feel the poignancy of the moment.' Bob Hawke, ousted, surges out into the brutal light of the media. He is smiling, but looks smaller, and the camera flashes are like a splatter of pockmarks on his face.

———

I did a mammoth bout of ironing, everything I own plus fifteen shirts of V's. I *love* ironing. I sing away, or think. While I was gaily working he opened the fridge and grumbled, 'The place is stripped. There's nothing here to eat.' I went to inspect and found it contained: tomatoes, eggs, carrots, a large plastic container of home-made soup and, right in the front, three beautiful French cheeses. I remarked in what I hoped was a neutral tone, 'There's some cheese in here.' 'Is there? Where?' It's not self-control I need to study, but detachment. This morning he kept returning to the annoying disappointment of finding 'an empty fridge'. I suggested we should change our household organisation so that food-buying was shared and he could have all the things he liked. He thought for a moment, then said he didn't really care about the fridge.

———

V tells me he called his wife for her birthday. She reported certain adventures abroad, then asked him, 'And what have *you* been doing? What's been happening in your life?' He replied, 'Nothing. Nothing much.' I was surprised. 'You didn't tell her you'd started a new book?' 'Listen,' he said. 'She's been in *Africa*, and *India*. Dealing with *elephants* and *tigers*. And you want me to say, "I've started planning a novel and been to the cricket a few times"?'

———

A letter comes from O. It is restrained, decent, deeply generous, deeply offended and hurt, and still attempting a literary response as well as a personal one. I'm sad. For having hurt him. I examine myself for guilt and don't find any. I find a hard nut of something in the centre of my heart. I find sadness but I do not find regret. I suppose this is a friendship lost. Destroyed. By me. How will I answer?

———

I don't know what angels are, but this book I've just written is full of them.

———

A five-year-old English boy came to dinner with his mother and stepfather. He was supposed to be watching TV and eating a chocolate frog but after a while he came creeping out to the kitchen. I set him up at the coffee table with a paintbox and paper and a glass of water. He began to work. Watching him dab his brush in the paint and sweep his upper body sideways towards the paper, V had to cover his mouth to hold in a rush of laughter, then he looked at me with an expression of astonishment and said, 'He's really *absorbed*, isn't he!' When the other adults left the room, the boy paused in his work and said to me, 'V's funny, isn't he.' 'Yes. He's very funny.' 'Why did you choose him, for your husband?' 'Oh…because I loved him. Because he's kind to me, and he makes me laugh.' The boy turned back to his painting, restraining a smile of embarrassment. I heard later that he has an IQ of 135.

––––––––

Chez Nous is going to Berlin. I have to find, before Monday, German equivalents for 'moll', 'dago' and 'fair go'.

––––––––

V thinks parents should speak to their children as Canetti's mother did to him. In an orchard she screamed at him, 'You know *nothing*!' Imagine the bumptious, opinionated creep the little Canetti must have been.

––––––––

G's first wife outside the fruit shop. We embraced. She's been working in Vientiane for two years. 'It was beautiful. I lived in a house next to a rice field. I got around on a little motorbike, or a pushbike. I'd look around me and I'd think, 'This is *good* for me. It's good for my soul.' Pedalling on to work, I realised the point of this meeting: she was an angel to remind me that *things pass*. Ten years ago she shoved a tarot card at me through my car window—a body face down with seven swords stuck in its back—because of a story I'd published about G. Now we kiss when we meet, and talk quietly, using the word 'soul'.

V reports a call from Z, who spoke to him about my book. 'Did he seem to, um, like it?' 'Aw, he said it was "rich", or something.' On our walk to the coffee shop he speaks disobligingly about the Polish philosopher, to whom he had taken quite a shine until last week when she apparently expressed to him several unacceptable thoughts after having read his first novel. Trying to exercise my new mode of detachment and self-command, I merely acknowledge with a friendly murmur that he has spoken. Short silence.

V: 'What's the matter?'

H: 'Nothing. I'm just practising not being "argumentative", "rude", "touchy" and so on.'

V: 'Oh.'

Short pause.

V: 'But I'd really like to know what you think.'

H: 'Well, I wasn't there. But she's so clever, and so sensitive, that I find it hard to imagine her saying anything stupid or offensive.'

V: 'Sometimes I can't be bothered summing up someone else's argument with as much nuance as you seem to want—I just sum it up.'

H: 'But if the argument *involves* nuance, isn't that a distortion?'

V: 'Look—I don't think her ideas were much better than hackneyed.'

And on we walk to the coffee shop, under our little cloud of trouble.

What the Polish philosopher said to him, she told me later, was that in his conversation she finds warmth and sympathy that are missing from his work. She suggested that what's blocking the access of it into his work are his severe theories about what art is or is supposed to be. I agree with this. So does the great reader. But he won't listen. He reads Canetti with immense admiration, and my heart sinks. But also—relief: that I'm not alone in my famous refusal to *'be told'* what's wrong with me and my work.

'...We live only with what we do not love, with what we have brought to live with us only in order to kill *the intolerable love*...'
—Proust, *The Captive*

1992

E's pretty new hat: a darkish lavender, of heavy but flexible straw. She didn't want to swim in the waves, and went back to sit on the sand. I dived and floated on my own. Once I turned back to glance at her sitting on her towel. I raised one hand and instantly she waved back: like a mother. She told me she'd seen O. Although he had been very hurt by my story, she said, he fully endorsed my right to have written it.

———

Fantasy. Someone asks me, 'Why do you write such terrible things about O?' and I say, 'Because I love him.' Then they ask O, 'Why does Helen write such terrible things about you?' and he replies, 'Because she loves me.'

———

'He worked a great deal from memory, using everybody he knew.'
—D. H. Lawrence, *Sons and Lovers*

———

I toil over a reply to O's letter. I try to express my admiration for his generosity, grace and sweetness of spirit. I point to the depth and power of his shaping influence on me over our long, long friendship. 'It was with you that my whole outlook as a young adult, my early attitudes towards literature, study, drinking, politics, football, films, music, people—even my sense of humour—were formed.' I say my dearest wish is that one day he might find in the story the love and respect I believe are in it, as well as the struggle and anger and frustration.

———

Z told us how he'd had an audience with the Queen, for winning the Commonwealth Literary Award. 'But Z,' I said, 'you're a republican!' 'Commonwealth,' he replied smoothly. 'Even if we were a republic, we'd still be in the Commonwealth. She's head of the Commonwealth.' Everyone laughed.

———

The characters that people I know become when I write about them are, to me, almost totally separate from the people themselves, once I've finished the piece of work and put it aside, or published it. It's as if I've extracted or borrowed from the real person the aspects of them that I needed to struggle with, and the character consists only of those aspects. I can return to the real person with no sense of overlap. Cold comfort.

———

Hot sweats wake me through the night. I'm so touchy—on a hair trigger. Everything makes me angry and I don't know why. I'm cooking a pasta sauce, V comes and stares into the pot and says, 'There's not much there. There's not enough.' I fly off the handle and we eat wretchedly (there *was* enough, it was rich and there was plenty). Can I find any kind of excuse or reason in the fact of menopause? Yanking weeds out of the grass after dinner, we try to speak reasonably to each other. Am I discontented? I say it bothers me that he has taken over the house, that I can't be at home during his working hours without feeling I'm trespassing, and there on sufferance. He says, 'Everyone needs a clear space, to work.' 'Yes, a room that's theirs. But a whole house—that's an immense luxury.' 'What about Proust?' he said. 'Flaubert?' He says I should come and go as I please, that he will try to adapt. Then I am filled with guilt, as if my claim were unreasonable. Also, I know he doesn't mean it.

———

O replies. 'Amicably and equably' he sends his good wishes to both of us. I read his postcard as a justified dismissal, a farewell. I think I will also choose to see it as a blessing, the sort that might come from an exhausted father who finally throws up his hands, stands back from the complaints and attacks of a daughter, and says, 'Go in peace.'

———

First time alone at Primrose Gully since before I moved to Sydney. Crows, to the south. A wallaby sat up on its haunches, holding an apple to its mouth with both front paws. In the evening a koala began to snort and rumble. Kookaburras. Rain in the night, though I slept so deeply I hardly noticed it. Magpies when I woke: the morning birds of childhood. I swept the house and polished the windows. Everything I saw through them was distinct and glossy, moving in the cool air. I'm happy up here. A better person. My movements are slower and more leisurely. My whole *rate* slows down.

———

A clear, hottish summer Sunday. After breakfast at Marios we walked in the Botanic Gardens. V, smoking his weekly Havana, discoursed with sombre pleasure upon the naivety of the Anglican women deacons who had *actually believed* that the Bishop would ordain them, who said they were 'devastated, stunned and in pain' when the court injunction was granted. 'They're utterly naïve,' he said, 'about *power*. I've realised, from my reading over the last few years, quite a lot about power. It's what makes men unpleasant, but it's also what they *are*. It's what they've *got*. Perhaps it's all they've got.' I suggested tentatively that perhaps women who've been at the mercy of power had as good an understanding of it as did the men who were wielding it, since in order to survive under it they'd had to learn about its ways. He flatly rejected this, and restated his thesis. I floated the idea that if all men had was power, it was not surprising that when they were about to lose it, they panicked. 'I don't see much panic around,' he said superbly, puffing away. 'It's in art, too, in a slightly lesser way. Now that painting's no longer important, anybody at all can have a go. More women are…accepted.' I kept trying to listen analytically—I mean, I tried not to get lost in my dismay. I wanted to be sure I wasn't imagining it. The Havana he was smoking was a prop in a performance: as if some unmodulated male principle had come to inhabit him. He was a mouthpiece to an archetype.

————

The Latin American kids dancing cumbia: blankly single-minded on their fluid legs.

————

A visitor went out our kitchen door and said, 'What a beautiful back garden. It's full of air.'

————

I'm reading *Jane Eyre*, adoring it. V tried to make me get off the bed late in the afternoon and come for a walk along the creek but I clung to the mattress edge with my free hand, saying, 'Wait. Wait. An anguished cry has just rent the night in twain.' I was only half joking but he doubled over.

————

The first capsicum appears, a firm green shiny lump as big as a walnut.

————

It was a warm summer night and we talked for a long time without quarrelling. V said he had to have 'an asbestos suit on' in order to criticise my work. We came at this vexed topic from several angles, lying on our bed beside the open windows. I said, 'I know I'm hypersensitive and unpleasant. But I've been trying hard lately to be more reasonable.' 'Well, it has got a bit easier, but I'm very wary of it.' I tried to explain that I would readily accept his criticisms if only he would preface them by telling me whether the work had affected him, whether it had touched him in any way. He said he'd told me something in the book was 'quite moving'. I think I would have remembered that, but maybe I'd had a moment of deafness; anyway I privately seized on 'quite moving', knowing it was all I could ever hope for. I said that I had a very high regard for him as a reader, and deeply respected his literary opinion, but that after his technical comments he'd never mentioned the book again. He'd dealt with it briskly, like an obligation, and buried it. I said that I kept hoping he might mention something that had stuck in his mind or made him laugh—but he never did. I said I was disappointed that he hadn't been more...comradely. He listened, without interrupting. Then he said, '*I* would never expect you to respond to *my* work in the way you're describing.' 'But I did. Didn't I? When your book came out? I talked about it a lot. I said how much I liked it, I quoted lines from it, I remembered turns of phrase and things that were clever and funny—I *enjoyed* talking about it.' 'I do remember you being very nice.'

Oh, what's the point of all this—saying it in the first place, writing it down later. I don't know how we'll be able to live together as writers. I can't see a way, unless I drop all this craving for...what? These grudging crumbs he'll drop in front of me if I pester him? I long for him to let me see how my work affects him. Maybe it doesn't. Maybe it leaves him cold.

———

Whenever I lie down to sleep, night or day, tremendous hot flushes pour over my torso and limbs—not tremendous in temperature so much as in stiflingness, as if all my body's pores were blocked, a disagreeable sensation, like being trapped in a blanketing force that precisely moulds all my contours.

———

Last night, V sat beside me on the kitchen couch and took my bare feet on his lap and told me what he really thought about 'Recording Angel'—that it was 'a very strong story', but that O would have been shocked to read a description of himself at his lowest, in hospital after that dreadful operation: to be revealed and scrutinised while in that state. I began to feel the horror of what I've done. I heard myself jabbering the same old justifications, how I thought I'd done this and what I'd meant was that, and it made me sick. I broke off mid-sentence and got up and walked over to the sink. He said, 'What's up, sweetheart?' I said, 'I'm sick and tired of myself, that's all.' He came and put his arms round me and gently kissed me. The awful truth is that no one can help you carry the consequences of your behaviour. You are required to carry them on your own.

———

As I rushed down Lygon Street, the biographer came walking up it, all in white, smiling and strolling on her own. I called out her name. When she turned and saw me her face broke into her familiar sweet and beautiful smile. We kissed. I babbled out my destination and ran on. Today I got a note from her: 'That was a moment of pure love and it's still with me. Dear old Lygon Street on a sunny day, dear you, and dear me!'

———

The producer told me that when *Chez Nous* was screened in Berlin, they laughed. Out loud. And at the end they stood up and applauded. And people said to the director, 'What have you done to Bruno? He's so *warm*!' Maybe I'm not such a dog after all.

———

Woman after woman, five of them in a few days, came up to me to say they liked 'Recording Angel'. And each of them said a version of 'It's full of love.' I'd better get used to this. Men see it one way, women another.

———

V has a cold. He's outraged that he's ill: 'How did I *catch* it?' 'Same as everyone else. A germ was flying along and you got in its way.' I make an unobtrusive fuss of him, clean sheets, an extra blanket, vichyssoise, but he insists on getting up at the usual time and sits all morning at his desk with bowed shoulders, honking and groaning.

After lunch he lies on top of the bed with his shoes on and one hand over his eyes.

———

Got knocked off my bike on the footpath up near Natural Tucker by a middle-aged woman in a Volvo that came surging out of a lane. I sailed sideways through the air towards the gutter, hearing myself emit a long cry of protest, and landed comfortably on the pad of muscle of my left upper arm and shoulder. My front wheel was all twisted and buckled. Thoughts passed thickly through my head. The driver was very upset. I said in a clear, authoritative tone, but with a dream-like slowness, 'I'm not hurt. Don't worry. I shouldn't have been on the footpath.' She gave me her phone number, apologised over and over, and drove away. That's when I felt like bawling with foolishness and shock, all forlorn on the pavement with my mangled bike and nobody to help me. Trundled it to the bakery and bought a casalinga.

———

Mum and Dad came to the literary lunch. I went down to say hello. Dad called me 'dear' and introduced me proudly to several strangers at their table. When I was called to speak, he took my wrist and said in a soft, good-natured tone, 'Don't criticise me too much, will you.' I could have howled and laid my forehead on his shoe. I said as many respectful things about him, and Mum, as I could think of. I even thanked him for his 'strong character'.

———

Morning streets so quiet, all we could hear was a dove calling and calling. V polished off a terrific piece about boxing, and then we went for a walk along the Merri Creek in the autumn sun. He smoked a cigar. We collected eucalypt wood for barbecues and chattered away merrily as we scrounged.

———

G and M-C here to stay. He vagues out on her, she is sharp with him at the table. G confides in V, M-C in me. V says they're about to part. Out in the yard G says to me, 'I want what you've got, Hel.' 'What?' 'I hear you two talking and laughing in bed, for hours. That's what I want.'

———

Reviews of *Cosmo*, some excellent, others bilious (I am 'pretentious' and so on). I have recovered my equilibrium; V and I read the bad ones out loud and laugh meanly. I really hardly care at all. Must have attained satori. The Cretan called: he wanted to 'rush out in the street and kick its critics right up the bum, so they'd have an orgasm and then *die*.' The young guy in the bank told me the balance of my account, then added, 'But it'll be a few dollars more by Friday, because I'm going out today to buy your book.' Meanwhile I keep my copy of *Paradise Lost* in the outside toilet. Staggered by its *worked* quality, the beautiful placing of the feet, their weight and balance.

———

While I was cleaning the bathroom basin V came in and we had an interesting discussion. Leaning against the door jamb with his arms folded, he advised me that it was time for me to stop writing 'about the 70s'. Oh? Why's that? Because the 70s was a 'period of bullshit, of clapped-out theories that Victoria is now bearing the brunt of.' Apparently G shared his opinion; indeed he had told V that he'd already had 'a little talk' with me about it. I said we hadn't spoken about this as far as I recalled. Shifting my energies to the bath, I pointed out that certain social changes had occurred in the 70s that people had been deeply affected by—that this could not be scrubbed out of either my characters or me, and that to attempt it would not make sense. I said that his work was coloured by different assumptions because his ideas were formed in a different era and through different experiences. I said that whenever I read him I felt that I was in the 50s. He said that much of his work was set in no-place and no-time. I said that it was in the relationships between men and women, and in the underlying assumptions about these, that period still made itself felt. He asked me what I thought about what he'd said. I said, opening the toilet lid and attacking the rim of the bowl, 'I don't think anything in particular.' He pressed me harder. I said, 'I understand the point you're making. But I can't say how it will affect me, until I sit down to write the next thing.' I forbore to point out that in the simple fact that I was on my knees scrubbing the porcelain as we talked, and in the fact (which he had only the other evening admitted publicly without shame or remorse) that he has 'never cleaned a lavatory in his life', resided a thundering piece of…whatever it is we were talking about: a whopping great assumption about men, women and domestic labour which dates him, and judges him, as accurately as does any misplaced nostalgia that I have been reproached with.

———

Some mornings in our street I hear a birdcall that I can't identify: a liquid sound, like a string firmly plucked under bubbling water.

———

Went to a general yoga class last night. Much harder than the beginners, different in tone: people were calm, silent, ready to work, a sense of organisation and purpose in the room. They fell quickly into lines, certain basic things were taken for granted. I followed awkwardly but I *followed*. Riding home in the warm dark I thought, I'm nearly fifty and I *kept up*.

———

I proposed to the *Age* a piece about autopsies. They're lining it up with Coronial Services. V said he'd like to come too. On the phone to the professor I talked him in as 'a colleague'. It won't be just me and the situation. Well, it can be, if I make it be. I've got that female habit of filtering everything through what I imagine my male companion's responses are.

———

Today we saw a dead man's body cut open, and his organs stowed into a plastic bag and sewn back into his abdominal cavity. We saw the corpse of an old woman slit from neck to pubic bone, disembowelled, skinned; her scalp peeled forward over her face like a hairy cap and her skull sawn in half as one halves a hard-boiled egg.

————

When we got home I found a message from the *Age* to call the Coroner. He was furious that we had been allowed to go into the mortuary when work was in progress—when *detectives* were there. He said severely that I was to come back to the mortuary at the first available opportunity, 'put on mortuary clothes', and watch an autopsy from start to finish, with a pathologist present to explain each stage of the process as it was done. 'Yes, Mr Hallenstein,' I said meekly, biting back a shout of joy. 'I can come tomorrow morning.'

————

I hardly know how to write what I was shown. A young man with a narrow, dark red trench where the ligature took his weight. A little boy who had fallen out of a ute, his slender body and huge swollen half-shaven head. A woman in her sixties, as if asleep, her expression of patient resignation. A tiny baby on a metal shelf, perfectly swaddled in a pink cotton blanket. The demeanour of the people who work there, their quiet efficiency, their respect and modesty, made it possible for me to witness these things without fear or revulsion. I felt such affection for them. I can say, here at least, how calm and grateful, how *happy* I was in their company. Almost as if I belonged there.

————

At Queenscliff I slept all night beside two enormous open windows. Magpies sang in a particularly ornate and leisurely manner. Huge skies covered in thin pale clouds.

————

'I think you should learn the second Czerny,' said my piano teacher. 'They make a pair. You've been on the first one long enough.' 'Okay. I love boring exercises.' 'I've noticed,' she said. 'You must be looking for something deeper in the music. Something spiritual.' We laughed but I wasn't *quite* sure whether she was teasing me.

———

I've been offered a job reviewing movies for a monthly magazine. Out of the depths of my ignorance I take it. The editor, gossiping about a certain journalist, says, 'Like all bullies and authoritarians, he's very easily wounded.' Later I report this to V. 'Yes,' he says, 'that's good, isn't it. Did you, um, think it might apply to you? A bit?' 'Yes, I did,' I said, hanging my head. And the more easily wounded one is, the more bullying and authoritarian one becomes. To protect the shivering chasm at the core.

———

At dinner V fed Dad questions and played the eager listener; Dad blossomed. In fact he talked without stopping for the entire evening. Not one question did he ask, not one hint of interest in anyone else's views of life or experience. To hear that slow voice grind on and on, hour after hour—I had to keep getting up and 'going to the toilet', for relief from the voice. I could have torn out my hair.

———

Easter morning. He is risen. A steady quiet, outside. A dove calling. All those bodies down there, in the House of Death and Justice and Science, the House of Patience, are only remains. Their spark has fled. The wind gets up. A mild shifting of the plane leaves. Sun comes through in patches. Dry bitumen.

———

At Wilcannia my nun and her friend (girlfriend? I don't ask) live for free in a tumbledown, abandoned old house with walls a foot thick and an immense yard that backs on to the Darling River. From the kitchen door you can hear its soft flow. Last night when I staggered out to the dunny, fighting my way past the three dogs that live in the yard, the Milky Way crackled overhead in a huge arc.

———

I called home. V has a bad cold. Why does he get sick whenever I go away?

When I sit on the outside dunny the brown kelpie pup, Tex, shoves his front legs under the door and madly rummages with them, like a burglar going through a drawer. He likes me. I dream of turning up at home with a dog. For V. To put life back into him. The guy who's minding him said I couldn't take him because I live in a city: 'I wouldn't do that to a dog.' Crestfallen, I hide in the bottom of my suitcase the blue leather collar and webbing lead I'd secretly bought at the store. But the nurse says, 'Of course you can have the pup. We need to get rid of him. No, I won't take any money. I'd love you to have him.' I practise teaching him to sit and stay. He learns fast. He is beautiful and clever. My wrists are covered with bite marks from our wrestling bouts.

The women are busy all day with the overwhelming bureaucratics of their work here with the Aboriginal people. They don't look after themselves, so I do the washing, I iron things, I cook, I do the dishes, I fix broken gadgets, sweep the yard, scoop up puppy shit. I cut an apple and make the nun eat the peeled and cored quarters. She looks up surprised when I place them on the arm of her chair. She eats them obediently.

Out here they pray for rain. The drought is shocking. The land is degraded. It's blowing away. 'When Kidman built his mansion on the Darling,' a farmer tells me, 'he had forty-seven Chinese gardeners.'

I've got a cage booked at Broken Hill airport, the space booked at Ansett Adelaide, and three Dramamine pills from the priest to keep him calm en route.

Rain at night brings the Merri Creek up a foot or so. V and I happily walk Tex along the creek path and watch him frolic and gambol. He likes to race up a rocky outcrop and pose on its peak, gazing nobly into the distance. We call it 'Tex's Look-Out'. He sleeps calmly on his blanket on the back veranda. He has a merry, patient nature. He never complains. But he needs two *enormous* walks each day.

————

J's won his second Miles Franklin. That's a prize I know I'll never win.

————

The great reader's old school friend paid tribute to the great reader's mother: she said that during the war, when they were young women, they used to ask each other, 'Who would you tell if you had a black baby?' The great reader's mother was the only name that came up. This made V laugh terribly. So, the following evening, did F's imitation of Pompidou. V laughed so much he couldn't get his breath.

————

Dreamt that every time I turned over in bed, $400 was added to our electricity bill.

————

'Dear Mr and Mrs Watson, here is the card from the Lost Dogs' Home vet, where we took Tex for his shots; also the worm pill packet, so you'll know what he's had. I'm very sad to give him up, but I know it's the best thing for him, and I'm sure you'll be good to him and he'll be happier in the country. Thanks for taking him. I felt very down in the dumps about him last night but today I cheered up. We ate the carrots and the silverbeet last night, they were delicious. It was really nice to meet you. I hope your CAT scan results are good, Mr Watson. Thanks again for everything. Yours sincerely, Helen.'

————

We read about a kelpie cross called Trixie who, when her master had a stroke and lay paralysed in his bed for nine days, kept him alive by soaking a towel in her water bowl and the toilet and draping it over his face so he could suck the moisture.

V pointed out again, as we walked along the creek, that I had an obsessive interest in 'death, rape, murder and so on'. I wonder if it's true. And if it is true, what it means. Is it wrong?

———

We hear that Tex is happy. He runs about the farm collecting items for a museum of objects that he likes to toss and catch—old bones, cow horns etc. One day they saw something brown among his treasures. 'That's not a piece of horn.' It was a dead tiger snake. I felt a pang. But life without him and his mad working-dog energy contains less guilt.

———

Sometimes we talk about getting married.

———

Two letters from people who hated my articles about the morgue. 'I sincerely hope, Ms Garner, that when I die, my body will be free from your perverted gaze.'

———

I like the prayer that says, 'Forgive us all that is past.'

———

I planted a little daphne bush, dug out the old herb patch, composted, mulched, moved the sage plant. V came out with two coffees. Proudly I showed him my handiwork. He glanced in its direction, blank-faced. I tugged at his sleeve. 'Doesn't it look terrific?' He put on a voice: 'Yeah! It looks groovy! *Cool!*' I soldiered on: 'And we'll still go to the tip this Sunday, will we?' 'Oh, *I* don't care.' He trudged inside with the cups. I stood in the shed among the kindling, looking down at my muddy boots and controlling my 'melodramatic', 'hypersensitive' 'overreactions'. Then I went to have another look at the broad-bean patch. Every morning for weeks I've been rushing out to check and there's never anything there. I stared at the line where I'd parted the mulch for them. I was about to walk away when I saw a pale green dot slightly off-centre in the lumpy dirt. I crouched down. It was a bean shoot. Curved over on itself like a bent wrist. Struggling up to the light, shoving aside the clods.

———

Brett Whiteley has been found dead in a motel room at Thirroul. Whisky, needles and drugs nearby. The owner had heard nothing from the room for twenty-four hours, except the TV.

———

My nun's therapist told her that her right hand was stiff because she 'wanted to punch someone'. My nun believes her daily migraines and even her leukaemia are due to this frustrated desire, to a lifetime of suppressed fear and rage.

———

The people at Coronial Services invited me to the opening of the Donor Tissue Bank. They said they'd liked my articles so much that they wanted to frame them and hang them on the wall in the building. I blushed bright red. 'Oh! I'd be proud! I'd be honoured!' The Coroner approached me with his hand out. 'Hello Mr Hallenstein!' 'Hal's the name,' he said genially. When I told this to V later he cracked up. It was my happiest day in journalism. On my way home, standing on the cold tram stop dreaming of my hour of glory, I had a wonderful fantasy of being allowed to follow the Coroner around the bloody, violent scenes of his daily work, and when anyone asked him who I was, he'd say, 'She's the Coroner's Poet.'

———

Y asked me what my nun 'gave' me, i.e. what was the point of being friends with her. Her idea of nuns as pinched-lipped straiteners surprised me. She got crisp with me because I didn't understand the difference between the mass market and literary arms of a publisher.

———

My sister and her band had played with some Colombians, who to their joy told them they had 'soul'. 'Playing with Latin Americans,' said her partner, the trumpeter, 'is so different. They don't have any cynicism, the way Australians do. They're not ironic. They just want to laugh and dance.'

———

V marched into my room and without a word banged down on the desk a bundle of typed A4 sheets. He was already gone by the time I'd turned them over and realised it was the opening of his new novel. An impressive density and complexity of texture. And a kick of curiosity at the introduction of the man, Holland, arriving in the town and standing like a tree in the middle of his paddock.

———

I met G up in the Cross. His father has died. Everything in his own life before this death, G said, now seems frivolous, unserious, a waste of time; and he realises there's not much time left. We wondered if the death of V's father when V was twenty-four might have had the same effect on him—turned him into a serious, severe person at an early age.

———

At the Sydney International Piano Competition I sat in the second row where one can see the sweat splashing off their noses and chins and soaking the hair on the backs of their necks. I'd been in a mood for never hearing Mozart again, but a Frenchman played a rondo with such airy clarity and creamy smoothness that I nearly passed out. People in the audience become intimate friends with strangers. By the next session they have completely forgotten each other.

———

Dreamt of a climbing rose that was flourishing gaily, its leaves glossy green with reddened edges, and tiny white buds everywhere, ready to open.

———

Alone in the great reader's small, sunny flat in Double Bay. V will be here tonight. I'll be glad to see him. But one day I'll live on my own. It holds no fears. I even long for it. Maybe I can only have this fantasy because of the emotional stability, the safety, of being loved.

———

In the queue for the last piano concert V reports a conversation with R. 'I told her that everybody from Tolstoy down wrote about real people. She said, "Yes, but he finds it hard, out there in the open." I asked her about you. She said you went through her life like a breath of fresh air. But you're very strong. She said it was part of her growing up—she felt she had to move on.' I was grateful to him for asking. I imagined they must have said much worse things about me as well. Let it be what it is.

———

Alone at home all evening, polishing my rave review of *Wayne's World*. A brilliant, high, cold full moon in an inky sky. Watched a wonderful TV doco about the history of Australian vaudeville. Some of the acts threw me into fits. One of the old stars regretted the passing of entertainment that could make whole families laugh: 'I remember a man who had to be taken to the doctor. He laughed so much he hurt his neck.' Wiping away the tears I thought of O—it was the kind of foolery he loves. Now I've slashed him out of my life I've lost thirty years of shared laughter.

———

The story about going to Wilcannia. It has no *motor* to drive it, no reason to exist. The dog brought a rush of energy, but it faded. I'm giving up.

———

My editor called to say *Cosmo* hadn't been shortlisted for the Victorian Premier's Award. I was surprised that she'd even thought of telling me. I said cheerfully, 'Oh, I don't care! I've decided never to give a prize another thought.' A short pause, then she said, hotly, 'Well, *I* care!'

———

V and I went out to Mum and Dad's to tell them we were getting married. I didn't raise the subject until I'd cooked up a series of excellent spinach and ricotta crepes (unremarked upon: Dad, after guzzling his share, went out into the kitchen and started to make himself some toast). I said, 'Actually we came out to tell you some news—we're getting married. On August 14. And we're inviting you to come.' Mum said, 'Oh! That's nice!' Pause. V said, in a light, jesting tone, 'It's usually the role of the bride's father to provide a tremendous banquet.' '*Huh*,' said Dad. 'Not for the *third* time, *thank* you very much.' Pause. I said, 'It's at the Registry Office. So far, apart from you, we've only invited M.' 'When did you say?' said Mum. I repeated the date and time. Pause. Still possessed by the idiotic hope that one of them might say something, the sort of thing that normal people say on such an occasion, I sat stiffly on my chair at the end of the table. Pause. Dad said, 'We had a lot of really good food, on our trip. Specially at Brissago, and in Nice.' Mum showed us her photos of Hong Kong. And so the topic was dropped. At the door Dad said, 'See you on the 14th.' I wanted to scream and smash things and shout, 'Why don't you ever MAKE A FUSS OF ME?' I seem to have no resources at all to deal with the parents I've got. All the way home I yelled and cursed. This morning I woke up ashamed, as if after a tantrum.

———

V cheered me by reading from Nathaniel Hawthorne's lost note-books: 'The Abyssinians, after dressing their hair, sleep with their heads in a forked stick, in order not to discompose it.'

———

We walked along the creek this morning. Wind very sweet and balmy, a drying wind. High, creamy clouds, burst through by sheets of sparkling sun. The first spring-like morning. The green shoots clearer on every tree, and everything seems in motion, standing up to the wind in good humour.

———

V wakes from 'a terrible dream. I was on a huge ladder, against a twenty-storey building. The whole things swayed, it all began to go. I grabbed hold of a gutter. Someone I knew who was above me wasn't helping. Could be a dream about getting married, do you think?' 'Are you sure you want to go ahead with it?' 'Yes. 'Why?' 'Because,' he said, 'it'd be conservative not to.' He's off his own turf, down here. We'll end up back in Sydney, I know.

———

The Master of Ormond College is up on a charge in the Magistrate's Court. He's accused of having 'squeezed a student's breast at a dance after a vice-regal dinner'. It went to *court*? Crikey. Isn't that overkill? Aren't courts for rape and violence and murder? I wrote the guy a letter. Hope I won't regret it.

———

Lancelin, even in winter, the presence always of light. Life is organised with the power of light in mind. Trees are full of it, they flash and flicker. A yard without a tree is ugly and shelterless. High fields of cloud in the morning. Each dab of cloud has its own pearliness as well as its top of fierce brightness.

———

Flu. V waits on me kindly. He brings me some Cyril Connolly to read, then goes into his room and bashes away on the portable typewriter he got in a swap with Shiva Naipaul.

———

Gardening, a slow, plodding, dogged state. You don't stop, or think of anything more than the task at hand. I used my hands rather than a tool to loosen up the soil round the beans and lettuces. I dug in the compost with my fingers. I stopped caring about keeping my wedding ring scratch-free.

———

The Polish philosopher reports her conversation with Dad at the wedding.
  PP: 'And so, you are happy that Helen is married?'
  D: (*pulls a face*)
  PP: 'What? You are *not* happy?'
  D: 'It's the third time.'

PP: 'In Powland we say, "The third time is lucky."'

D: (*shrugs*)

PP: 'But *she* is happy, they are happy together—don't you think?'

D: 'They're both writers, though.'

PP: 'They will understand each other.'

D: 'But one day one of them will write something that the other one doesn't like—and there'll be trouble.'

PP: 'They are together already several years. Don't you think they have already read each other's work?'

D: (*shrugs*)

PP: 'Anyway, you like V, don't you? Don't you think it would be nice to show Helen that you are happy for her?'

D: '*She* doesn't care.'

'At that moment,' said the Polish philosopher to me, 'the official speech started, so I could not continue.'

He thinks I don't care. Once I would have got upset. Now I put it down and walk away.

———

The Jungian psychoanalyst James Hillman says on *Late Night Live* that Eros strikes always so that one falls in love with 'the wrong person'.

———

V no longer tries to dissuade me from going to Primrose Gully. We make each other laugh a lot, lately. He chucks a hunk of plastic into the creek for Tess, the blue heeler we're minding for M's boyfriend, and she bombs in after it with a splash as colossal as if someone had dropped a washing machine off a bridge.

———

Dreamt I was a teacher. My class was unruly. In vain I shouted abuse. A boy stood up from his desk and walked forward to where I stood. He was wearing a headdress of great delicacy and beauty: a shimmery concoction of silver wire and pearl drops that seemed barely attached to his head and hovered around it, quivering.

———

Three writers came to dinner. V was talking admiringly about something European. Absorbed in what he was saying, I asked, 'Do you wish you were European?' He swung round at me: '*No. No, I don't.*' My question was sincere but he was offended and I didn't know why. I started to stammer out an explanation, but the American poet spoke across me in a dreamy tone, 'What do I wish *I* were?' The sting went out of the moment. I looked at the poet's droll, pugnacious face and thought, 'You've got manners.'

———

The writers' festival. It's like being barbecued. The New Zealand novelist and I drank glasses of water in her forty-fourth-floor room. Outside, dark, rain, thousands and thousands of lights in street patterns. We agreed that at such a height we entertained thoughts of jumping. On my way home, buskers were playing jazz outside Flinders Street. A little boy threw himself into the space and galloped to the music in joyful turns and rolls. His father spread out the kid's parka and coins rained on to it. Everyone was laughing and shouting.

———

My favourite scene in *Strictly Ballroom*: Barry Otto seen through a window, dancing by himself under a harsh, ugly white light— something fluid and Hispanic—absorbed in his own movement. The secret dancing-life of men.

———

A day in the Magistrates' Court. The Ormond Master's appeal.

———

C told me about applying to become a member of the synagogue. She had to fill in a form: two Jewish families who'd vouch for her, the Hebrew names of her children. 'I looked at the form and felt *lost*. I felt as if I'd got lost a long time ago.' She began to cry. 'We used to think we could do without the family. But now I believe it's all we've got.'

———

Four men and four women entertaining themselves round a table. Someone posed a question: 'What change would you like, to your physical self, if you were granted one wish?'

'Thinness.'

'Yes. Thinness.'

'Thick, long, black hair.'

'Smaller ears.'

'A bigger mouth, with voluptuous lips.'

'Thick black hair and a thick black moustache.'

Then the oldest man at the table said, 'A body that was completely adequate, so I never had to think about it and could appear in a bathing suit without a thought.'

The last of us, a woman, said, 'Same as him.'

––––––

Reviews of *Chez Nous*. So various that except for the plot details you'd hardly know they were all talking about the same movie. 'Lugubrious.' 'The fine, stern edge of truth.' 'Fatuous.' I stop reading and shove them into the filing cabinet.

––––––

The trial of the guy who beat the toddler to death. The little white body garlanded, festooned with bruises. On day four the tough, tattooed journalist beside me took her glasses off and burst out sobbing. I hung on till I was riding home. Every outbreath made a weird moaning sound. I crawled along the vegetable patch and pulled out weeds, yanking and weeping, making a lot of noise.

––––––

It started with one young woman in the jury box. She leaned forward, opened her mouth, and let out a stream of loud, tearing sobs. It ran along the front row in a wave, five women crying and a man too. Their sobs echoed off the walls. They can't reach a verdict, and are dismissed.

––––––

Time magazine wants to run what I've already written, but V firmly urges me to hold out for the retrial. He is generous, patient and right.

———

I cut up a Christie's catalogue V gave me and made fifty postcards. Messing around for hours with scissors and glue—straight edges, crooked edges, torn edges against the white rectangle of the card. Is this what they call 'a hobby'?

———

Mum and Dad here for dinner. They drank a fair amount of red wine. V made a little wire barbecue and cooked chops. Pleasant evening. Mum mentioned several members of her family and Dad said, 'Your family had a rather tragic history.' He listed their losses. Her youngest brother, barely nineteen, shot down in a flying battle in 1944 near the border of Holland and Germany. 'He was a ter*rif*ic bloke,' said Dad. 'He was like your *twin*.' A cousin lost in a blizzard, her body not found till the spring, and *her* brother had some sort of crack-up after the war. 'I went to lunch with him one day,' said Mum, 'and he was in a terribly jittery state. He couldn't sit still.' An uncle fiddled the books of the family firm and when found out gassed himself in his car. Another cousin caught polio as an adult, they took him in his iron lung to the football at the MCG, he caught a chill, got pneumonia and died. These stories, several of them news to me, seemed drawn from them by V's presence, the quality of his attention, his ability to ask for a detail at the right moment.

———

My piano teacher quotes Wilfred Bion: a psychoanalyst must embark on a session 'without memory, desire or understanding'. I can't even mention this sort of thing to V. He goes berserk.

———

The imagery V uses in ordinary speech, loaded with reluctance. 'I'll dump you off at work.' 'I said I'd cart her round the bookshops.' 'We'd better get rid of' (i.e. eat) 'those potatoes.' 'I suppose I'll drag m'self into town.' As if the ideal were stasis.

Michael Ondaatje came over, after his publicity tour in Sydney. The *Herald* journalist had interviewed him without either tape or note-book, and had invented all kinds of things for Michael to say. He laughed about it. A very warm, quiet bloke, with a gentle manner.

The two young complainants in the Ormond matter don't want to speak to me. 'Without them there's no book,' says Y.

Storm clouds formed. Thunder ran absent-mindedly round the sky, like deep thoughts not yet focused; then it chose its topic and began to crackle more narrowly. The air was a sharp blueish grey, yet very clear. Fat, flat drops fell in a rush and with regret I ran inside.

At the painter's place two of the men were scathing about 'religion'. The painter roared that it 'should be stamped out'. I lost my temper then sat in a gloomy sulk. Tried to pull myself together and construct an argument but lacked the energy (or skill) to heave the discussion on to a territory where I could say what I thought. The men (except V, who tried valiantly to create a civilised ground) drank and shouted. Y fell asleep in her chair. The painter's wife was attentive but mostly silent. On the way home V rebuked me for my lack of interest in politics. I said there was a hierarchy of topics at any dinner table, and that politics was always at the top; that people not interested in politics had to sit through aeons of shouting and table-thumping without protest because of this unspoken consensus. V: 'Why are you so angry?' H: 'I don't know.' I did know, but it was too late in the evening to open that can of worms.

'It seems,' says my sister, 'that women go mad and men have heart attacks.'

H: 'Would you say that most of our difficulties are basically due to me?'

V: 'Well…I do think that for the most part I'm pretty…blameless.'

———

I asked V what he 'really thought' of my work. He said he thought it was very good but that I should get beyond the subject matter that limited me, 'those households, what are they called? That you always write about?'

———

'Marriage,' said the Polish philosopher, 'is a very powerful symbol. Perhaps your sadness, and depression, might stem from an unconscious fantasy of what marriage could do, or be—for example, that you will have total approval and support. Perhaps you need to locate this fantasy and replace it with a more appropriate idea of marriage.' When I got home V suggested we should see a movie and eat out. We did. I looked at him with a kind of shame and a new affection.

1993

Federal Election. I voted, with clenched teeth, straight down the Labor ticket. V as always destroyed his vote by writing on it a protest against compulsory voting.

———

My nun's leukaemia has become acute. The platelets they are giving her twice a week are being destroyed, by the cancer, within fifteen minutes of each transfusion. I feel the first stab of fear.

———

My lovely cheap new sprinkler. On low pressure, a bud of water, then as I open the tap further, a hollow onion; then a wide fountain.

———

A visitor speaks about having brought her ageing mother to live with her and her family. 'It's hard, yes. Hard. If anyone else came in and said, "I've made a cake. Sit down and I'll bring you a cup of tea", I'd love it. But because it's my mother I sort of can't accept it. I won't allow her to do any cleaning. No, none at all.' 'Why not, if that's what she'd like to do?' 'I won't have my mother being a servant.' Next day she calls and says she'd felt as if she'd been 'expertly interviewed'. I was dismayed and began to apologise. No—she didn't regret anything she'd said—it was rather that she'd said things she hadn't known she thought, or felt.

———

Dreamt of a large house in whose garden were discovered thirty-five buried typewriters.

———

I called a tutor I knew at Ormond College and asked if she'd speak to me about the events there. She blew up! She ripped shreds off me. She was so furious, rapping out accusations and challenges, that I started to laugh. After she'd slammed down the phone I had to lie on the couch to get my breath back. Is there something crazy in this story? I think I'll slog on.

———

'Now listen,' said V. 'Your father's got cancer.' Multiple family ring-arounds. The two nurses say that ninety-nine per cent of men over sixty have prostate trouble and he'll probably die of something else before the cancer gets him.

———

It's nearly O's birthday. I wrote to him and said I missed him, and that I was sad that I'd broken our friendship, and lost him. I said I hoped that one day he might be able to forgive me for what I'd done, for having offended him and made him angry, and hurt him.

———

I don't want to go to New York and leave my vegetable garden, and my mulch and compost.

———

Dreamt I was dancing with a gay man from my French class, on an enormous timber floor. We danced in perfect accord, firmly clasped with our whole fronts touching, arms high in classic ballroom position. A thrilling sense of power and mastery. At first I was so dazzled by his grace and confidence that all I did was follow. Then after a while I ventured to press my leg against his as a hint to change direction. He picked it up at once and smoothly incorporated it. I realised with joy that we really were *a double act*.

———

O replies. A restrained letter of such subtlety, generosity and readiness to laugh—and to make *me* laugh—that what was left of my huffy defences dissolved. He even used the term '*folie à deux*'. He opened all the windows and let the breeze flow through.

———

A big lumpkin of a Down-syndrome boy is lying on the concrete path outside my friends' kitchen window while I wash up. He peeps up just as I'm glancing out. Our eyes meet. We both dart back to shelter, then slowly inch out for a checking look and clash again. I hold up a soup ladle where my head was. He lets out a gurgling shriek. Next time I look he's holding up one fat bare foot. I start to let out operatic trills instead of making appearances. He mimics them in a surprisingly warm, true voice. Thus two strangers entertain themselves through a hot autumn afternoon in Murray Bridge, late in the twentieth century.

———

Reading Richard Holmes and then Camille Paglia. Comparing their tones is like matching against each other the two intellectual and stylistic influences of my life: the restrained, formal English and the brash, funny, noisy Americans. Maybe the tension between them produces whatever I've got that's mine.

———

Paglia momentarily takes away my fear, and replaces it with a kind of over-excitement that is almost defiant. What am I scared of? Going out on a limb. Arguing against feminists. Antagonising women. No, that doesn't go deep enough. I feel a weird dark anxiety. Distraction and fear. I told my nun I had night panics. Her immediate practical response: 'Babe—have you got a little Gospel?' 'Yes.' 'Well, Jesus said, about fifty-eight times, "Fear not". Look it up.'

———

I rush home from a critics' film screening, carrying a box of vegetables and fruit, and propose fresh broccoli for lunch. Alas, V is sick of 'grass and bloody boiled carrots'. Seems I cook in a bad spirit and he often feels guilty when he eats what I've cooked. No, not guilty that *he* hardly ever cooks—it's a fault in *my* attitude. And it's mean-spirited of me to want him to share the work of cooking. In his opinion cooking isn't 'work' in the way that drudgery, like washing dishes, is—it's more 'a kind of giving'. He says he's basically pretty pleased with the way he is, with the shape of himself, and he doesn't want anyone to require him to change—for him to start learning to cook, he says, would be an alteration in his *shape* and *nature*—it would make him less himself.

Still, this evening he cooked the dinner. He served, without eye contact and with disdainful flicks of the spoon, arranging it as unattractively as possible, a delicious rack of lamb with potatoes and capsicum. Why the hell was I sad? I'd got what I wanted, hadn't I? What more did I want?

———

A ten-page letter from G, in his minuscule hand. He is in the thoracic ward at St Vincent's with a collapsed lung. He'd been drinking way too much; M-C finally got fed up with him and the mess he was making of everything. She said she wasn't going to stay with an alcoholic, and moved out of their apartment and into her studio in the Cross. But then the studio burnt down and she had nowhere else to go, so she came back. Now she's pregnant. He feels 'like a plaything in the hands of fate'. He tells me to show the letter to V. I decide that this would be a mistake.

———

Late on a work day V called out under the window of my office. We went up to Lygon Street for a coffee. He said he was going out to play snooker with one of the painters. Hurray. House to myself for a couple of hours, and when he gets back from a blokes' outing I'll be really pleased to see him.

———

Q met a top curator at the National Gallery who told her that V was 'the best writer on art in Australia'. At home, adopting a 'level' tone, I pass on the tribute. He acts as if I hadn't spoken. I'll never understand this guy. I suppose it doesn't help that Q is a woman.

———

I wanted to use the word 'blowhard' so I called Mum. She was very pleased and interested, and made several fine discriminations that were useful to me. Hung up happy, feeling that for once our minds had connected.

———

I had a cold and V brought me breakfast in bed. I must slow down and remember him more.

———

Freycinet Peninsula, on my own, for a travel magazine. Dashed off the piece and faxed it. A roaring black night with a high sprinkle of stars. In the morning big gulls dive-bombed for fish. They soared into a tremendous wind, turned to let it push them over to the fish-field, then plummeted, wings half open, folding them only at the moment of entry. The *work* of being a bird.

———

Dreams of a river? A baby? A fire?

———

Got to get myself a Walkman so V won't scowl and say, 'What are you playing that loud, clashing music for?' (It was only Lenny Kravitz.)

———

I've got this NYU teaching gig coming up. Four months in New York. V presses me to fight the university for a flat that's big enough for him to work in all day but small enough to prevent visitors, particularly my family.

———

Midnight call from my sister in Bali: her husband has died in the surf, she is about to board a plane. Third sister and I drive across town to tell their daughter. We stand outside the dark house, exchanging looks of dread. A clear, cold, still night, sharp stars—a beautiful night.

Our sister wheels her trolley out of customs, her face distorted and flushed. We rush to engulf her, all weeping loudly, howling and wailing. I open my eyes and see a line of Japanese men staring at us, their mouths sagging, shameless in their shock and curiosity. Outside it's morning, not quite light. I put my big black scarf around her. She's babbling, sobbing, stumbling along between us. We'll take you straight home. *Don't leave me alone!* We'll stay with you, we'll look after you, we won't leave you alone. Between bursts of racking sobs she speaks with a sudden coherence: his car's in the long-term carpark, how much will it cost? I promise to deal with it. Moved by her, deeply impressed. I feel *proud* of her. The crying rolls through her house in waves. I hear someone in another room strike up again, sobbing and keening, but crying is now *what one does*, it doesn't occur to me to go and investigate or comfort. Soon it subsides. Stupor. Someone tells you something—a name, a task to do—you say carefully, 'Yes, right, okay, got that, I'll do it'—you turn to do it, you've already forgotten the entire conversation and you're in a chair by yourself in a room looking through the window at a bare tree branch moving in the wind. It was afternoon, the sun was low, she saw him coming down the face of the wave, she thought, it's too big, and dived under it, and surfaced, but he didn't come up. The sun was in her eyes. The water he died in was only waist-deep. She sits bowed forward with her head on the kitchen table. Under her cheek a cushion wrapped in a towel soaks up her tears.

—————

Never before has it been so important that birds sing at the end of the night.

—————

I said to Mum on the phone, 'I don't think I've got any tears left.' She was silent for a moment, then said, 'They'll come back again, when they're needed.'

—————

V has to drive to Sydney. 'Not a mile passed,' he says to my sister, 'when I didn't think of him.'

_____

A dear letter from V's mother: 'Try to carry on and look forward.'

_____

If you sit in a garden, you see that life goes on. It doesn't *end*. How could it end?

—

Manhattan. Another planet. There go the sirens, wild and determined—wailers, then the harsh hooters—get outa my way. Eighty-six degrees. In Woolworths 6th Avenue, everything disordered, plastic, cheap, dusty.

    H: 'Let's get one of those ice trays.'

    V: 'Ice? What for?'

_____

My borrowed office. Under the desk a dead mouse, its feet stuck to a square of superglue.

_____

A tall blond man with hair clipped short walks into the English department cocktail party wearing a striped, reddish-yellow sort of pyjama suit. An obscure Russian tutor beside me mutters, 'My Gahd. It's Yevtushenko. He's a national joke.'

_____

Why should I write anything? The world is huge and stuffed with books, and my mind is very small and stiff.

_____

Very late in the hot night, a quick smatter of explosions that sound like gunfire, followed by a shuddering echo, a brief silence, then a chorus of screams. We go back to sleep.

_____

How well-mannered the students are, so confident and relaxed in their approach to me, not at all shy. I can do this.

_____

V and I watched a show called *Seinfeld* that one of the students told me about. Something about a puffy shirt. Laughed. A lot.

———

The Institute for the Humanities has an electric pencil sharpener. You shove your pencil in, it whirs hard, you pull it out and return to your office to push the magnificent long sharp point fruitlessly across the paper. I can't find the spot at which to start this book. I've got to write it dashingly—use the rip and slash that surrounds me here—drop the self-righteous provincial poor-me-scorned-by-feminists tone.

———

At some people's place I got points for knowing who Kinky Friedman and Beavis and Butt-Head were.

———

In the Hassidic computer shop a man with a grey beard spreading all over his chest caught my eye in a friendly way while he was saying to his customer, 'There's a four. There's a five. Soon there'll be a six. *C'est la vie.*' I had no idea what he was talking about, but the beat between his last two sentences was so exquisitely timed that I had a little moment of ecstasy.

———

I want to write charmingly, using 'I' but without becoming grandiose.

———

The lower down the hierarchy the person is, the more likely they are to befriend you or to make efforts to put you at ease.

———

Even V, as the ferry surged away from the Ellis Island Immigration Museum, had a small red line above his upper lip, as if he'd been biting it with his lower teeth in an attempt to maintain its stiffness.

———

V slaps down in front of me, with relish, a big *New York Review* piece by Frederick Crews about Freud. H: (mildly) 'Why do you show me articles against Freud?' V: 'Because I think most of that stuff's *rubbish*.' Neither of us knows much about psychoanalysis, but I am by nature receptive to the idea of it while he is by nature repelled by it. And, for some reason, he feels an urge to attack and destroy. Anyone would think I was 'a Freudian', the way he goes on.

———

At the 92nd Street Y, Shostakovich's 24 Preludes and Fugues played by Tatiana Nikolayeva—a round ball of an old lady in a voluminous silky dress that billowed pleasantly, bringing to mind a breezy bedroom. She played with immense power that rolled down her hard, muscular forearms. The music, which I knew only as recorded by Shostakovich himself in an awkward, harsh, ugly performance, surprised me by its frequent sweetness and beauty. Susan Sontag was sitting a couple of rows in front of us. She applauded seriously but with enthusiasm, holding her large, dry-looking, dark-skinned hands high above her head.

———

A new hang at MoMA. For the first time I get why V is so crazy about Cézanne: a bather, modest, even quite small, and at the same time stupendous, elemental. I stopped dead before it. Twisted face, eyes downcast as if in thought though perhaps he is being careful on the stones. Hands on hips; great big buniony feet.

———

I sat in on the well-known poet's three-hour masterclass at the 92nd Street Y. He was trying to make them think like poets, not fiction writers. They resisted, one sulked, but he prevailed. In a neighbouring room, for the first hour, someone not much more able than I am played over and over Bach's first prelude from the forty-eight. The poets were too absorbed to notice it, but to me it was terribly moving and beautiful, the way it dipped and plunged. Imagine having a good piano in an empty room and no reason to stop—a piece of Bach not too monstrously difficult but always resisting your efforts to master it. It doesn't matter how clumsy you are, it is not possible to make that music sound ugly.

———

I've reached the point in the Ormond book where all I can do is start paraphrasing and arguing. I don't know how.

———

Janet Malcolm's big *New Yorker* essay on the biographers of Sylvia Plath: boom! She shows me that the things I'm too timid to write *can be written*—that I should trust the stuff that my inner censor has been telling me to scrap. Meanwhile, in the *New York Times* someone reviews a book: 'a model polemic, full of autobiographical detail, conversations with friends, family and colleagues, and debates the author has had with himself and critics.' Is that what a 'model polemic' is? I think maybe I can do that.

———

G writes. He has been present at the birth of the baby, a girl with 'long, splayed fingers: I think she could manage a tenth already, on a proportionately reduced piano. I'm dizzy with exhilaration and lack of sleep—exalted, absurdly happy. Is there a plan, Helen, or is it just women carrying on with life, civilising through that peculiarly feminine self-abnegating and unselfconscious love? In awe and wonder, your respectful friend.'

———

John McGahern's short stories. He goes in very deep, broaching a vast reservoir of sadness, passivity, hopelessness, despair. It excites me that he is so carefree about using 'I'. One guesses 'I' may be McGahern himself but what if it is? It's *not the point*.

———

I don't think I've got anything you could call 'an argument', in this book. But I do see how a thought can curve around and connect with another in a graceful flourish.

———

My story about the little murdered boy has won a Walkley Award.

———

Wrote myself off, accidentally, two nights ago, in various bars with my students after our final class. Poisoned myself with vodka and tequila and God knows what else on an empty stomach. Don't know how I found my way back here. In the bathroom I passed out. When I came to I was face down in vomit. Staggered into a metal shelf in the dark and drove my front teeth into my bottom lip. Blood and vomit everywhere.

———

I am a pariah. V incredulous, revolted: how could I let myself get that drunk? He says it's because I change myself and my behaviour when I'm with 'the young'—I alter my way of talking to be more 'groovy'. Too sick to defend myself. Asked him to go out and buy ten packets of chicken noodle soup. That's all I could eat for days. In bowls handed to me on a very long arm, face turned away. This morning he's gone up to Hartford on the train to visit the Australian art critic. I got out of bed and looked at myself in the mirror. Bruise along my chin like a five o'clock shadow, another under left eyebrow, one across bridge of nose. Mouth swollen, a half-inch open split inside my lower lip. I put on my coat and took a cab to the nearest emergency room. 'What happened?' asked the nurse. 'I got drunk and fell down.' She pursed her lips, raised her eyebrows. The young doctor, to whose blond crew-cut clung a shred of Christmas tinsel: 'Why didn't you come in sooner? It's too late now for stitches. What happened?' 'I got drunk and fell down.' A long, ironic look. I took a breath to explain, then thought, I'll never see them again, it doesn't matter what they think. So I stood still and said nothing, in the desolate freedom of a great city. Antibiotics $30 so I had to walk home. At least it wasn't snowing.

———

On the New York–London night flight we slept. Dreamt I sat on an open veranda where mosquitoes landed on the backs of my hands and stung me, with sharp, fine, very painful stabs.

1994

New Year's Day. We're both culture-shocked. V very snaky. Everything I do irritates him. I may not remark on the weather, what would *I* know about London weather? I'm like a bloody terrier, going on about buying two newspapers! *Nobody* buys two newspapers! I don't dare to ask what's wrong. Is it because he can't forgive me for getting drunk, or because he used to live here with his first wife when they were young and happy? Is he sad? Is he scared? I keep my mouth shut. Near Piccadilly we turn a corner and come upon a parade, people in strange uniforms, a band with drums and silver helmets, the thrilling gold of brass played softly. V turns aside into Simpson's sale and I stay on the street to watch the marching girls go by—a squad of them, long hair pulled back hard, in severe little black fitted jackets with sparkly silver belts, and long skirts with a top layer of black tulle—and each girl wielding a flag on a long, flexible pole. They march double time with tiny rolling steps, and twirl these blue and white flags, no smiles, just serious concentration and always the chins held high. Once they all, in perfect unison, drop into a dramatic pose, front leg bent, the other stretched sideways and back—and the flags are swung head down and laid for a beat or two on the pavement—something stabbing about the proud flags drooping and allowed for a moment to trail on the ground.

———

A great British publisher shows keen interest in V's novel-in-progress. I hope it might make him happier. No luck so far.

———

I say I want to live more merrily, with more spontaneity.

V: 'Do you think we should part?'

H: 'No.' (Was it a serious question? I couldn't tell.) 'You're disappointed in me, I know. What is it about me, that disappoints you?'

V: (*reluctantly*) 'Oh…your street-fighting qualities, and…'

I waited a few moments for him to ask me the same question, but he didn't, so I let it pass.

———

British Airways messed up our flight to Madrid and our English friends had to go on ahead without us. V handled the desk staff so brilliantly, never losing his cool, that he got us a refund for the whole trip, including the hotel, and we even still *went*, at BA's expense, though not arriving till dinner time. Astonished and impressed by the patient charmingness of his negotiations. H: 'We've really had a nice day, haven't we, in spite of our visa troubles.' V: 'Yes, and it's because *I* was in charge.' I laughed; but we're locked in an endless power struggle. When we see couples who are cheerfully loving we exchange sad, wry glances. I suppose he thought we would always be 'in love'. My next task: to pick up at speed enough Spanish to handle the weekend here, without threatening his need to be seen as running the show.

———

Prado. *Las Meniñas*. Thunderstruck. But my favourite is Goya. His speed, force, despair, horror, blackness. *Fight with Cudgels*. A series—an armed bandit threatens a monk in brown, who offers him a pair of shoes then wrests the gun off him and shoots him in the bum—the posture of the bandit as the shot strikes him—his knees sag, his arms fly up and forward, his fingers splayed with shock. Some too terrifying to be looked at. Execution by firing squad. In a park we saw a puppet show, an old woman with a foolish chook in a tutu, a wolf came, the old woman dug a hole and the wolf fell in, children mad with joy, their shrieks and warning cries.

———

What V needs, *en voyage*. At the breakfast table in Madrid: 'Have I had one croissant or two?' When I don't know, he is surprised and cross. He has a throat infection and a nasty cough, but walks about the winter streets with his shirt collar open and his coat unbuttoned. Unable to stand it any longer, I take off my woollen scarf and without asking wind it round his neck. His face softens and he says, 'That's very sweet of you. A rendition of love.' In Kew Gardens. Grand vistas and prospects. The rodent flowing of squirrels. We've brought the old Pentax K1000 only so he can take a photo of the famous eucalypt in the gardens, but once he's got his shot, he expects me to lug the heavy camera all day in my little backpack in case someone mistakes him for a tourist. Unless I'm mothering him—carrying his gear, taking responsibility for his health, his food intake, the state of his clothes—everything about me gets on his wick. He tells me that my way of interrupting him with 'sharp questions and urgings comes perilously close to trimming'. Ouch. All right. I resolve to get off his case.

———

Is this what marriage is? I mean, I need to know: *is* it?

———

My front tooth is dead. I have to have root canal. But I swam eight laps of the Fitzroy Baths. My arms were heavy. Tomorrow I'll do ten.

———

Since my drunken fall in New York I have hardly any sense of smell. I read in Janet Malcolm about a patient of Freud's whose sense of smell went away while she clung to unrealistic fantasies that her employer would return her love and marry her. I ask myself what my 'unrealistic fantasies' are, or rather, what I am declining to say bluntly to myself. And out it comes: 'I regret having got married.

I regret my loss of freedom.' Okay. I regret it. But I also accept it, accept my regret, and decide consciously that I'll try to stay married, and will make serious efforts to be more generous, less angry, less controlling, less *reducing*. I state to myself, too, that for all the faults I find in him V is a clever, funny, decent man who puts up with my craziness and tries to be kind to me. And that while there are thousands of 'wrong' men out there, there is no such thing as the 'right' man.

Of course there is an alternative diagnosis, the one given by my GP: that a nerve has been damaged and could take eighteen months to heal.

————

G, M-C and their baby come to stay. They are calm, smooth, gentle. All his panic, all her reproaches gone. The baby is a tiny, dainty button of a creature with blue eyes and a shock of black hair. In our kitchen, after work, I lie on the couch and contemplate her on M-C's lap, my head resting beside them on a cushion. I'm not hungry, not thirsty, not anxious. Her presence bathes the room in peace.

————

The book is coming round in its curve. I wrote an image of a fireplace that came straight out of the collective unconscious. Thought of the sax player who said, 'When I play badly it's my fault. When I play well, it's got nothing to do with me.'

————

A photo of a young soldier with his beaming, frothy, off-the-shoulder bride, who turns out to be already married to two other soldiers from the same barracks. Everyone's furious. She gets a two-year good behaviour bond. Maybe she just liked weddings. Having a reason to put flowers in her hair.

————

Delivered a rough draft of the book to Y. Now I don't know what to do with myself.

————

My nun's been talking about suicide.

———

On the train to Murray Bridge I think that my fantasies of a solitary life are possible only because I'm resting on a solid base of companionship. I see V's stability and how I've come to depend on it. I remember too that one day he will die. Full of gratitude for him, as the train rolls along.

———

I drive my nun to the hospital for her transfusion. Four bags. On the way home I wait outside the convent while she goes in for one of the consecrated wafers that the priest leaves there for the nuns. She emerges and produces from her pocket a single wafer, which she snaps in two. 'This is Jesus,' she says. 'All good things. Health, hope.' We ate the wafer. I was still chewing as I put the car in gear and pulled out on to the road.

———

At Mount Barker I met a five-year-old boy called Maurice Chambers. I asked him if I could take his photo. He sat very still, looking straight into the lens with a serious, slightly strained expression.

———

The woman in her eighties '…was always gentle, eager to please and prepared to disguise her own keen intelligence and sharp memory if these were to interfere with the general harmony. She had never married, never known the control a wife and mother exercises, the unsimple compromises a man and a woman make with each other.'
—Colm Tóibín, *The Heather Blazing*

———

On the station platform waiting for the Overland home I remembered the days when train windows used to open. It was a beautiful mild summer night, soft, with half a moon and the air thick with the smell of dry grass and sheep shit. And I was going to spend it in a plastic box.

———

A friend called: 'Listen, the shit's really going to hit the fan with this book. The street word is you're running the line that women who get raped are asking for it.'

In DJ's I found for my nun a beautiful white Italian nightie, in heavy cotton verging on the flannelette she had specified, but with swirls of flowers embroidered on the bosom. I loved it so much I longed to keep it for myself. I walked away with the parcel in my arms fantasising saying to her, 'And when you die I'd like to have it back.' Is everybody greedy and selfish and hard-hearted in secret? I hope so, otherwise I'm a monster.

In the hospice she couldn't seem to die, she was out of it, in a coma, the Aboriginal women had seen the message bird out on the lawn, the willy wagtail swinging its spread tail, but she gasped on and on. Her girlfriend called the old priest in Wilcannia: 'Is there a prayer to let her go?' and he said, 'Listen, you have to ask her to forgive you, and you have to tell her that you forgive her—doesn't matter what for.' The girlfriend went down on her knees and whispered to her, stepped out on to the balcony and came straight back in. Two minutes later she gave a big sigh, and died.

V didn't know why I'd even gone. He asked me what I'd found in her that attracted me. I stammered and stumbled. I said that when I was with her I laughed a lot and was happy, and that she had the God stuff worked out in a good way. He said she was melodramatic, and mentioned other dying people he'd known who'd behaved with more restraint and dignity. If I want to cry properly I have to hide in the yard, or wait till he goes out, or drive somewhere in the car.

I think he must be anxious and a bit wretched—struggles with a gallery about a retrospective catalogue he's to write—scared because his novel won't roll—I feel so sorry for what he's going through but

I suppose he would take it as unmanning if I expressed this. Years ago I stopped trying to comfort him with tales of my inability to write after the end of a marriage. One can't comfort a person who won't admit there's anything wrong. If I could just quietly be nice to him. But I've got my own anxieties and fears to get past. We're both battling, and our battles clash, as well as our two natures. I cooked a brilliant lamb casserole with capsicum, carrots, red wine and a lot of onions and garlic.

———

I'll shred this fucking book if things get too tedious with the law. The journalist was dying to tell me his sources. He was having to *bite his lip*. It was almost funny.

———

I hit a low point today. I felt I could not go on. It was like knowing that a free garden, calm and full of rest, lay on the other side of a wall. I knew where the gate was, I could walk through it whenever I felt like it. I was withholding release from myself. Then I had a coffee and a cake, went back to the desk, forced a solution, and kept going.

———

Gieseking playing Bach makes Gould sound like a brilliant machine. He makes mistakes, at times his beat is bumpy, but this makes the grandeur of the music less awesome, more…enfolding, I don't know. One feels that complexity and beauty are within human grasp. In V's workroom half a dozen superb Fairweathers are leaning against the walls. I wish I could go in there and sit among them for an hour or two.

———

My brother's little boy passionately wants M's boyfriend to come and visit him. He describes the house so he'll know it when he walks down their street: 'There's a tree out the front, with round things on it, it's a green, round-thing tree. And there are walls, and then things like *this*, and they're the roof.' The patient openness on the young man's face as he listened seemed very beautiful to me and in my heart I hoped he and M might marry and have children. I would love to be related to him.

———

V wants us to let this house and move into G's flat in Rose Bay for six months, while they're in Italy. Here we go again.

———

The podiatrist sat on the floor and made me walk barefoot up and down the hall. 'You're hollowed out here,' she said, 'and here. These bones are extremely prominent. Your left shoulder is higher than your right, that's the scoliosis. You swing your left arm more freely than your right, to balance the curve of your spine.' So I am twisted, imperfect, a prisoner of inherited forms—but also shaped and saved by my body's own silent, inventive history of adaptation, its ingenuity, its urge towards balance.

———

E's visit. I love having her in the house. 'When you get to this stage of a book,' she says, 'the knot of anxiety here, in your chest, goes away and is replaced by a sort of warmth.'

———

I am getting more cunning. But there are people out there who are a hell of a lot more cunning than I am.

———

I must learn to let V rant about things. He needs to rant. He should rant, and I should detach from his ranting. I hate to see his face go cramped and dark. A knot of contempt between the eyebrows. I remember what F used to say when I scowled and swore: 'Don't be full of hatred. It's ugly.'

———

At Piedimonte's the checkout girl hits the wrong keys and gives me a bill of $184.20. Seeing this vast sum on her screen she mimes horror and says, 'Don't show *this* to your husband—if you're married!'

———

A warm, dry, autumn wind sped over the landscape. Leaves seemed to change colour before my eyes. Worked well, reinserting the good bits that got lost in the ferocious cull, polishing the curves and slotting in small shiny details. Things will interleaf with each other, quite smoothly and appropriately, if I am patient and do not panic. After work saw a movie with V, then he walked and I pedalled along beside him all the way home. He still loves to reminisce about Tex. We laugh and sigh at our memories of his brief reign. At such moments I feel I am 'happily married'.

———

A phone call from a woman I was friends with at university. I recognised her voice before she even said her name. She's heard around the traps that there are plans to take out an injunction against the book. While she spoke, the room and everything outside it seemed to be slowly darkening. I cursed the day I had first heard about the case. My regret lasted about ten minutes. Then I got back on the horse.

———

V has read the book in manuscript. He said in a brisk, offhand tone that he 'couldn't be less interested' in the feminist aspects of it. The people I have interviewed he compared unfavourably with the ones in Janet Malcolm's book—Ted Hughes's sister, for example—and he discoursed for some time about how 'boring' 'young people' are. I maintained a faultless detachment. Having established the pointlessness and tedium of my project, he made several very sharp and useful editorial suggestions, which I incorporated.

———

We go for a walk most evenings at dusk, along the creek past Tex's Look-out. We walk briskly, sometimes arm in arm. Trees completely bare now. Tonight a yellow sky faded to the purest grey-blue. A moon almost full. Dogs, ducks, a few people.

———

How and when will he write his new book? The wonderful idea of it. What's stopping him? *Is it me?*

Yesterday I made a brick incinerator and burnt quite a lot of my early diaries. 'Felt' nothing in particular. Saved about fifteen pieces of paper, most concerning M. I'll make a small salvage book, perhaps. Very sad, ill-tempered, troubled by thoughts about the book and whether it will be published; about my false position with Y who is so terribly ill and with the publishers and lawyers, everyone is backing and filling and having secret meetings, nobody will tell me anything, even my agent can't get any sense out of them; and about my family and their unlikeable characteristics which, V points out, I too am disgracefully displaying. Not to mention anxiety about moving to another small apartment in Sydney, where V's right to our shared living space he will once again assume to be primary. He hates this subject but we manage to discuss it. He offers, with a stiff, unreadable expression, to be the one to rent an outside office. I accept. And at once feel guilty. This is why feminism had to be invented. This morning I ask him if he's still angry with me. 'Well… not really…but it does seems a bit odd that when I make a serious complaint about your rudeness and unpleasantness I end up having to move out of the house.'

E: 'Men's needs are *like air*.'

Drank a pernod with U in a ridiculous bar. She wore an ink-blue hat pulled right down over her thick curls. Its brim cast a stylish shadow across her pretty little giggly face. I admired this look immensely. We talked about angels and devils. We had both seen them.

A *journalist* called and told me my book had been put back to February next year. I finally spat the dummy.

J's in town with his new book. M is away but her boyfriend, with his dog, brings us calamari and swordfish from the market. J springs

up to meet a fellow-surfer, hand out, face earnest. The four of us
and the blue heeler walk for miles along the creek. The dog applies
her knowledge of physics to fetch a branch out of a pool and drag
it up a steep bank, scrabbling madly backwards for a purchase on
the crumbling lip of the drop. We applaud and she grins up at us,
dripping and spiky.

———

'Four Beds'—a story with no characters in it, only rooms, furniture
and light.

———

On the back veranda G and M-C's baby hears a birdcall. Her eyes
snap into focus and she tilts her head with a shrewd expression.

———

The mighty poet publishes a gratuitously sneering crack about me
in his magazine column. V maintains that it is not offensive. G and
M-L sit gaping at him. Under their incredulous pressure he goes so
far as to say it 'might be discourteous'. 'It *is* offensive,' says G firmly.
'It's an *insult*.' Since I am trying to cook an over-complicated meal for
eight I don't take part in the discussion but work on at the stove. V's
response stings more than the insult, but comes as less of a surprise.

———

V has sold to some mysterious tycoon two paintings I know he
greatly prizes. I ask him, several times and with sympathy, how he
feels about selling them. He replies with what he thinks. I wonder
if he does 'feel', or whether he has achieved complete dissociation of
heart from head. He says his book is going so slowly that he thinks
he ought to give it up. I say, 'Oh no! Keep going, sweetheart', but
with a pang of guilt. As if it were my fault. I try to examine this.
How *can* it be my fault?

———

Watching V's face soften and flush with laughter while he talked
with G on the phone, I thought that people need friends they can
adore, not ones they're afraid of and have to be false with.

V gets out of bed at 11.50 pm to answer the phone. Listens, then slams it down. 'It was some bloody journalist. Wanting you to comment on the closing of the Fitzroy *pool*.'

As a farewell present the old Armenian guy next door passes over the fence to us a small soda-water bottle of ouzo. We break out the glasses and throw back a couple of shots. After this we spend the morning packing in hilarious spirits, laughing and cracking jokes.

A red brick building on New South Head Road, a long, narrow, old, shabby apartment. Out every window a sunny stretch of water, silk-blue and riffling, or else a terracotta tiled roof and large palm fronds. Somewhere a power saw. Crows call, melancholy and harsh. Constant clinking of masts. A mile or so away the Manly ferry goes sliding.

At E's dinner I met R. I said to her, 'I want to talk to you about envy.' 'I,' she said, 'want to talk to you about everything.'

Y speaking on TV about the government's cultural statement. Yes, she looks thinner, paler, but terrific—more dramatic, handsomer, sadder, more knowing. The face of someone who has suffered.

Two magazine editors, women, invited me to lunch. They were fresh and clever and interested in people and the world, and they want me to work for them.

The harbour. I can hardly comprehend its constant differentness from itself. Today wide slow ridges, ten feet apart, move towards me at a slant and softly collapse against the low stone wall. Taking notes—this little discipline—is a defence against the blank word-lessness that overcomes me when I stand at the window and look at the water. Why do I feel I have to conquer this state, subdue it, flail away at it with my vocabulary? In fact it is a tremendous gift. A chance at the soul.

———

The lawyers see the book as defamatory on five points. V keeps saying, as if checking, 'You do feel it's worth publishing, do you? That the general subject is important enough to warrant the effect on him? To me it's a much less interesting and important subject than it is to you.'

———

A photo in the paper of Edna O'Brien, hand on bosom, eyes raised to heaven. V deeply impressed: 'She's all woman.'

———

Thunder like someone running across the corrugated iron roof of a shed.

———

I lay on the couch after V had gone to bed, and watched the Queen's Christmas message. Her ghastly rigid hairdo, the big spectacles, the stream of dull clichés, and worst, at the end, her heart-breaking little attempt at a smile.

———

At last I got to talk on the phone with the defamation lawyer. He was flexible, lively, imaginative. He said at the start that he 'couldn't put the book down', had started reading in bed at seven last night and stayed awake till eleven, 'reading on and on'. After this of course I thought he was the best lawyer in the whole wide world.

———

This morning on our walk we got to within sight of the Watsons Bay lighthouse. I was excited and said, 'I reckon that by the end of this week we can get all the way there.' 'Why would you want to get to the lighthouse?' I must have an eager beaver quality that causes blokes to dig their toes in. I *will* get to the lighthouse. It's only a mile further on.

A plumber came to fix our blocked shower: a boy with dark curls who shook V's hand at the door. We stood outside the bathroom marvelling at his industry. I said, 'You're the first tradie I've ever seen clean up after himself.' He said he would feel embarrassed to leave a mess, that he liked working, in fact preferred work to everything else. He wanted to make enough money to buy a house. He squatted by the plughole pouring water down it from a bucket. I said anxiously, 'Is it fixed?' 'Oh yeah,' he said, 'it's sweet. I just like to see the twirl.'

During the auction E and I waited for V in a bar. An hour and a half later he came briskly walking in and sat down. His face was rather pale. 'Did you get it?' He leaned back and gazed off to one side, with an ironic smile. 'Did you? Did you get it?' At last he replied: 'Yes.'

My agent calls: 'It's on. I'm going to the TAB to place a bet.' To tell the truth I felt not only deflated and slightly drab, after all the adrenalin of waiting, but also a kind of dread about the next mountain, the outcome of it, what publicity I'll have to do.

Y has left publishing. Apparently people are going round saying I 'abandoned her when she was dying'. Oh, for God's sake. No defence is possible against this crazy shit.

1995

New Year's Eve fireworks off the Harbour Bridge. People called out comparisons. Chrysanthemums! Lilies! Tapeworms!

———

Our new neighbour one floor down is a hilarious China scholar with a massive mop of extensions. She says she and her flatmates, young musicians, play a lot of Scrabble—any time we feel like a game...On my way up the stairs I hear them laughing. She drops in to model for us a hat she's found in an op shop: a tiny black cowpat with a curving line of green sequins on the front and a little puff of black veil over one eye. After she leaves, V expresses gloomy concern that this building might be 'too young for us': he says he is planning a serious, quiet life.

———

The first journalist who interviewed me was very skilled. He knew how to present an opposing viewpoint in exactly the right tone of disinterestedness to make me examine my own thoughts more critically.

———

V has, of course, never again mentioned his offer to be the one to work away from home. And I lack the mettle for the fight. My agent borrows me a friend's flat in Bellevue Hill for a month and away I pace each morning, in my runners and straw hat. When I get home he's lying on the couch in the cool, watching the cricket. Home.

What is home. Home is the place one may enter and leave whenever one needs to. Since 1988 I have not had one of these. I don't know by what means I am able to be in such good spirits, to be spontaneously generous and efficient, shopping and cooking and serving, while the little virus of displacement nestles itself more deeply into my vitals.

———

The Pope's in town and the drought has broken. On Channel 9 News they showed a meteo map of a moving rain cloud in the shape of a cross. Even I let out a burst of scornful laughter.

———

The owner of the borrowed flat is back. Over in Bondi Junction a hot little sex bomb called Ronnie showed me a tiny north-facing room above a pharmacy on the mall: 'For $50 a week the owner'll paint it any colour you want and put in a new carpet.'

———

The adventurous beauty tells us about her lover in India.
    V: 'What are his good points?'
    AB: 'He's deep, serious, moral…'
    V: 'What are his bad points?'
    She hesitates.
    H: 'He's deep, serious, moral?'
    She laughs.
    AB: 'Exactly. He doesn't much like to *play*.'

———

Our London friends are going home. I helped them move out of their flat. While we were doing a final clean the husband began to sing in the bedroom and his wife joined in. They had ordinary, tuneful voices. I rushed in and we all warbled away merrily, remembering the words of 'It's Only a Paper Moon' and 'Buttons and Bows'. Something wonderful about this—something I've lost without even realising it was gone. Imagine—cleaning together! *Singing* together!

———

Cool morning, with clouds. Our new flat is calm, with leafy windows and plenty of space. The only thing missing is being able to step out a door and stand near some plants. H: (*eagerly*) 'We should open the windows.' V: (*levelly*) 'What for.'

———

He flopped a new short story on to the table in front of me. Within a few lines I could see it was good. It was beautiful. All the weirdness of his early stuff but also a warmth, I could almost say a tenderness. I went to congratulate him. He writhed, turned his face aside, strode out of the room.

———

In Bondi Junction mall I bought a 70s disco compilation and Steely Dan's *Greatest Hits*. Skipped home, crouched in a corner with the headphones on and played my best tracks over and over. Can't wait for him to go out so I can DANCE.

———

The Cretan's had a little heart attack but he's home. His wife, who has the pretty freckles and dainty feet of an Irish dancer, is a woman you know would be brilliant in a crisis. He looks smaller, paler, thinner. His dark-brown eyes glow fiercely.

———

Dinner out with V and a couple of journalist friends of mine from way back. The white-haired one turns up without his wife. 'It's got nothing to do with *you*,' he says cheerfully. 'She just couldn't stand to go out with *me*.' V: 'Do you and your wife have many arguments?' 'Yep. Lots. All the time.' V: How often?' 'Oh...we'd have a major argument about...once a fortnight.' V: (*shocked, fascinated*) 'But those aren't *arguments*, if they're once a fortnight, are they?' The other journo, the husband's close friend, leans in and says, 'Oh, they fight all the time. It's a Jewish thing, maybe. It's not embarrassing or anything, if you're there. Someone'll rush out of the room in tears, and ten minutes later come back in and sit at the table as if nothing had happened.' The white-haired husband laughs and shrugs, and we all reach for the menus. I notice V flicking him furtive looks.

———

Dreamt I drove past a big square two-storey house—had I once lived there?—that had been gutted, its insides stripped away and burnt. The block of land on which it stood was bare, not a blade of grass to be seen. The house was only a shimmering framework, still erect, but fragile.

———

I bought a phone/fax/answering machine, a Brother, for my office. $870. It has functions beyond my wildest dreams. I don't even know what they are, and am almost afraid to find out. In case I don't need them.

———

The daughter of a family who befriended M when she was working in France—she hung out at their house, went on holiday with them—is coming to Australia next month. M writes to ask if she can bring her to Sydney and stay two or three nights. First, the shot of happiness at the thought of their company, and of returning the family kindness; then the clenching gut. Looking out the kitchen window from the sink I see a small, sunny motel on the other side of the lane. Perfect. I'll book them a room there. They'll be out all day, and they can eat with us in the evenings—I won't have to do that nerve-racking juggling of guests' sleeping and waking and tiptoeing around V's work. When he comes back from a cigar-smoking walk I tell him my brilliant plan. He flips. From his position on the sofa he starts to shout, throwing back his head and clutching his temples. 'This is *mad. You're* mad! *Mother*-mad! This is the kind of thing that drives men *crazy*! It's completely *insane* for you to contemplate *paying* for their *motel*! There's something weird about your relationship with M! Why do you go peculiar and behave in these exaggerated ways when she's about to visit, and when she's here?' And so on and on, rolling his eyes and clicking his tongue and groaning when I try to put my case, until he's completely drowned me out. I drop it mid-sentence and say in a dull, exhausted voice, 'Why does this make me feel so awful?' Silence. I get up and go into the kitchen and start preparing the meal. After a while he comes in, puts his arms round me and says, 'Don't be unhappy. There isn't a problem.'

———

The GP calls. 'There *is* something on your ovary. I'd like to send you to someone who knows more about ovaries than I do.'

———

The Ormond complainants are going for an injunction. And they're requesting access to my interview tapes, notes, and working journals. Lying in bed in the dark, remembering the journals, the record of my labour, the extreme *personalness* of what's in them, I feel grit start to harden inside me.

———

The wary, carefully blank face of the defamation lawyer when he's listening. If the complainants succeed in getting access, he says, he sees no reason why they should need to be shown anything other than the book itself, since that's all 'we' plan to publish. He says that in the last few years five journalists have been jailed for refusing to reveal their sources. Privately I resolve to become number six if I have to. They are not getting those notebooks.

———

The gynaecologist, someone told me, is famous for being a former captain of the Wallabies. I am not a hundred per cent sure who the Wallabies are. He looks to be in his late sixties, with a pleasantly wrinkled face, and the slight remoteness of the old-fashioned doctor. He tells me that my right ovary is enlarged. There's a cyst. Probably been there for a long time. He doesn't think I've got cancer, but he would like to take it out. These things can be bilateral, he says, so he'd take the other one out as well. 'What about the uterus?' 'Well, it's no use to you any more, post-menopause. It's a site for trouble. I'd like to take *it* out as well. You'd be in hospital for a week.' I sit there in a stupor. So it's going to happen to *me*: 'a clean sweep from the waist down,' as women of Mum's generation used to quote their gynaecologists saying; and we'd all laugh. He said, 'We'll put you into George V.' This also meant nothing to me. I took the train back to Bondi Junction and sat in my office. After a while I called V and he came and got me.

———

The publisher calls. 'We won. With costs.' Two hours later: 'They're seeking leave to appeal to the Full Bench of the Victorian Supreme Court—tomorrow.'

———

Our lawyers had to work till late into the night, work wasted, for in the morning the complainants withdrew. Maybe somebody said to them, 'What are you *doing*? There's nothing in this book that identifies you! You haven't got a case!' Maybe now they'll hold their fire till the book's out, and then go for me. Maybe this hysterectomy is rather well-timed.

———

I was buying *Remembering Babylon* in the Tullamarine bookshop and spotted my book on the Picador rack. Heart got smaller and sank into my ankle boots. I walked away from it and sat reading a *TLS* at the departure gate.

———

The doctor gets out his leather-covered pocket diary and I get out my spirax. I propose a date. 'Yeeeees,' he said, 'I'll be around then. I'm babysitting that weekend.' 'Who are you babysitting?' 'Two grandchildren,' he says with a proud smile. He says that the removal of the uterus doesn't make the operation more serious. 'If I made an incision and just sewed it up again, your recovery time would be exactly the same as if I took out your ovaries and your uterus.' So it's the abdominal wound that's the trouble. I go downstairs for a blood test. While waiting I read an article in a magazine about a Californian girl who fought off a serial killer. He raped her and she talked her way out—asked him to *kiss* her (he was someone she knew), talked to him for hours, faked emotion for him, talking and acting and persuading—this against a six foot four man armed with a big kitchen knife. Eventually early the next morning she persuades him to leave because she has to go to work. This ghastly story—but what a woman! 'I remember saying to myself, *Think*!' I was filled with awe.

———

Days of media interviews, back to back. In the boardroom the publishers drink beer and I, timid in my fatigue, stick to orange juice.

———

Dreamt that on a street a young woman came walking towards me. She passed me without a greeting. I saw she was weeping, holding one hand up to her face as she hurried along.

———

At Mildura Writers' Festival the mighty poet was surprisingly friendly to me. No doubt he had forgotten having fanged me in his column so I forgot it too. After the evening session he asked me to walk back to the hotel with him. We paced along slowly. He said he had lost three stone and had to lose more. And that he had always hated feminism. I made a few awkward jokes. We both laughed. He said, 'Well, I've been seen with you, and you've been seen with me.' Over our heads, wonderful desert stars.

———

I met a glorious short-haired pointer on a bridge.

———

I estimate that last week I received about fifty letters about the book. They kept arriving in bundles, forwarded by the publisher and *Good Weekend*. They are mostly favourable, but more interestingly, they are often many pages long—accounts of confusing sexual or semi-sexual experiences that the writers have had, that they long to understand ethically and psychologically. I sat on the floor last night ripping open envelope after envelope, taking out stories of sexual and moral bewilderment, many of them beautiful and touching in their candour.

———

A middle-aged woman came up to me at the Edgecliff Centre and said, 'I haven't read your book yet, but I'm going to.' I said, 'Thank you. I hope you'll like it.' 'It doesn't matter whether I like it or not. I congratulate you for having opened up the debate.'

———

A rather wet radio interviewer gave me nothing to push against, and I found myself charging out into the space she was leaving. I spoke with aggression about certain of my critics and their intellectual dishonesty. Afterwards I felt I'd behaved foolishly, like a boxer all kitted up and dancing around shouting, 'Come on! Hit me!'

———

Breakfast radio with an eminent feminist historian of my generation. The young interviewer screeched at me: the techs in the booth had to turn her down. She seemed to be almost manic. The historian registered this and sat back. I did the same. Like two tired mothers we withdrew our energy and let the girl pour out her spleen: I had set feminism back twenty years, and so on. I must have said something but I don't remember what it was. Time was up and she dashed away to 'the launch of a new T-shirt'. Out on the street I got one of those scary stress attacks I used to have: my mind raced and swerved, I didn't know what country or city I was in, whether the stuff that surged through my head was real or imaginary. I came home very carefully on a bus, crawled into bed, and passed out for a couple of hours.

———

In a cafe in Bondi Junction four or five young women, maybe students, pass my table on their way to the register. Moments later I get a feeling someone's looking at me from outside the door. I glance up. One of the women is facing me foursquare through the big street window, right up against the glass, glaring at me with cold loathing. She sustains the death-ray full blast till I turn back to my food. Which has slightly lost its savour.

———

The hostile letters are coming now. Many of them are from university students with big heads of steam and a lot of women's studies jargon. Some of them loved *Monkey Grip* and feel I've betrayed them. The huffy ones are sort of sweet—sanctimonious and very young. They're going to get rid of all my other books off their shelves. They aren't going to buy my book, they don't want me to get their money, it really shits them that it's on the bestseller list, it's not my story, I've stolen it, I'm making money out of other people's troubles, anyway they haven't read it and they aren't planning to, but they know EXACTLY what the book says and they're outraged. I think I'll try to answer all of them. It's a calming exercise, trying to visualise the person and slide an answer round her shield of righteousness. One older woman calls me 'an immature "bloody" idiot' and abuses me for three pages, then adds, 'You are welcome to respond.' I want to vomit insults but instead dash off a card thanking her for her 'courteous and thoughtful letter'. Turning the other cheek. It gives a small but very enjoyable rush of power. Over myself.

———

The magazine asked me if I wanted to cover the backpacker murder trial. Two pieces, or more if the trial lengthens. I went down to the court. It was almost empty. Preliminary proceedings. Down at the front the accused, in a dark suit, sat beside his barrister with his back to the body of the court. How harmless and respectable a man in a suit can look. I took a seat ten rows behind him and sat watching him for fifteen minutes. When he turned his head to speak to the lawyer I saw the sharp line of his cheekbone and brow. How much of that cold shock was I projecting? I knew right away I did not want to find out.

———

I had prepared for Radio National's *Books and Writing* by rereading the book on a famous 1955 university sex scandal that the academic who was to interview me had published. I was imagining an energetic discussion of both our books, but not until I'd sat down alone in the Sydney Tardis and put on the headphones did I realise I'd been ambushed, that it was going to be only about my book, and that she was on the warpath. The sleazy, story-stealing book she was deploring did not sound like the one I had written. I was on the back foot throughout, shaken by her aggressive, carpet-bombing style. My rational arguments deserted me. At one point my voice trembled. Silences fell. It was a rout. After the theme music played I sat in the Tardis, appalled at myself. A pause. In my head-phones the host of the show spoke softly to me from Melbourne. 'Are you still there?' 'Yes.' 'Are you all right?' 'No.'

———

This morning I sat down to a fresh pile of letters. As I began to answer the first one, it occurred to me that the furious Ormond tutor was probably getting lots of letters too. I almost laughed. Two skinny little ladies, writing away like mad.

———

Easter. I went to St John's Darlinghurst. Hundreds of people. Someone told me that the vicar 'conducts at least three funerals a week, for the boys with AIDS'. At the first hymn, a frightful squawk behind me: a very old lady, trying to sing. I think this is going to be my church.

———

Nearly Anzac Day. A fresh, bright morning. On the bus I sat next to three jolly old blokes with sun-wrecked skin. They told me they were brothers. 'What? I don't believe you! Show me your licences!' Laughing, they dived for their wallets. The eldest, Henry, said he had been in Changi, 'but I weigh fourteen stone now'. Another said he was a farmer, and would march in Cootamundra. They rattled on about themselves as the bus chugged along. Halfway up William Street Henry said, 'But we haven't asked about you! What's your name?' 'Helen.' 'Helen!' he cried, and struck a poetical pose: '"Helen, thy beauty is to me—"' I chimed in with the second line: '"Like those Nicean barks of yore..."' and they all cheered. 'Is that Wordsworth?' asked one. 'More like Shelley,' said Henry. 'Where do you live, Helen?' 'Elizabeth Bay. I'm getting off at the next stop.' I went to press the button and he said, 'I've already pressed it for you.' I scrambled out over their legs. They waved, and the bus keeled round the corner. As I walked home along Ward Avenue I dredged my memory for the rest of the verse, and found it: '...That gently, o'er a perfumed sea/ The weary, wayworn wanderer bore/ To his own native shore.'

———

Turns out that not only will the transcript of the *Books and Writing* massacre be run in the next issue of *Australian Book Review*, but guess who has reviewed the book for them? The carpet-bomber herself. The editor calls and in a subdued voice tells me the issue is about to be posted out—do I want her to fax me a copy of the review, 'just so you'll have read it before everyone else sees it?' My mind scampers over the terrain. 'Oh, that won't be necessary, thanks. Just send me a copy of the magazine, if you wouldn't mind. But it's good of you to make the offer.' Spew spew spew. I'm so terminally *nice*.

———

V has found someone in Melbourne who wants to buy my piano. He's worked hard to persuade me that I won't be needing it again, that there's no room for a piano here, where on earth would I put it, a piano in an apartment building is an impossible thing, it would be outlandish, and imagine how much it would cost to truck the bloody thing up the highway. I listened, my arguments dying on my lips. I know that what he's really saying is, 'You're not a pianist, you don't sound good when you play, it's not really music, and I don't want to have to listen to it any more.' I can hardly mount a case against *that*.

———

The review. Isn't the editor of the magazine her *friend*? Shouldn't she have persuaded her to lose the embarrassing first third of it, the clunky accounts of our meetings in coffee shops, not to mention the way she sarcastically refers to me as 'the famous novelist'? I'd expected better from her, something coherent, not these insults and distortions. When she wheels on the phrase 'vagina dentata', about my admiring description of one of the complainants, a beautiful young woman in a low-cut evening dress, I was more than anything mortified for her. 'Madam. May I correct one point in your contributor's review of my book? The coffee I drank at our meeting was not a short black. It was a short macchiato.'

———

'Of course, Helen's motivation was purely commercial.' Somebody I know actually *said* that to someone else I know, who repeated it to me. Is that what people really think, or is it just a mean thing to say? Scared I'm so overloaded that I might make a serious tactical blunder. Main thing is to keep my temper. And drink a lot of water. Walking up the hill with V, I saw a page of the *Herald* lying blown against a wall. On it my face, very small, and my name in white caps: 'Garner faces her critics'. Kept walking.

———

Finished my article about the cruise ship. I laughed so much, writing it, that I had to walk around the room and put on lipstick. Then I knocked over my movie review, and filed both stories. V teases me when I say 'file'—he says it's like in old movies when the reporters in the news room shout 'Copy boy!'—but I like 'file', it makes me feel I'm the real thing, and not just 'making a guest appearance as a journalist', as another of the feminist academics wrote in her scathing review. By Wednesday when I hit George V I'll have cleared the decks.

———

I'm not exactly scared. To lose what's left of my reproductive organs. I'm ready. But from time to time I imagine with a cold thrill the scalpel blade slicing through the muscle of my abdomen.

———

I've stopped vomiting. Time passes with surprising slowness. Night-times I wake, trundle my drip to the dunny, piss, trundle back, press the button that delivers a hit of pethidine, sleep, wake, trundle. Towards morning I look in the mirror. The shape of my nose has changed. Flattened bridge, like a boxer. I must be imagining it. Over hours it gets worse. Sun comes up and I've got two black eyes. Must be from tubes the anaesthetist put in yesterday morning after the staples popped out of the wound. The nurse was sponging me, one of them pricked her, she panicked: 'Have you got hepatitis?' 'No, and I haven't got AIDS either.' Her voice went up the scale: 'I'll have to get a blood test.' The Wallabies guy had to come back and put in a new lot of staples, in theatre, with a second general anaesthetic.

———

Very bright, dry morning. Warm. Quality of light in the room makes me think I'm in a country town. The nurse checks my pethidine. 'You've hardly used any of this!' Proud of myself: I thought I'd used heaps and would be addicted. Lower abdomen a glory of bruise, a railway track of metal. Left hand purple, and puffy as a toad. Rather happy. Can't read, too dopey.

———

People come, I don't remember who, I guess I fall asleep because when I wake no one's there.

———

V brought me a brown paper bag. Oh, boy—mandarins! O made me laugh so much my stitches hurt. E came, and R, and the Cretan. The born-again brought me a C. S. Lewis book from his brother.

———

Something in a dream, something about my mother, made me cry hard and woke me. I came to, with my head turned towards the window. 5.45 am. I got up, just to move my body, and shuffled out on to the balcony. Still dark but the air soft and the city moving. Light entered the sky like a pink hem on stage curtains. A woman screamed. I hobbled to the rail, another scream, someone on the floor below, a muffled window with yellow light, someone's having a baby. On and on she screamed, over and over: Aiii-ah! Aii-*ahhh*! I leaned my chest on the rail and the tears kept quietly running out, something hard and stoic in me dissolved, I tried to pray, to *be* with her, I had no technique for this, it was only an idea, but I felt very close to her and somehow satisfied—a feeling of deep rightness and gratitude. I crept back to bed. Even with the window closed her cries and long howls reached me until the day of the ward began and there was too much other noise for me to hear her any more.

When I woke it was full daylight, and a middle-aged deaconess in a green shirt was sitting by my bed. She was earnest and humourless. She questioned me about my life and my family. I gave dutiful answers. 'Would you like me to pray for you?' she said. I thought she meant 'when I'm back at the church' and in relief I said thank you, I would. But she took my right hand between her small, dry, ridged palms, and began to address Jesus here and now, on my behalf. I was rigid with embarrassment, afraid some sceptical friend would walk in and laugh at me. She told him who I was and why I was there, how far away my family lived and why my parents couldn't come to see me. 'She is your child, Lord,' she said, and some further barrier in me went down. She blessed me and left the room. No one else came. I cried for a long time, and then I fell asleep.